THIS BELONGS TO:

AREEN DESIGN SERVICES LTD
AREEN HOUSE
282 KING STREET
LONDON W6 0SJ

Tel: 0181-748 8088 Fax: 0181-748 3475

Cortijo El Esparragal
(Photo Vincent Gyselinck)

With special thanks to our photographers

Bieke Claessens
Jan Dirkx
Phile Deprez
Vincent Gyselinck
Patrick Verbeeck
Donald Woodrow

&

Paul Kusseneers
Concept & Lay-Out

&

Printed by De Plano

Compiled by :Luc Quisenaerts
Concept & lay-out: Paul Kusseneers
Printed by: De Plano
Written by: Owen Davis
Publishers: D-Publications
List of photographers:
Bieke Claessens & Donald Woodrow:
Puente Romano, Marbella Club, Arts, Gran Hotel Bahia del Duque, Casa Imperial, Parador de Carmona, Parador de Jaén, Parador de Granada.
Jan Dirkx:
Parador de Santiago, Parador de Jarandilla de la Vera, Villa Real, Santo Mauro, Landa Palace, San Roman de Escalante, Parador de Sigüenza, Parador de León
Phile Deprez:
La Residencia, Finca Ca N'Ai, Palacio Ca Sa Galesa, Hacienda Na Xamena.
Vincent Gyselinck:
Hacienda Benazuza, Casa de Carmona, La Bobadilla, Alhambra Palace, La Cala Golf Resort, Cortijo El Esparragal, Parador de Zamora, Parador de Zafra.
Patrick Verbeeck:
Claris, Mas Pau, Mas de Torrent, Parador de Cardona

ISBN 90-76124-21-3   D/1999/8101/8

© All rights reserved. No part of this publication may be reproduced in any way whatsoever without written permission from D-Publications.

First Edition

HOTEL GEMS
OF
SPAIN

COMPILED BY

LUC QUISENAERTS

WRITTEN BY

OWEN DAVIS

PUBLISHERS D-PUBLICATIONS

THE SERIES 'HOTEL GEMS OF THE WORLD'

Dear Reader,

After 'Hotel Gems of France', 'Hotel Gems of Great Britain & Ireland' and 'Hotel Gems of Italy', this 'Hotel Gems of Spain' is the fourth book in a unique series.

Each book will describe the rich and fascinating hotel heritage of a certain country, a group of countries or a continent.

Each country will be described from a very special, original angle.

By enjoying the hospitality of the people of a country for one or several nights, one can taste the history, the culture and the cuisine of such a country in a deeply personal way.

Therefore, we thank all the hotels, who co-operated in this project for offering their hospitality, which is usually reserved for the guests who stay there, to the readers of these books.

In the following months and years, we hope to offer you a whole series of new voyages of discovery to the most fascinating hotels in the world.

We intend to enable readers to 'walk' through all these gems, to discover their unique nooks and crannies, by leafing through each book.

That is why this series, and each book in itself, can be considered a valuable archive containing a piece of the wealth and beauty of a country, created by the passion of all those people who put their souls into it.
…

HOTEL GEMS IN SPAIN

"This is paradise on earth and this is where I want to be buried and start my journey to heaven…" Emperor Charles V, in the first half of the 16th century ruler on which kingdom where the sun never set, had every good reason to spend his final years in castle Jarandilla de la Vera, which has now started a new life as a *parador*, and which offers its guests an unforgettable stay.

His words are a perfect illustration of the link that can be made between the once so powerful Spanish empire and the wealth of the cultural and historic heritage of the modern hotels in Spain.

Although it was one of the founders of Europe and an age-old beacon of western civilisation in the world, this southern country with its specific character was still very much influenced by Moorish civilisation.

In this book, we roam through bright white Andalusian *haciendas* that shimmer in the sunlight. We stand under Moorish arcades in the quiet courtyards of beautifully restored palaces in the old city centres of Seville, Palma and Madrid, and listen to the refreshing sound of fountains.

We admire the splendid architecture and wisely-chosen locations of centuries-old monasteries in the countryside, and feel the medieval atmosphere of majestic strongholds which, built on hill tops, dominate the landscape. We taste the pleasant, cosy life at the *fincas* on rural Mallorca, and the refined atmosphere of luxurious hotels of upmarket Marbella. And we return to the reality of modern life in the trendy designer hotels of Barcelona and Madrid.

If he were still alive, Charles would have a much harder time now choosing the place in Spain where he would live out his last years …

Luc Quisenaerts
Editor

THE COLLECTION

Casa de Carmona	10
Parador de Jaén	18
Mas de Torrent	24
Santo Mauro	30
Parador de Sigüenza	36
La Cala Golf Resort	40
Finca Ca N'Ai	44
Parador de León	48
La Bobadilla	52
Casa Imperial	56
Hacienda Na Xamena	62
Parador de Zafra	68
Alhambra Palace	72
La Residencia	78
Parador de Carmona	84
Claris	90
Palacio Ca Sa Galesa	98
Parador de Jarandilla de la Vera	104
Hacienda Benazuza	108
Mas Pau	116
Landa Palace	120
Parador de Zamora	126
Puente Romano	130
Parador de Granada	136
San Roman de Escalante	142
Parador de Santiago	146
Marbella Club	150
Villa Real	156
Gran Hotel Bahia del Duque	160
Arts	166
Cortijo El Esparragal	170
Parador de Cardona	176

Casa de Carmona

*'Desde mi habitacion
oigo la fuente.*

*Un racimo de la parra
y un rayo de sol.
Señalen hacia el lugar
de mi corazón.'*

*'From my room
I hear the fountain
A vine-tendril
and a ray of sunshine.
They point at the place
of my heart.'*

F.G. Lorca

Set in the very heart of poetic Andalusia, the Casa de Carmona is a romantic hotel that embodies all that one might imagine of a 400-year old *palazzo* in this Moorish-influenced corner of south-west Spain - a place of tranquil elegance, passion and particular beauty.

The fiery poetry of Frederico Garcia Lorca seems to hang, like promise, in the languid shadows of a timeless summer evenings, a soulful gypsy guitar might at any moment be borne to your open window on a soft jacaranda-scented breeze.

Carmona can be found on the high road linking Seville and Cordoba, a scant 15-minute drive from Seville airport. Both these famously intriguing historic cities are within easy reach - and you shouldn't miss either. Give each of them a day, at the least. But Carmona itself, as you will soon discover, is an ancient and captivating little town, easy to fall in love with.

Secret behind its discreet façade lies the five star Casa de Carmona Hotel, a wonder of tasteful design. Lemon trees stand sentries in shadowed courtyards where fountains endlessly play, there is a lovely; swimming-pool shaded by the fronds of a huge palm, a seductive Arab garden, a library, even a chess parlour… and 33 air-conditioned guest rooms of great refinement, each individually furnished with fine antiques, rugs and curtains, providing every modern luxury - fullly equipped bathrooms, CD players, videos and satellite television. Once we'd been shown to our expansive and light-filled room, we sat back and enjoyed the beautiful surroundings: the large bouquet of dark blue and sweetly-scented flowers on an old mahogany desk, the stunning and unusual antique bedstead and the oriental rugs laid across te floor, alive with the warm dark reds and blues.

The day before, we had visited the wonderful secret gardens of the Alhambra, and now we sought out the hotel's own Arab garden. While we sipped a pre-dinner cocktail, we listened to a little singing fountain of clear water and fell into one of those dreamy moods when time seems to stand still. I think that many of our fellow guests shared this quiet pleasure with us.

That evening, we had a superb dinner at the world-class restaurant at Casa de Carmona, run by masterchef Fernando Peña. Savouring the delights he offered us, we decided that there could not be a better way to conclude a day of wonderful discoveries in breathtaking Andalusia.

Hotel Casa de Carmona is situated in a former palace in the historic town of Carmona, a stone's trow from Seville.

Parador de Jaén

The luxurious Parador of Jaén was built right next to the castle of Santa Catalina, and it stands on top of a hill that once played an important part in world history. According to legend, Hannibal built a tower here when he and his impressive army of elephants were on their way to conquer Rome. According to the same legend, Hannibal married Imilee, an Iberian princess who came from this area. Over the centuries many buildings rose and crumbled. Together they formed the 'Castolli Viejo' (old castle), a stronghold with many Arabic influences. It was the Christians who founded the present castle of Santa Catalina, in memory of the taking of the city by the army of Fernando III. The castle was meant as a defensive stronghold, and its construction clearly shows this: it is surrounded by a massive stone wall with many towers. The castle contains many interesting parts, such as the 'Plaza de Armas' (Arms Square), the 'Torre del Postigo de la Llan' (Tower with a View over the Plain) and the charming little chapel.

'Some oil and garlic are all I need to give flavour to the produce I cook with', is a wise old saying. The cuisine of Jaén is tasty, varied and creative. The secret of its success certainly has to do with the use of good quality oil, and with the great variety of fresh produce: asparagus, potatoes, white truffles, capers, wild carnations, cardillo (a kind of thistle that is used in salads) and wild beans. Then there is soup, made from a mixture of meat and vegetables, and the tasty local fried breadcrumbs. The Pipirrana, a salad of tomatoes and cucumbers, is called 'queen of salads', but the regular thistle or tomato salad is just as tasty. Then there are simple but wonderful dishes such as salad with cucumber, melon or partridge, made with the very best local ingredients, or black pudding with - what else - garlic. Gourmets will not fail to appreciate the authentic cuisine of this hotel.

According to legend, Hannibal had a tower built here when he was on his way to Rome with his army and his elephants.

Mas de Torrent

Crossing the French border into Spain at the eastern end of the Pyrenees is no longer the adventure it was to me, back in the late fifties, a solitary young man using his thumb to discover a Europe only barely back on its feet after the war, but it is still exciting enough, and different enough, to call up the pulse-beat of romance.

The Costa Brava has become a mecca for holidaymakers seeking their two brief weeks of sunshine, blue seas and hot beaches… but there is another side to the area that a discerning traveller will appreciate: medieval towns, unspoilt and original still, like Pals, Peratallada and Toroella de Montgri, and the old quarter of the larger town of Girona. At Figueres you'll find the Dali Museum, a comprehensive gathering-together of the surrealist artist's paintings, drawings and sculptures - and in L'Empordà, in the very heart of the Costa Brava, the lovely Mas de Torrent.

Built in 1751, it began life a little more humbly, as a simple farmhouse. Perhaps I walked by it, in that very guise, on my early impecunious travels, 40 years ago. I would not advise you to pass it by today. It has been transformed, renovated and much extended to become a prestigious and luxurious five-star hotel, though its peaceful rural setting remains just as it always was. Since 1991, Mas de Torrent has been a member of Relais & Chateaux, a confirmation of excellence the hotel is clearly proud of.

As soon as you set foot in the hotel's welcoming front hall, with its oaken reception desk and autumn aromas of woodsmoke, apples and fresh flowers, you know that Mas de Torrent will be something a bit special.

25

Each room is sweetly named after a flower and, like each flower, is entirely individual and harmonious, with antique furniture and all the latest devices to make life easy - air-conditioning as standard, direct-dial phones, a minibar and satellite television. Each of the 20 suites has, in addition, a small and elegant private garden of its own.

The ground-floor restaurant is made up of three spacious rooms that look out across the flower-filled gardens. The cuisine is sublime – traditional yet individual, subtle and made with the freshest local ingredients and choicest sea food.

In summer, tables overflow onto the terrace and you can dine *al fresco*.

Before continuing south, you must, of course, make your way to Figueres to see the Dali Museum, and while you're in town, look out for Spain's only Toy Museum. It is full of nostalgic charm and a useful antidote to a surfeit of surrealism!

Santo Mauro

Madrid is an exciting city to wander in. There's the Prado museum, of course, full of marvellous paintings, worth many hours of your time, and there are the charming squares with café tables set out under the shade of trees, just right for a welcome rest on a hot day.

Everywhere, there's something to catch the curious eye: and old man sitting thoughtfully on a bench, a stunning blonde at the wheel of an open-topped sports car, a group of bright-eyed laughing school girls, a plump waiter resting an brief moment against the door-jamb of his café, a silver tray against his thigh… cities are as much the variety and liveliness of the people, as the tall and imposing buildings that tell their fascinating tales of histories half-forgotten, ignored by most of us in the headlong rush of modern life.

What the visitor needs, of course, when the sun begins to fail and shadows begin to lengthen, is a place to briefly call home, somewhere welcoming, with a cosy bedroom, a deep and steaming bath, and a good meal waiting in the softly-lit surroundings of a fine restaurant.

Luxurious and intimate, traditional and modern, the five-star Santo Mauro is one of the very best hotels you could find for yourself in the Spanish capital, answering all the requirements the guest might hope for… and it is conveniently close to the centre of things.

Built over 100 years ago and, over the years, the distinguished address of various embassies, it has now been completely renovated with many elegant and subtle touches. The contemporary furniture blends surprisingly aptly with the traditional aspect of the building. Along the walls sedate old engravings hang side by side with daring examples of avant-garde art.

The Santo Mauro has 37 rooms, which include a wonderful presidential suite and several high quality junior suites. Many have fireplaces of Italian marble, and they all have colour television, hi-fi and a CD player. There is a duplex suite where the old stables were once, with curtains and a bedspread of wild silk.

The restaurant has been placed, with great originality, in one of the oldest, original rooms - the library, and the choice of fresh gourmet food is so extensive that it may be wiser to invite the chef's own recommendations, as I did, and have an accompanying wine placed on the table also of the expert's choice.

Afterwards, I joined others who had made their way outside onto the terrace, to watch the ascending moon and sip a last cognac, as a welcome cool breeze played amongst the dark leaves of the nearby trees. For that night, and the next, I was indeed at home.

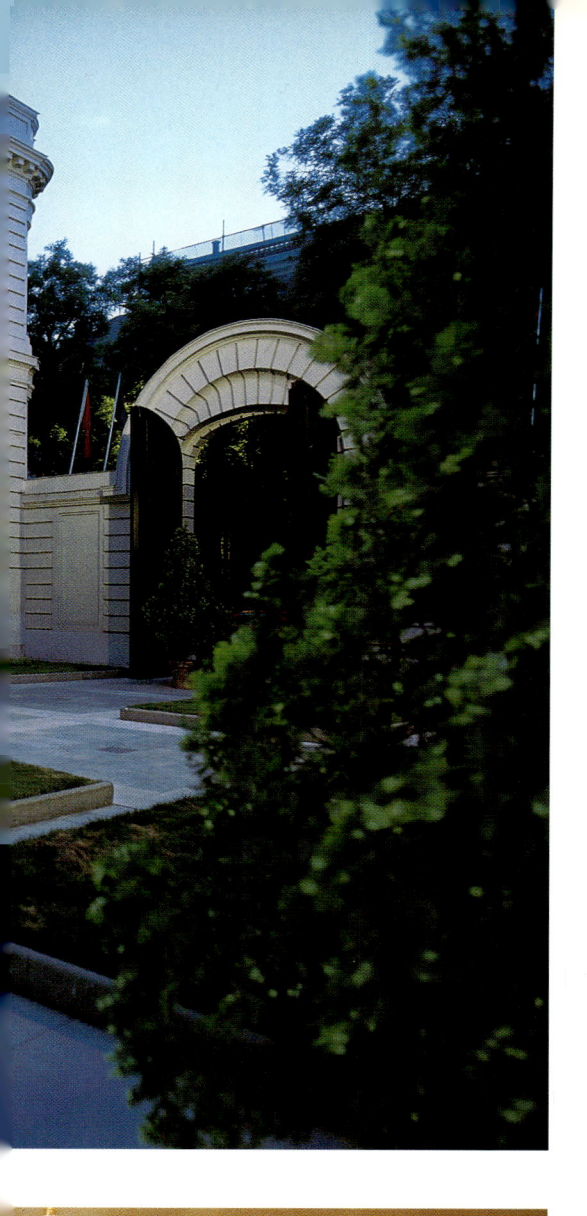

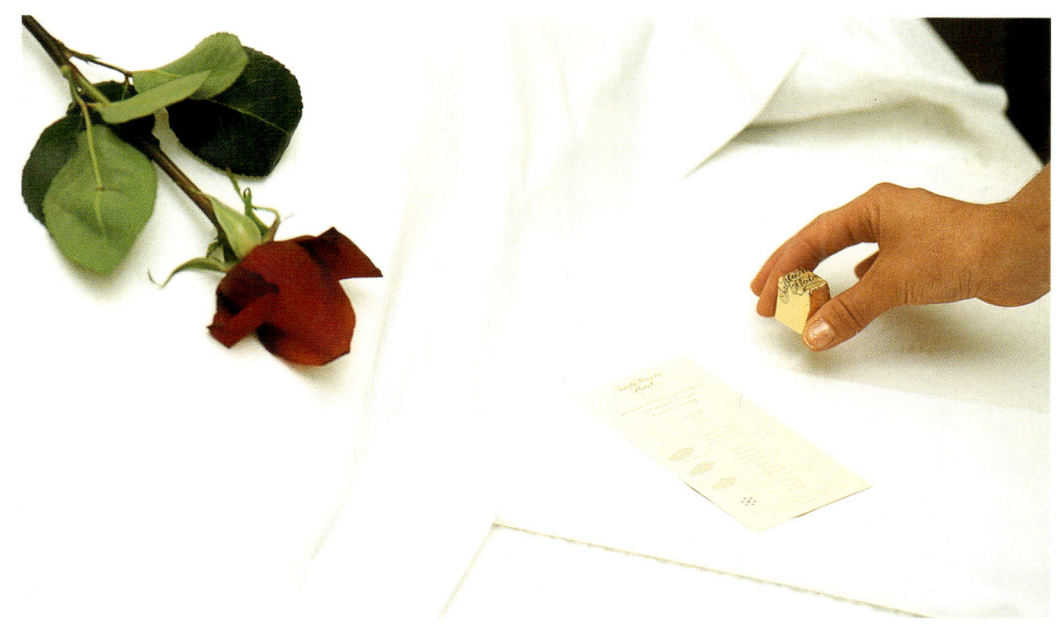

Once, several embassies were housed in this 100-year old palace in the centre of Madrid.

Parador de Sigüenza

This charming, medieval castle lies in the highest part of the town. It was completely renovated in the 'sixties, and became one of the Parador group. This castle, once a residence of the bishops of Sigüenza, was originally a Celtic Ibero-Roman stronghold and shows quite a few Gothic and Arabic influences. Since the town was re-conquered in 1124 and the Saracens expelled, the castle has constantly been renovated and enlarged. A succession of noblemen and bishops lived here, until it finally became derelict in the 19th century.

Before you reach the main entrance, you pass through a courtyard surrounded by a meter-wide wall. By way of a large staircase, flanked by two identical towers, you reach the entrance hall, and from there you proceed to the impressive central courtyard, with its wooden galleries and antique well.

The hotel itself contains a magnificent throne room (Salón del Trono), which once served as a judicial courtroom, and the Doña Blanca room (Salón de Doña Blanca) is nowadays a suitable venue for numerous exhibitions, conventions and banquets. Other historic gems are the beautiful Roman chapel and a tiny room where, as legend has it, Doña Blanca of Bourbon was locked up by her husband Petro I 'The Cruel'.

A building with a rich history, walls that have been witness to important decisions… the castle has many intriguing tales to tell, which are presented to visitors in a pleasant, original way.

Local cuisine is famous for its abundance and variety. There are, for example, many kinds of fish: fat river trout and tasty carp. There is also a great deal of fowl and game on the menu. Cheese, wine and honey are abundantly used in the very individual regional cuisine. '

Some specialities of the chef are a stew of ground pig's liver, a recipe from the kitchens of the ancient and noble Molinés family, cod with mushrooms and cheese in the mode of Trijueque, roast kid from Barreña and the famous Flores de Cabanillas. At Parador de Sigüenza, you will be spoilt for choice.

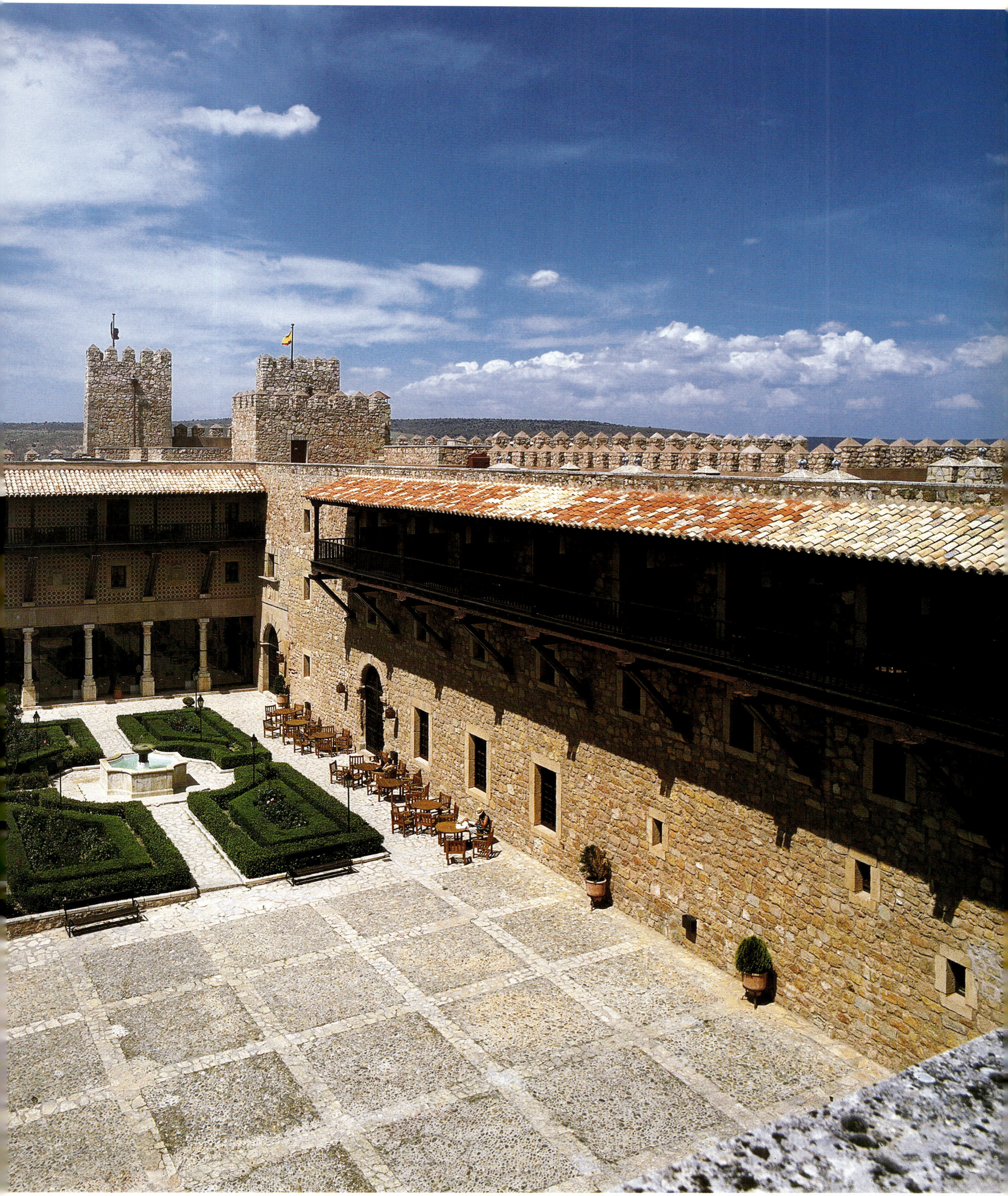

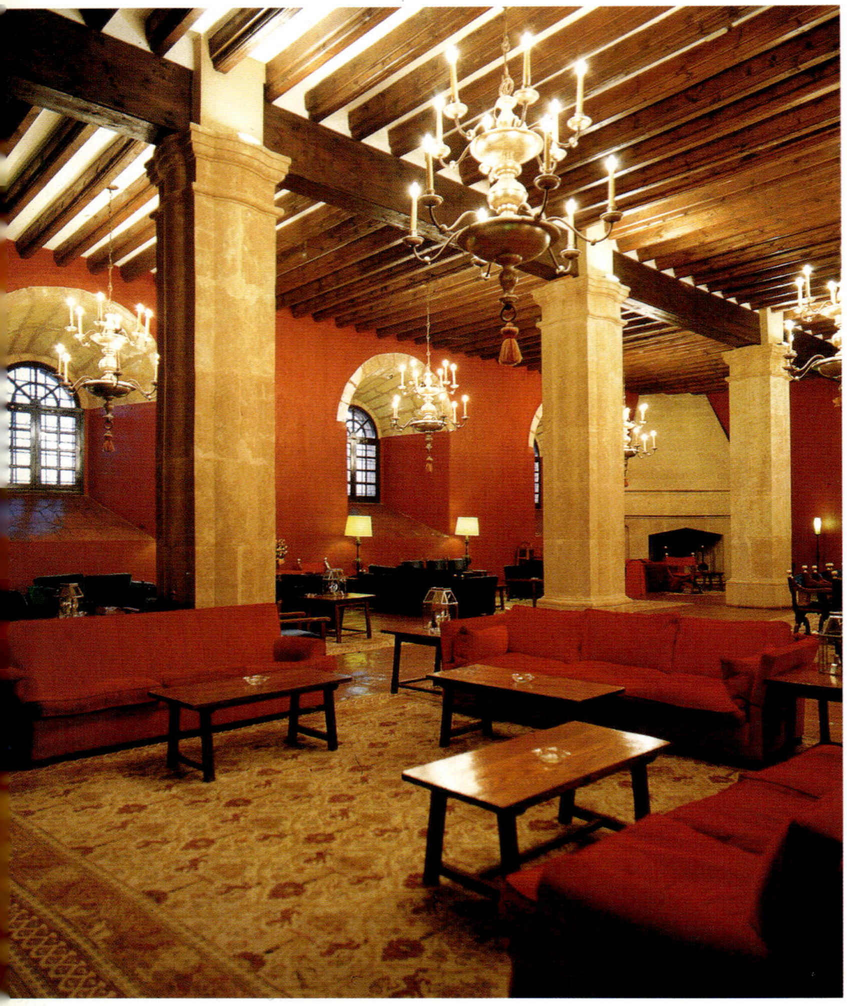

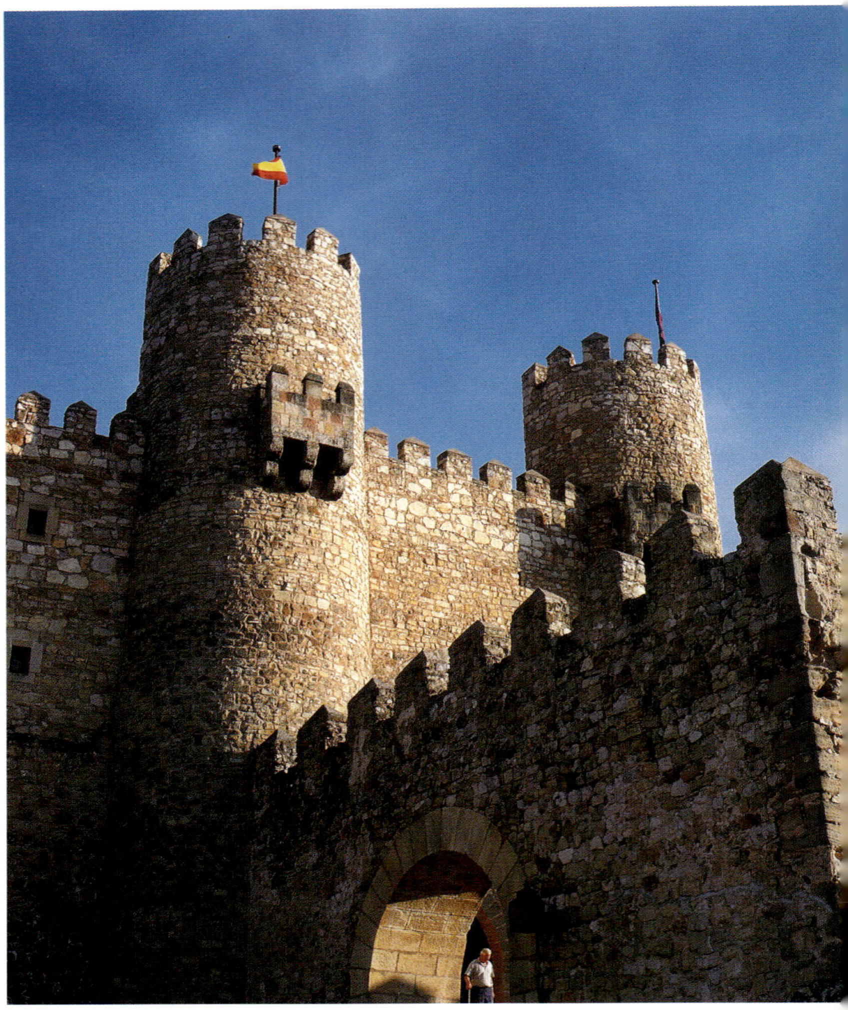

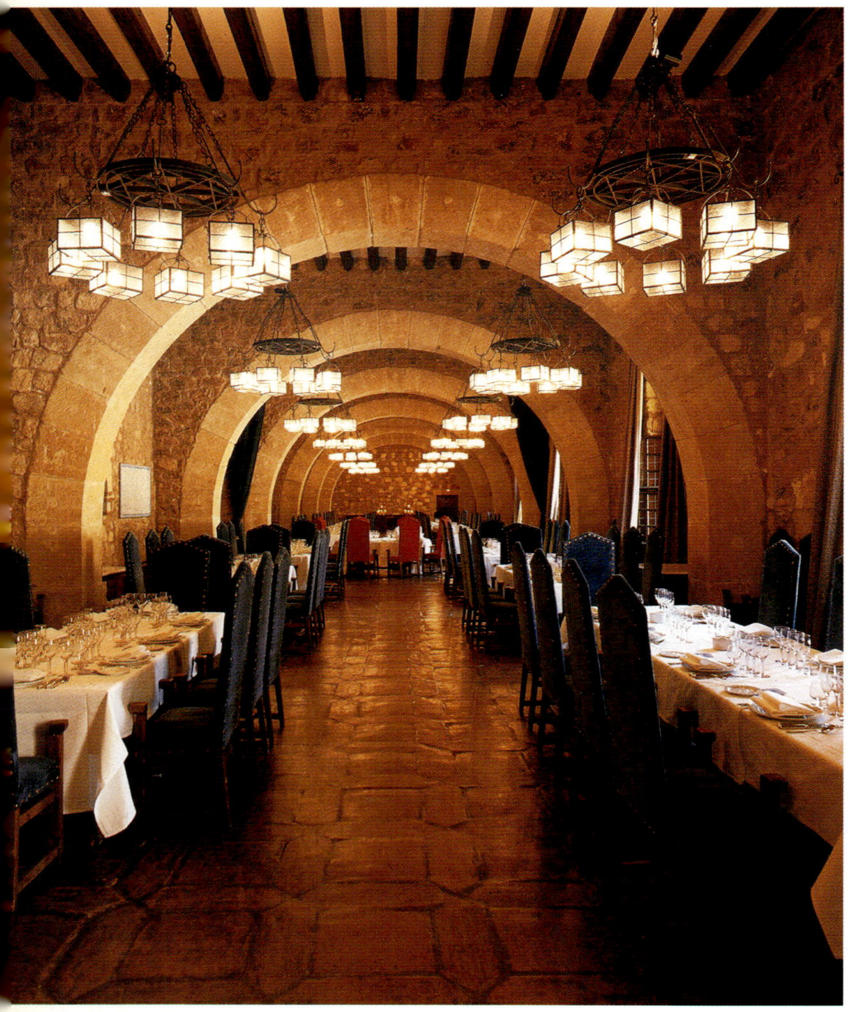

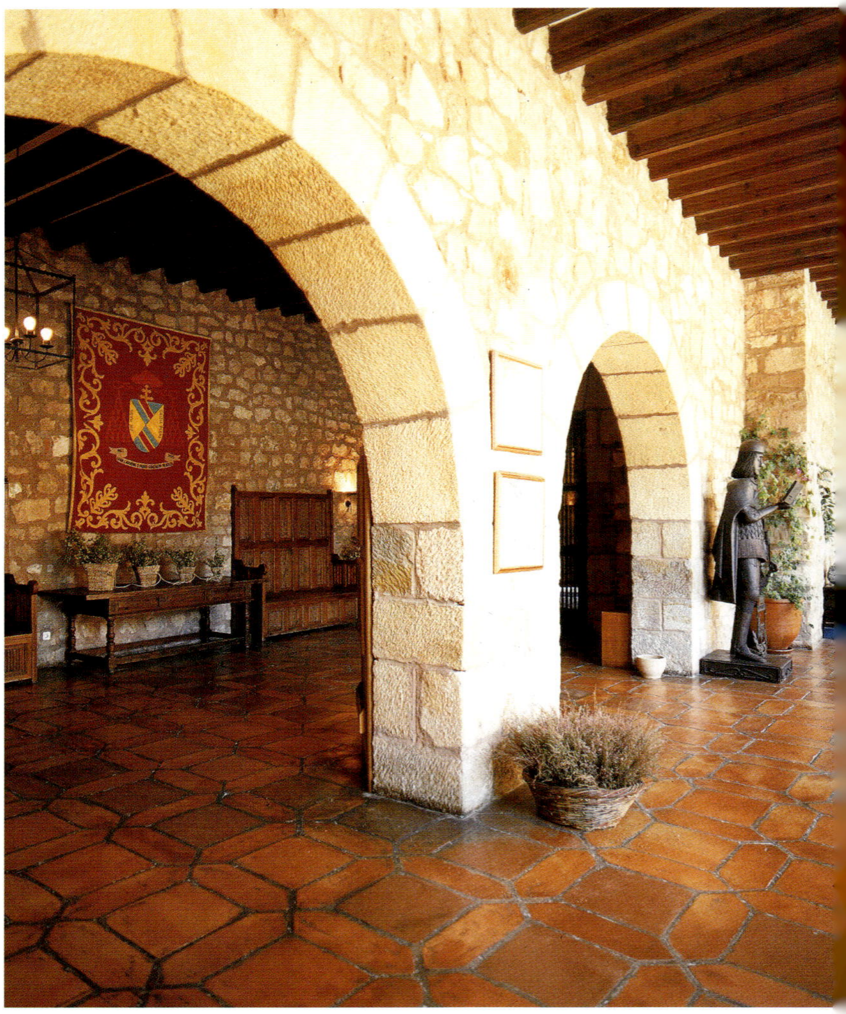

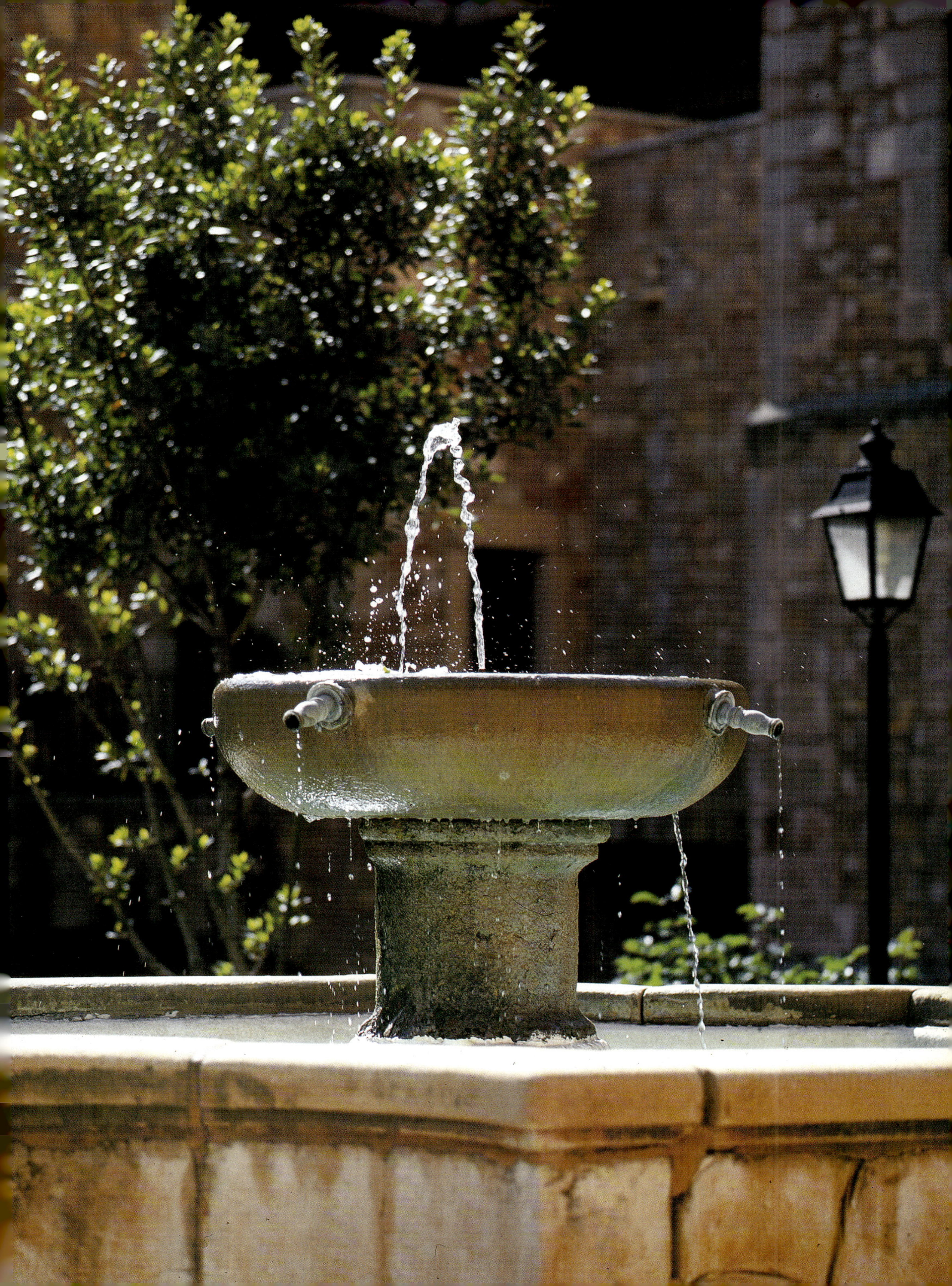

La Cala Golf Resort

La Cala, a little inland from Malaga and not far from Marbella, is a golfer's paradise. It lies precisely between two spectacular professionally-designed 18-hole championship courses of its own, it houses the prestigious David Leadbetter Golf Academy, has a driving range, a pro shop, a clubhouse restaurant, Los Olivos, and it offers a shorter six-hole 'executive' course.

La Cala is a five-star hotel, but that's only part of the story. It calls iself a resort, but I'd call it a country club.

Apart from the fine golf to be had, guests can choose from swimming (there's an indoor and an outdoor pool), tennis, billiards, a work-out suite, mountain biking or horse-riding, and even athletics and team games such as rugby and football. You could even… do nothing at all but sit on a terrace, read a book, doze off, or watch other people pursue the sporting life.

Whether you've come to La Cala to dash about or do nothing, when evening comes there's something special to look forward to; a gourmet meal at Los Olivos, or the equally fine La Terraza, situated in the hotel.

La Cala's hotel, designed in a traditional Andalusian style, has 83 de luxe double rooms, which all have a great view over the South course.If the idea of a golfer's resort appeals to you, then there are opportunities to purchase your own villa, townhouse or apartment. At this stage, there are even unbuilt plots still available. La Cala would be an inviting proposition for anyone considering a second home in the sun, which may eventuallly, when the time is right, make a wonderful retirement home, where you'll find any amount of like-minded friends to share the active life avalaible all around you.

It's hardly surprising that La Cala is also proving to be a popular venue for business conferences. Meeting rooms can be tailored to the size of your group and can offer all kinds of completely up-to-date visual aids and the usual back-up services. But whether you come for business or for pleasure, you will find La Cala a most wonderful experience!

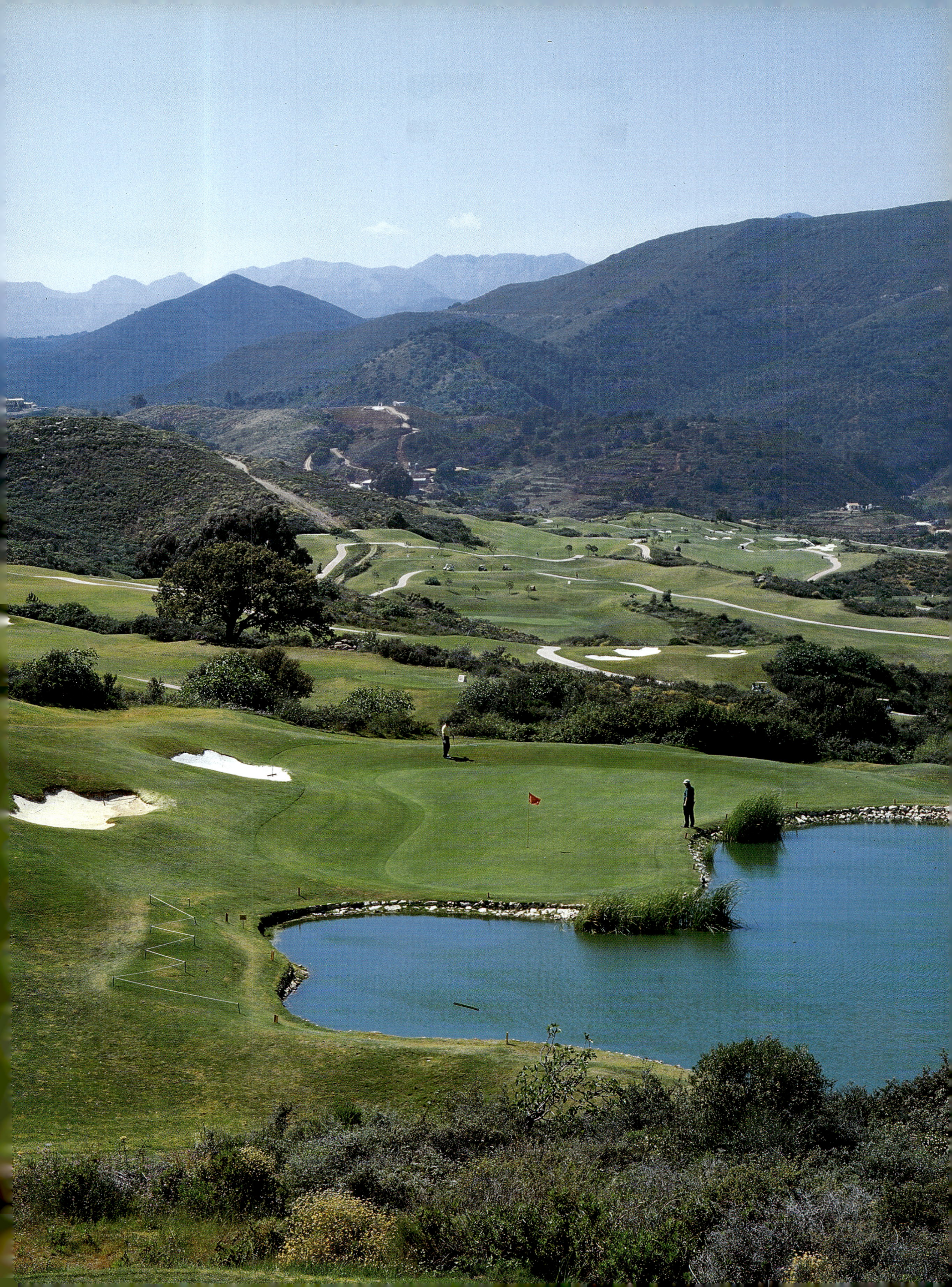

La Cala Golf Resort: a jewel, hidden by the mountains behind Malaga.

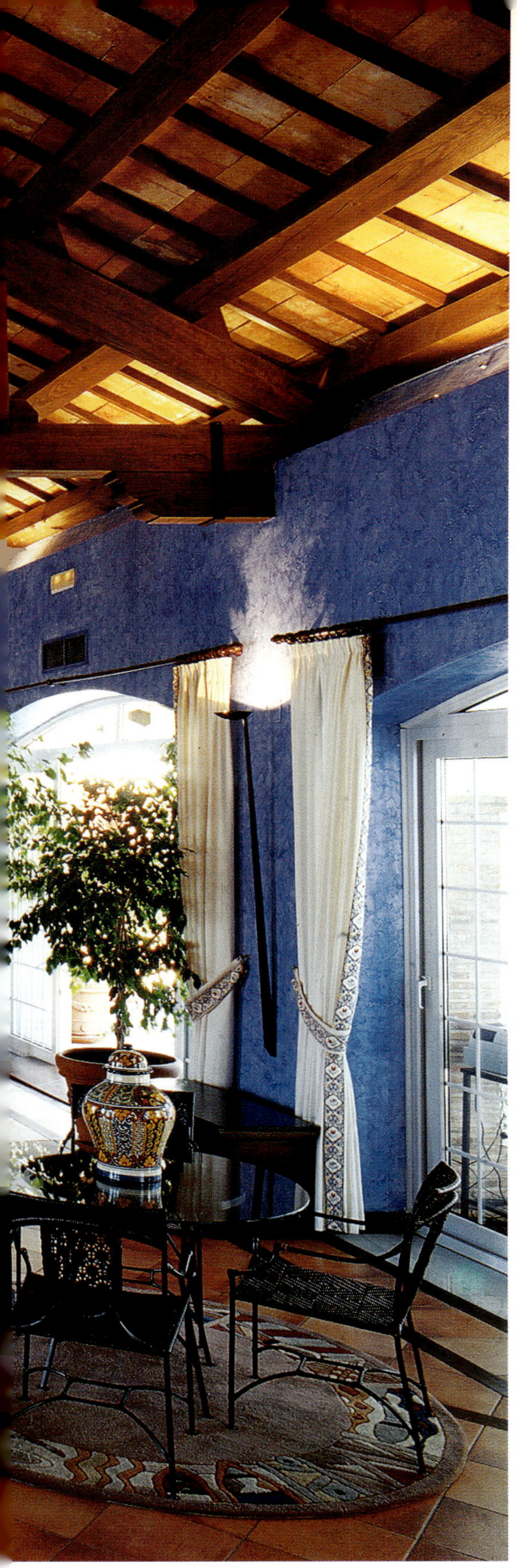
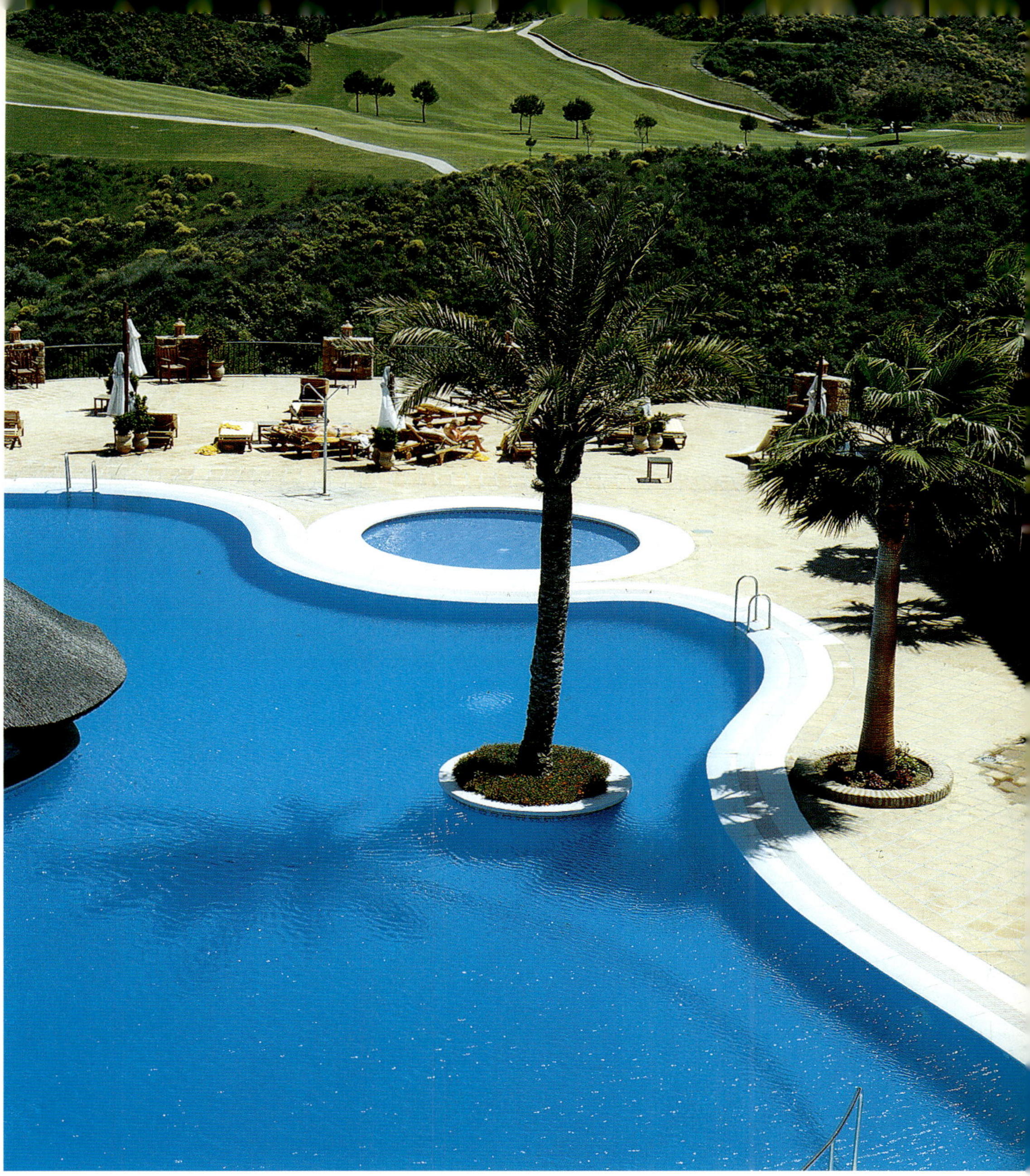
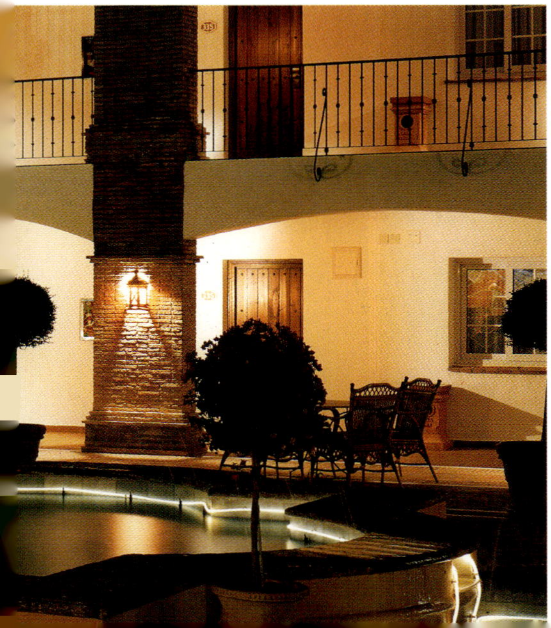
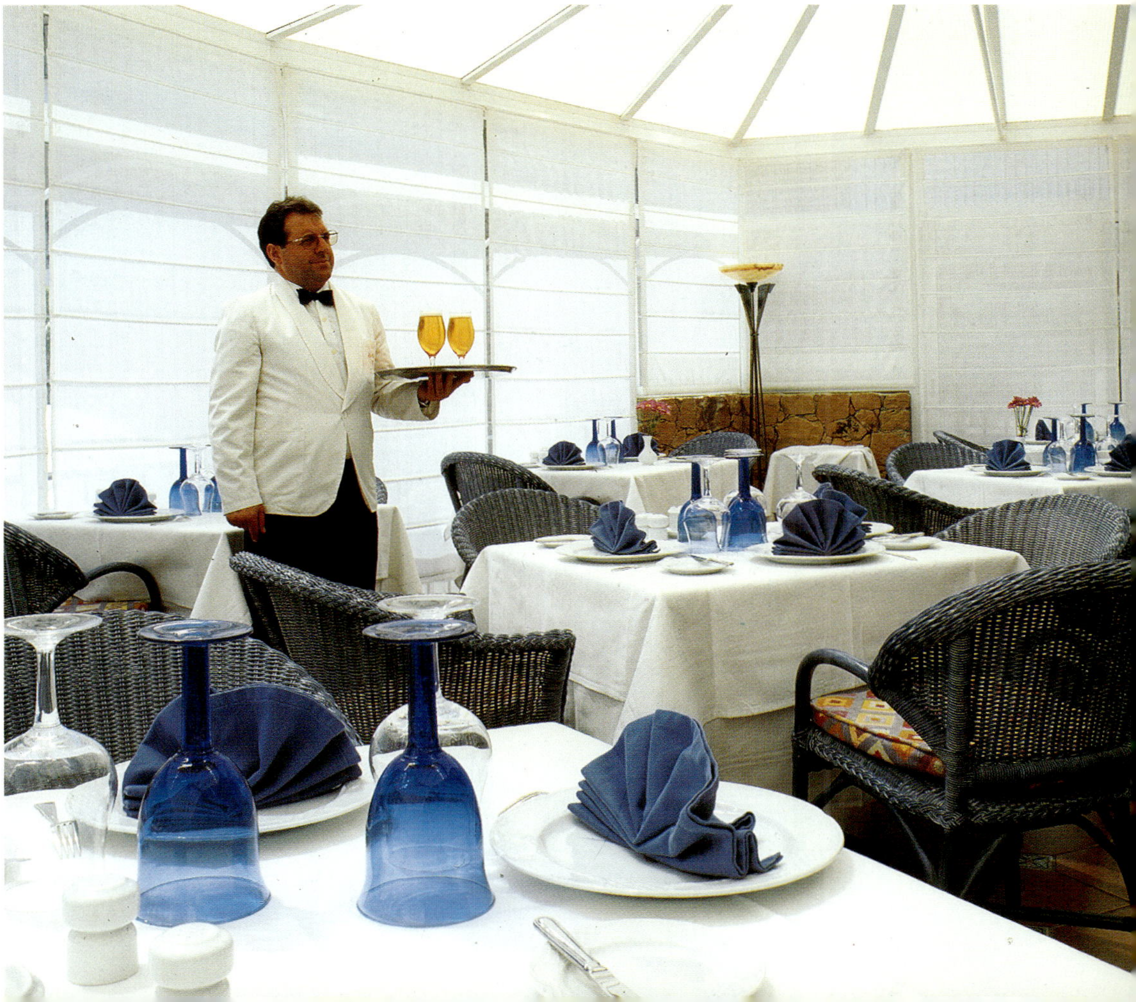

Finca Ca N'Ai

Visitors to Majorca are intent on discovering not very much except exactly what lures them to this popular Mediterranean isle - sandy beaches, warm blue seas and lots of sunshine. After patiently suffering a long north European winter and a capracious spring which often enough delivers less than it promises, who could blame them?

But there is more to Majorca, of course, and the canny traveller should look beyond the first stretch of summer beach. The interior is picturesque in the extreme, at any time of year, though my favourite month is surely May, early May, when the hordes are yet to come and blossom perfumes your every step.

As the road winds northwards through rising hills, the weathered mountain spire of Majorca ahead of you looks formidable and intriguing… And there, in the valley, you'll find an hotel of considerable antiquity and tremendous charm, homely, peaceful and very elegant, the Hotel Finca Ca N'Ai.

Finca means 'estate' and the hotel began life as the manor house, the principal residence of a wide farming estate, probably developed first by the Saracens, who were clever farmers adept at creating waterways to feed their crops. These still exist, and everywhere you stroll in the surrounding groves and gardens of Ca N'Ai you'll be accompanied by the satisfying murmur of little streams, carrying nourishment still to more than 5,000 orange trees, which envelope the hotel with shade and with fragrance.

The building has been painstakingly and skilfully restored to a high standard to provide every modern comfort and yet retain all the ambience of its historic past. There are little corners everywhere, and far, magnificent vistas. Everyone will seek out which spot suits them the best; beside the millpond, perhaps, where you can listen to the water-wheel turn and splash, or under the great 200-year-old linden tree, its leaves never still.

It is a rural idyll that has drawn the rich and famous to Ca N'Ai's door; even royalty have paused to take a meal here. The restaurant is proud of its far-reaching reputation, confirmed by its well-earned Michelin mention.

Here, you can taste natural produce which comes from the farm itself, an example of ecologically-aware agriculture in the service of gastronomic refinement. 'Refinement', is also the key word for the luxurious suites at Ca N'Ai: no two are the same, but each of them are like an oasis of peace, a unique combination of comfort and exquisite taste. Allow yourself a longer stay here, you would hardly be disappointed… there is the wonderful outdoor pool to be enjoyed. The sea and those sunny beaches are really not so far away, either. And there is a special tram that will transport you there, and return you safely back, in time for your unmissable evening meal.

But I love to wander through those endless orange groves and up into the pine-scented foothills of the sierras that cup the hotel's serene valley, accompanied only by swirling butterflies and the songs of quick and secret birds.

The world, sometimes, seems perfect. Its labours a distant memory, and its rewards, like the Hotel Finca Ca N'Ai, nearly infinite.

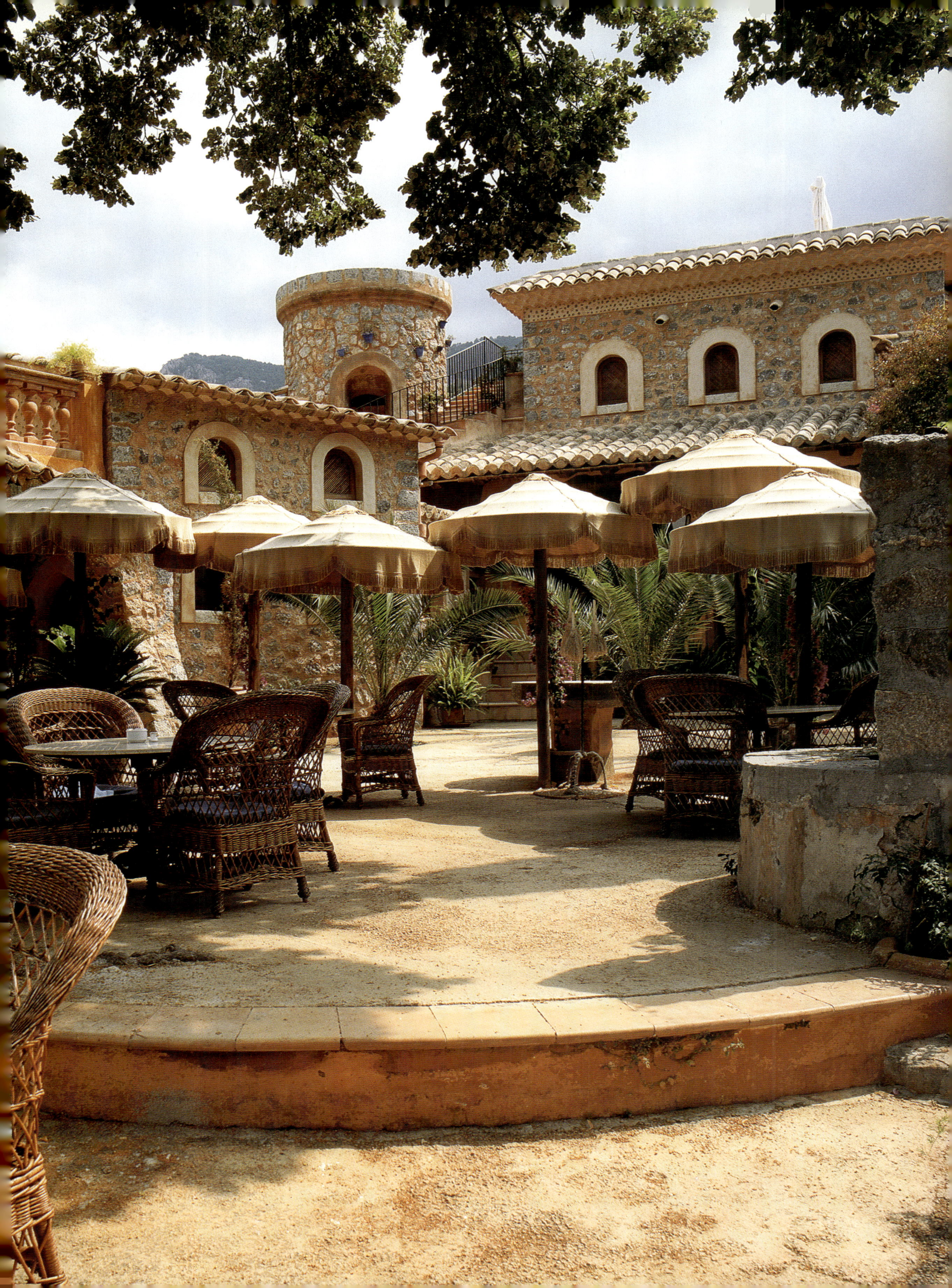

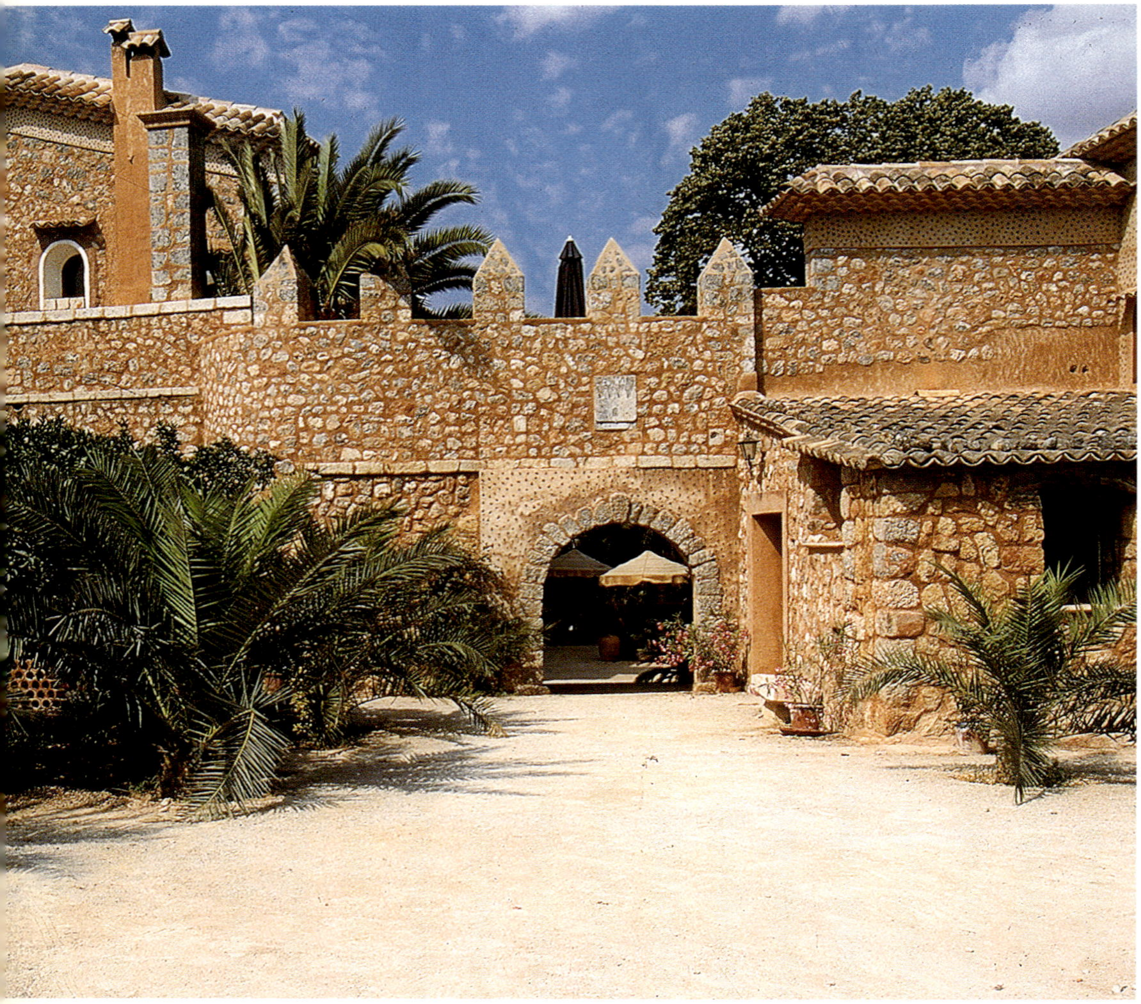

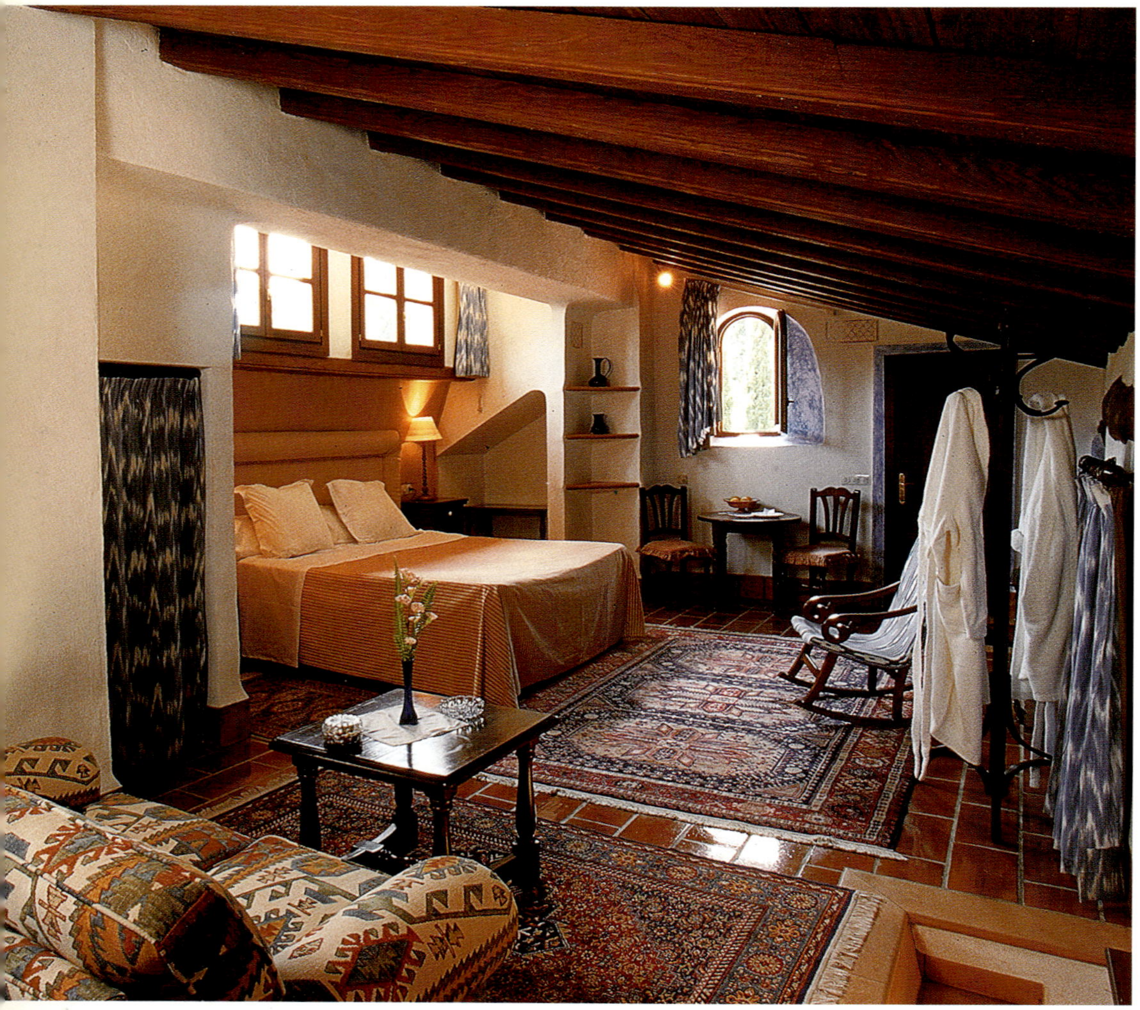

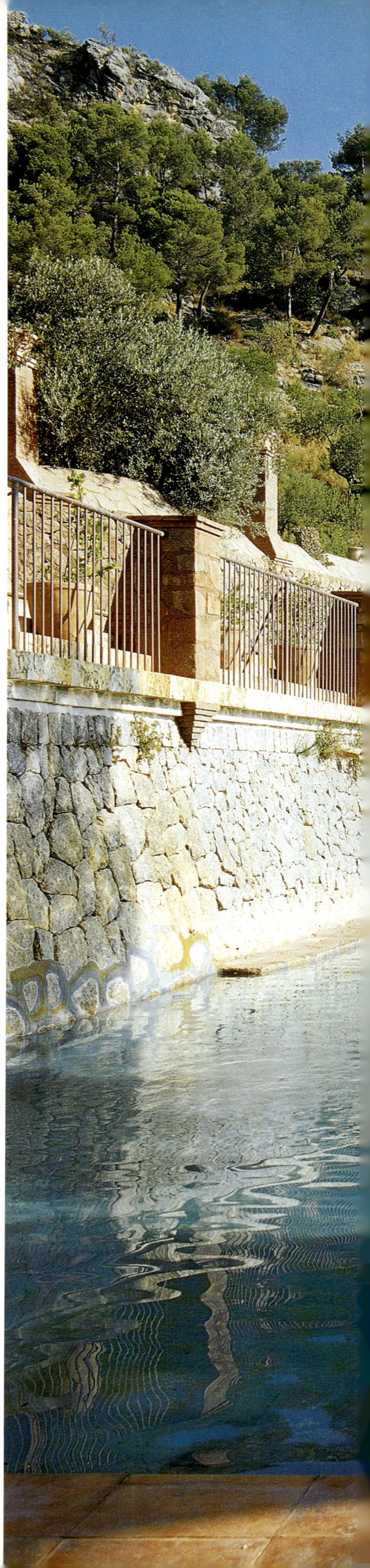

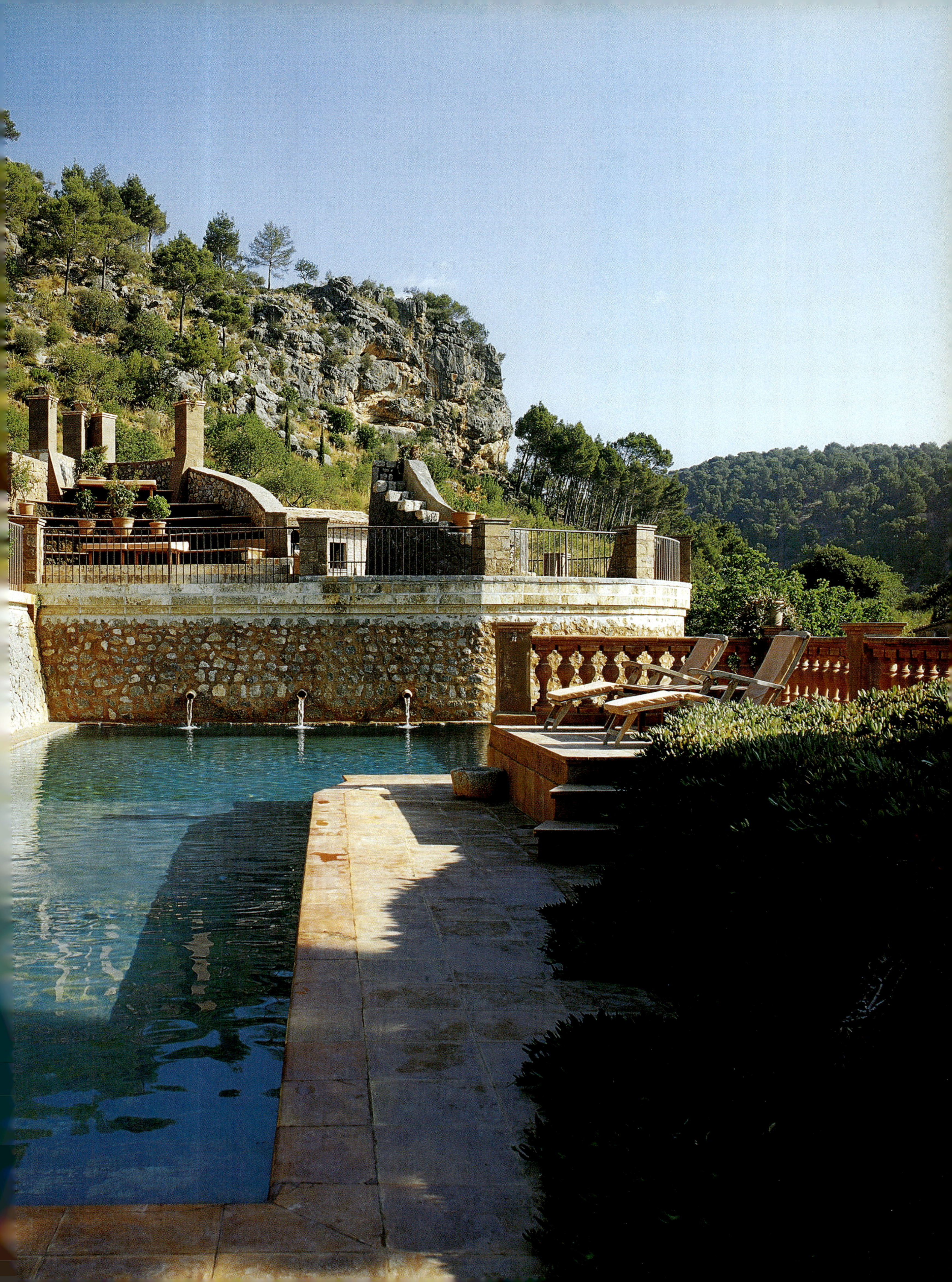

Parador de León

Where Parador 'Hostal de San Marcos' now stands, was the San Marcos Hospital, founded in the 12th century by the compassionate Doña Sancha who wanted to give homeless people shelter. Later, it became a refuge for pilgrims. Later still, it was the monks of Santiago who used it. The old medieval hospital was demolished at the beginning of the 16th century and room made for the edifice that is now the hotel. Some great names who contributed to the renovation over the years are Juan de Badajoz, Juan de Juni, Pedro de Ibarra and Guillermo Doncel.

From the 19th century onwards, the building was used for various purposes: it was a school, a hospital, a prison and soldiers' quarters; and in 1965, after extensive restoration, it became a Parador.

However, there are still traces of its religious past to be seen. Visitors can admire the beautiful church with its ornate sacristy, choir-stalls and cloisters. Here, ancient elements are stylishly combined with modern touches, and every possible kind of luxury provided without the building losing any of its original dignity.

Some highly recommended dishes here are the famous regional stews, frog's legs, veal and the famous sweetmeats. Moreover, the restaurant serves wonderful Bierzo peppers and beautifully cooked trout from the rivers around León. And do try the La Bañeza beans, combined with local meats. But leave some space for dessert, which will be hard to choose: flan from León with a crunchy round roll, the 'tocinillo de cielo' (a dessert made from egg yolks and sugar or syrup), chestnut pudding or the famous San Marcos cake, which is known all over the country. The restaurant provides for the most refined tastes, and will leave no pilgrim hungry.

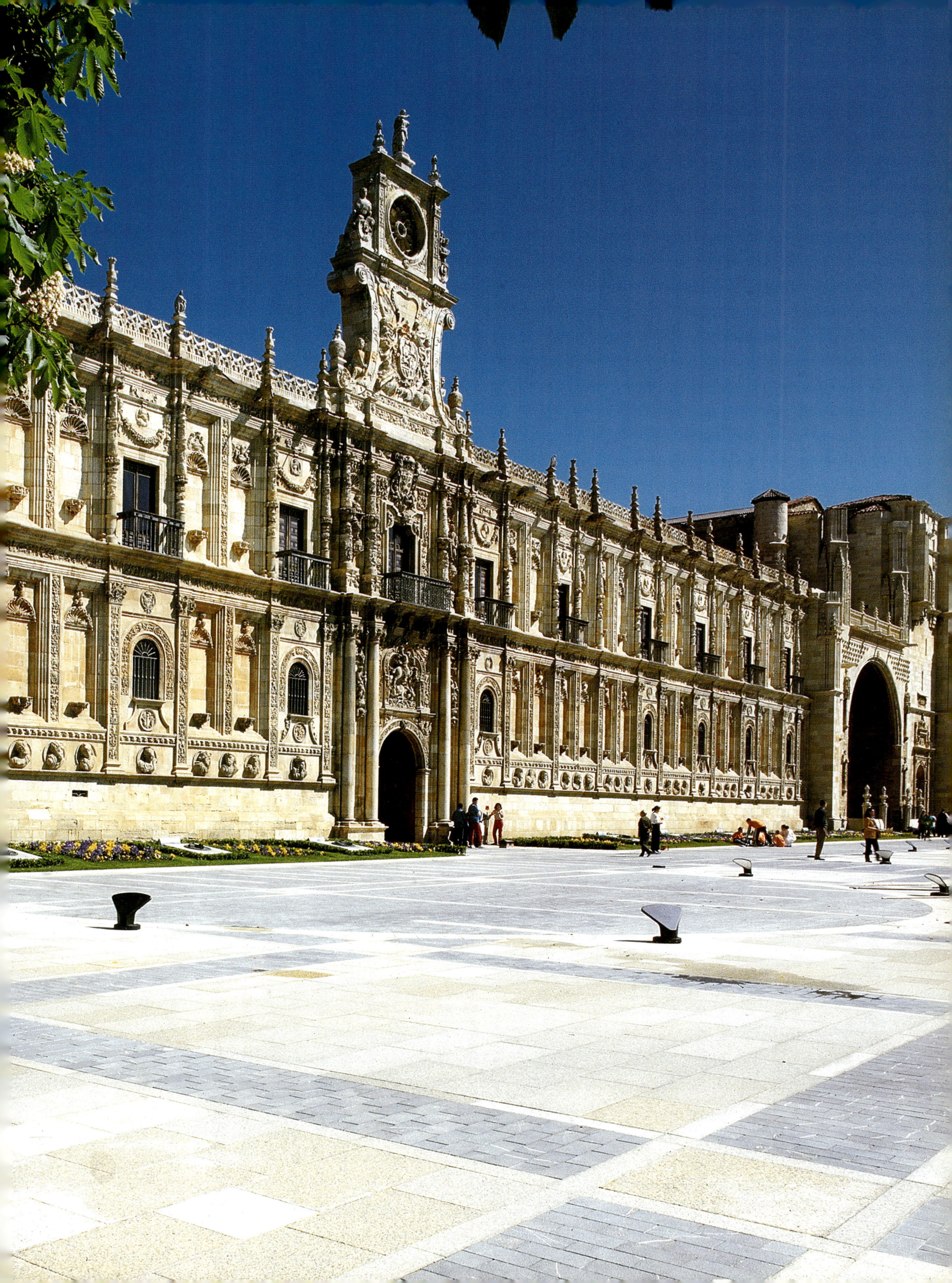

50

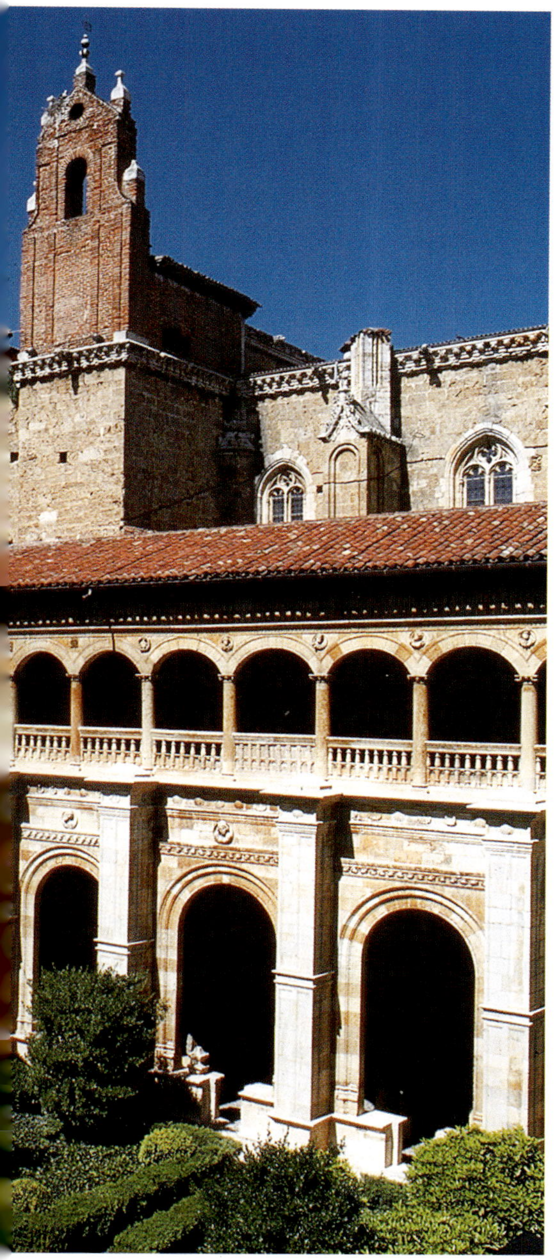
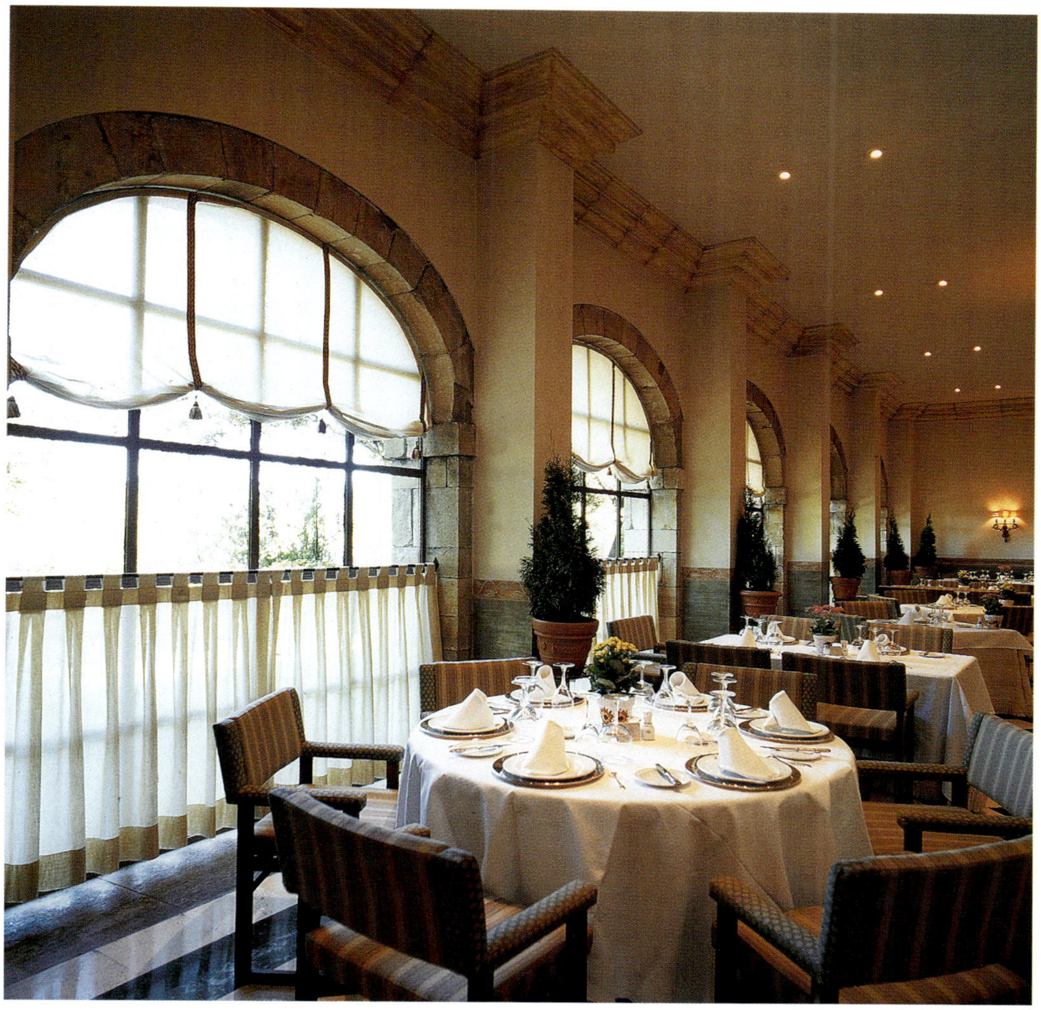
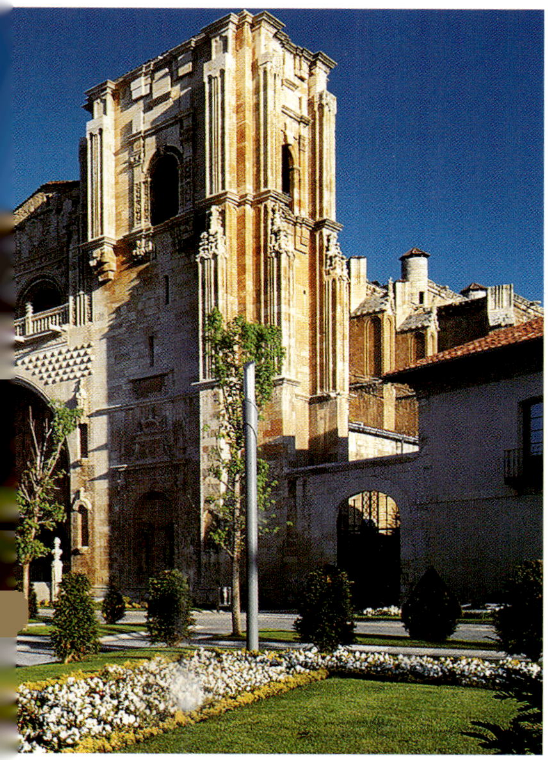
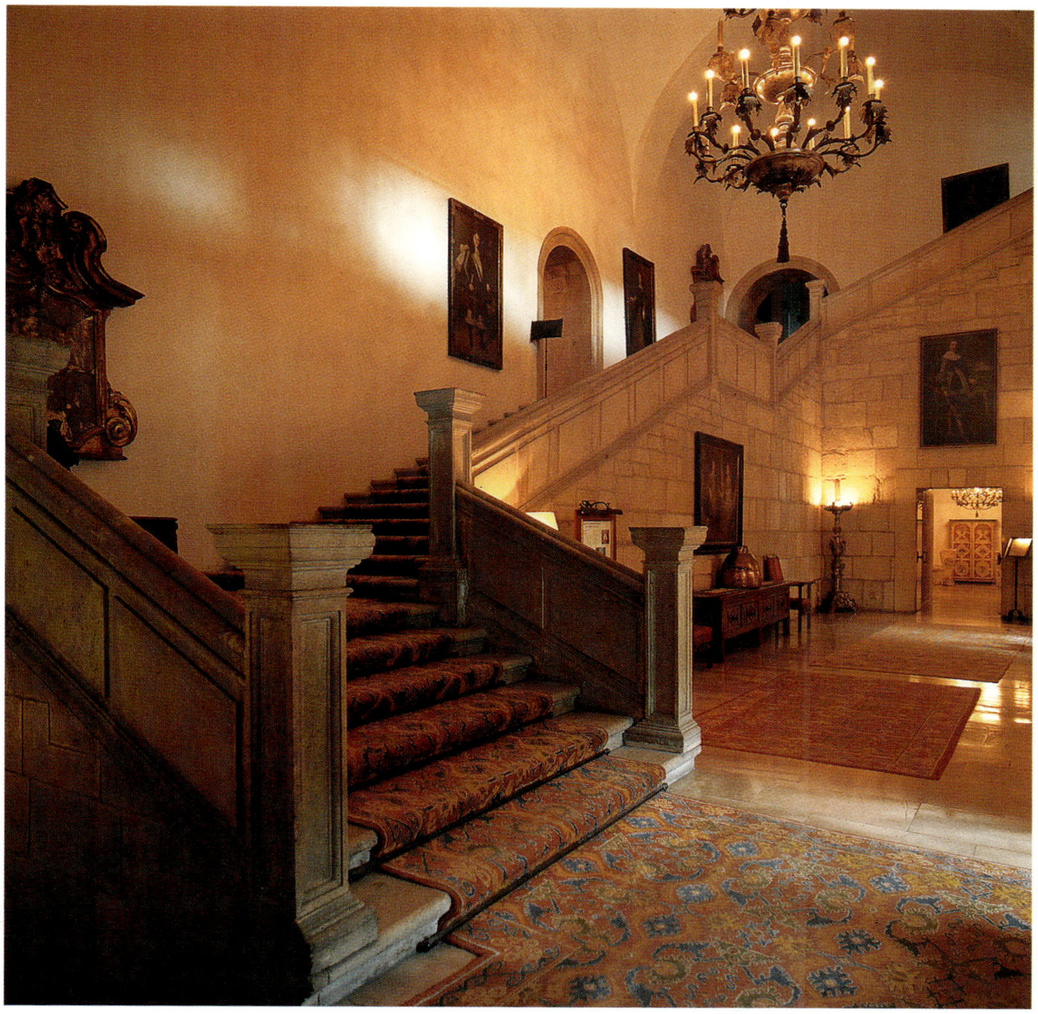

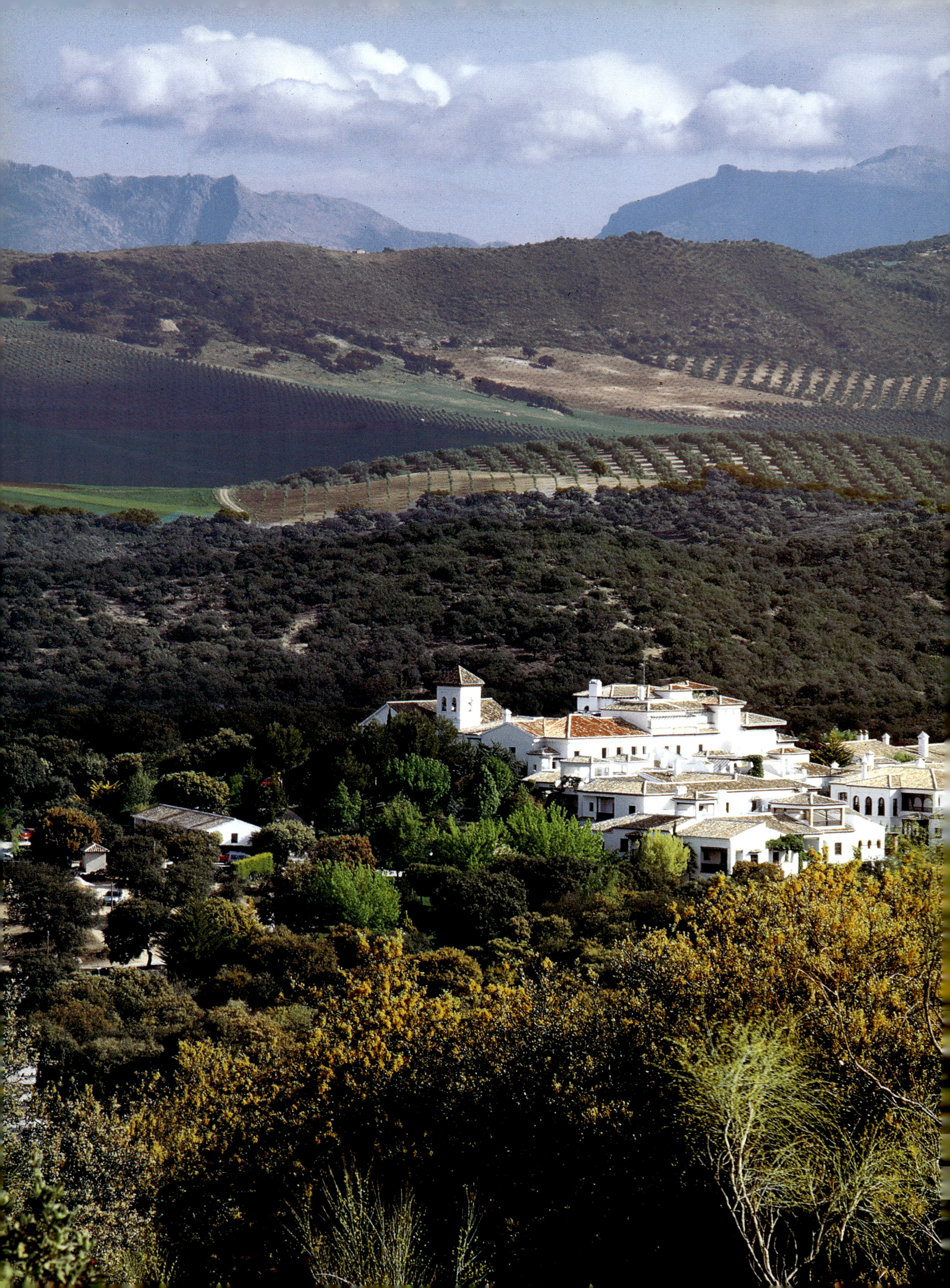

La Bobadilla

It was late spring, the air warm on my face, the distant peaks of the Sierra Nevada were snow-capped still. Before I could re-discover the romantic, cobbled streets of Granada, I had a special visit to make. I turned east into the setting sun and was soon in Loja, where I paused briefly at a café-bar and, along with my coffee, drank in the gorgeous views before completing my journey.

I was about to taste the very special charms of Hotel La Bobadilla, hidden from the stresses of modern life in wild countryside, thick with old, dark trees. A winding lane found its way downhill; ahead of me, looking more like a medieval Moorish village than a hotel, was La Bobadilla, all white walls and terracotta roofs. A clutch of elegant Andalusian horses, out of pure *joie de vivre*, galloped in a circle, throwing back their heads and sending up scuds of dust.

The entrance hall was grand and serene, pillars and arches dramatically lit, romantic candelabra set about on glistening floors… echoes of the alluring Grand Mosque at Cordoba, no less; an impression hard to live up to. But choose any suite at all, or any room - there are sixty in all - and the sense of grandeur and luxury is cleverly sustained. Each of them is different; some catch the morning light, others the soft gold shafts of evening, but all of them are designed with impeccable taste, providing every luxury you'd expect to find at a five-star hotel. Pieces of sculpture are set in niches, original art hangs on the walls, bowls of fresh flowers stand on antique tables.

My own suite boasted a fine, heavily-draped four-poster and a magnificent deep bath-tub… but I wanted to go exploring, first around the interior and then, as the evening sun touched on the hills, into the estate beyond, with its wandering pathways, two tempting swimming-pools, and the wilderness so close by that I turned a corner and caught sight of a deer making off into the undergrowth.

I sought out the bar and, sipping a cocktail, contemplated the evening's menu. There are two restaurants - La Finca, which serves a widely-celebrated *haute cuisine*, and El Cortijo, the one to choose for traditional Spanish dishes, deliciously prepared.

Next morning, bright and early, I consumed a buffet breakfast much larger than I should have, before bidding adieu to a memorable and very friendly hotel. As my car climbed slowly out of the cool valley that cups La Bobadilla, the same white horses that greeted me, were lined up placidly, as if to say goodbye, their long tails gracefully fanned by the morning breeze.

54

55

Casa Imperial

When you're travelling back into history, walking centuries-old cobbled streets, standing in the grandeur of shadowed cathedral precincts and stepping into museums full of timeless artefacts, there is something very appropriate and satisfying about staying in an hotel as old and steeped in the past as anything else around you. So it is with the Hotel Casa Imperial, in Seville. Its is a building so replete with Moorish influences - arched cloisters, serried columns, galleried verandahs full of deep poetic shadows, cool courtyards with formal walks and a central tiled fountain - that one might at any moment expect to come across a black-bearded vizier in curled slippers seated in furrowed contemplation on a stone bench.

The five-star Casa Imperial is perfectly situated in the very heart of Seville's old quarter. You could hardly find yourself more conveniently placed. It was, probably, though I neglected to enquire, the palatial residence of a Spanish nobleman, a grandee in a well-trimmed goatee beard making deals with plump merchants offering exotic goods arrived from the New World. Just across the street is the celebrated Casa Pilatos, ancient palace of Alfonso Villafranca.

Today one is more likely to hear the distant and muted sounds of traffic than the clip-clop of mules, but history lives bright as the morning in the streets all about the Casa Imperial. This kind of building is most likely still to be in private hands, so the guest is fortunate to have the opportunity to actually reside within its walls, sit in the pleasant and tranquil shade of a tree in the courtyard, and dine magnificently as the sun sets, in very much the same manner as those who lived here over the centuries.

The 24 rooms and 14 suites are superbly appointed to the most exacting standards, and extremely comfortable, with very individual furnishings, exquisite *azulejo* tiles, and distinctive bathrooms. Some have romantic roof terraces. Altogether, a most fascinating hotel with a magical atmosphere.

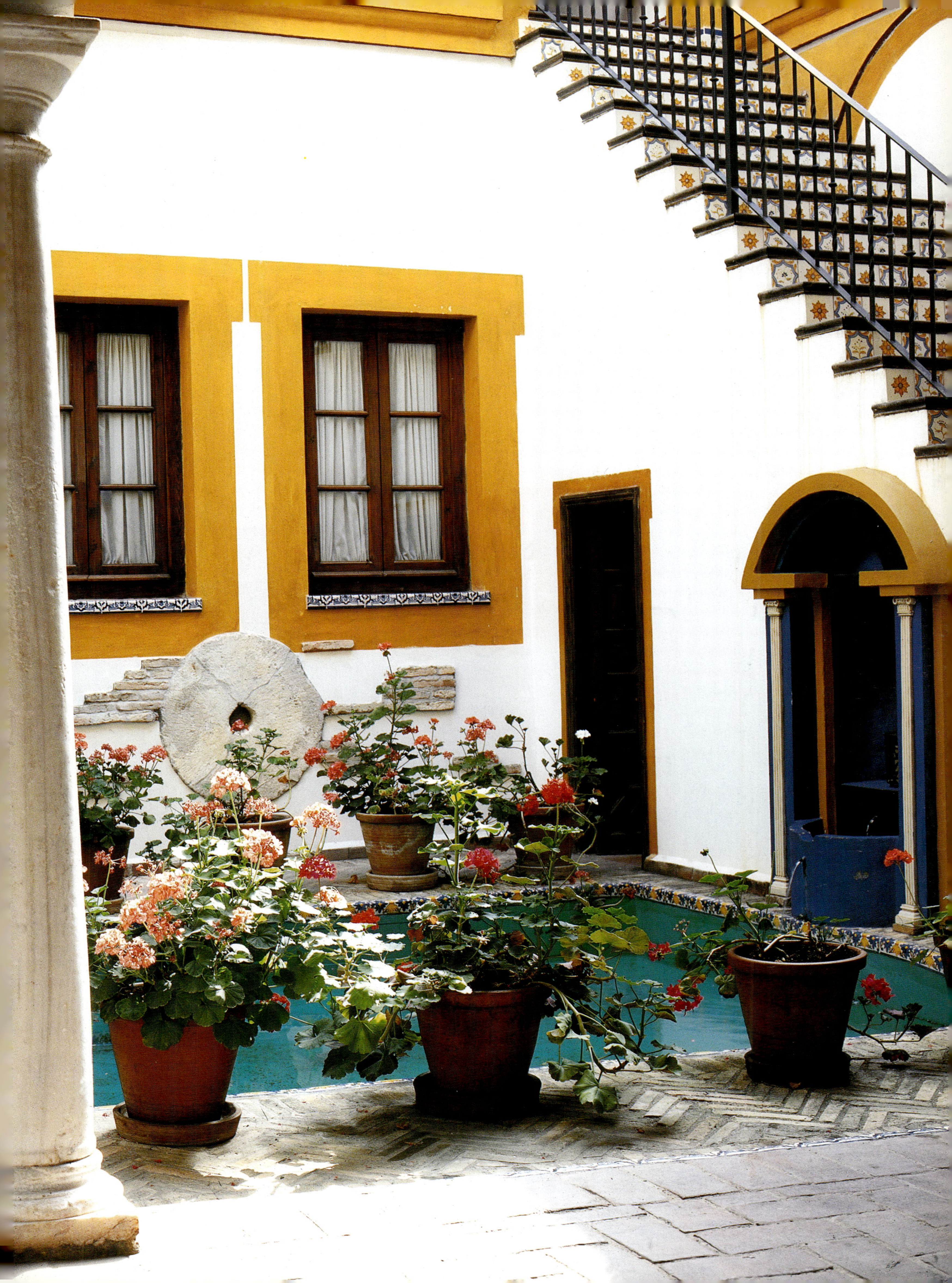

58

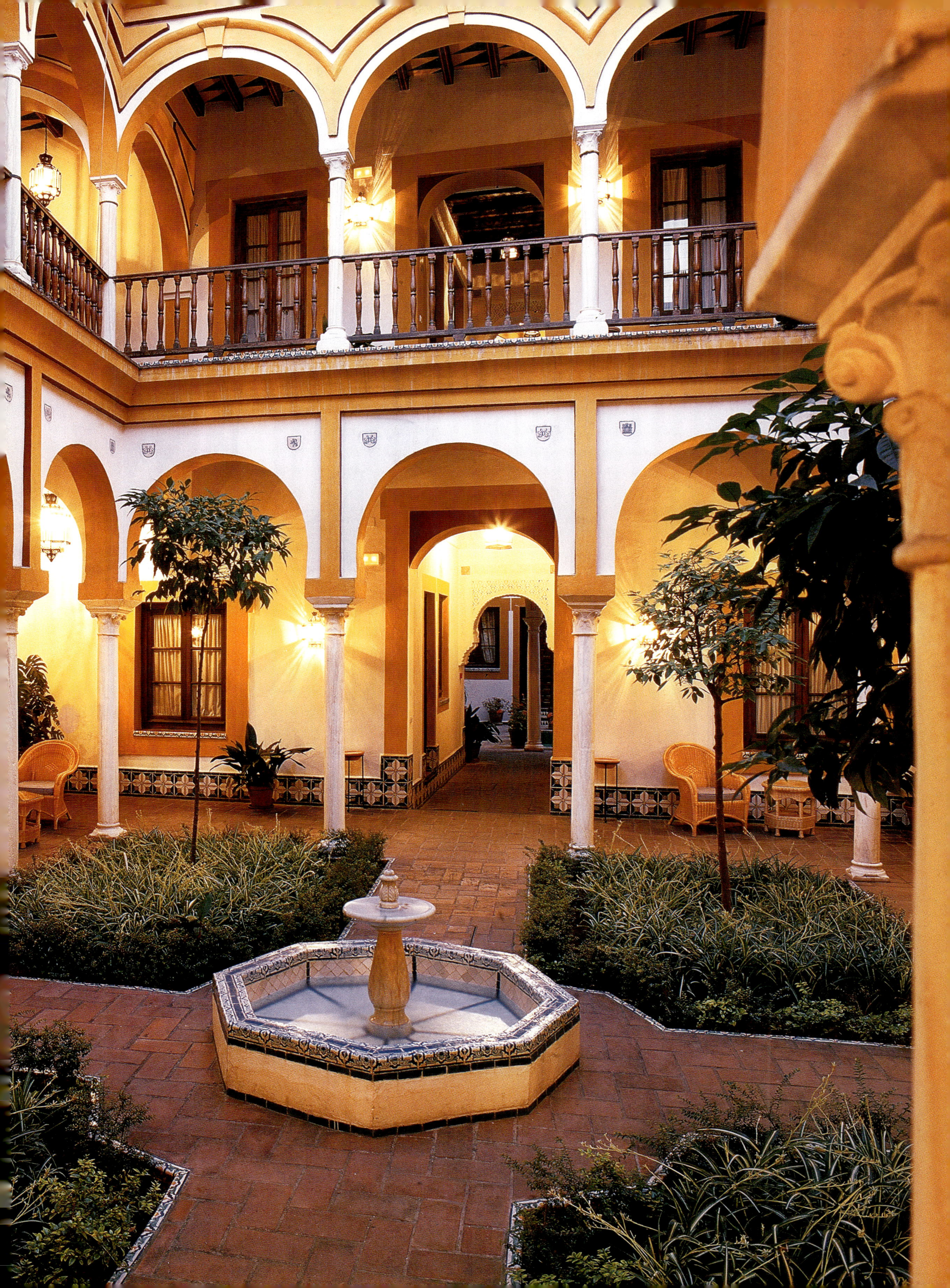

60

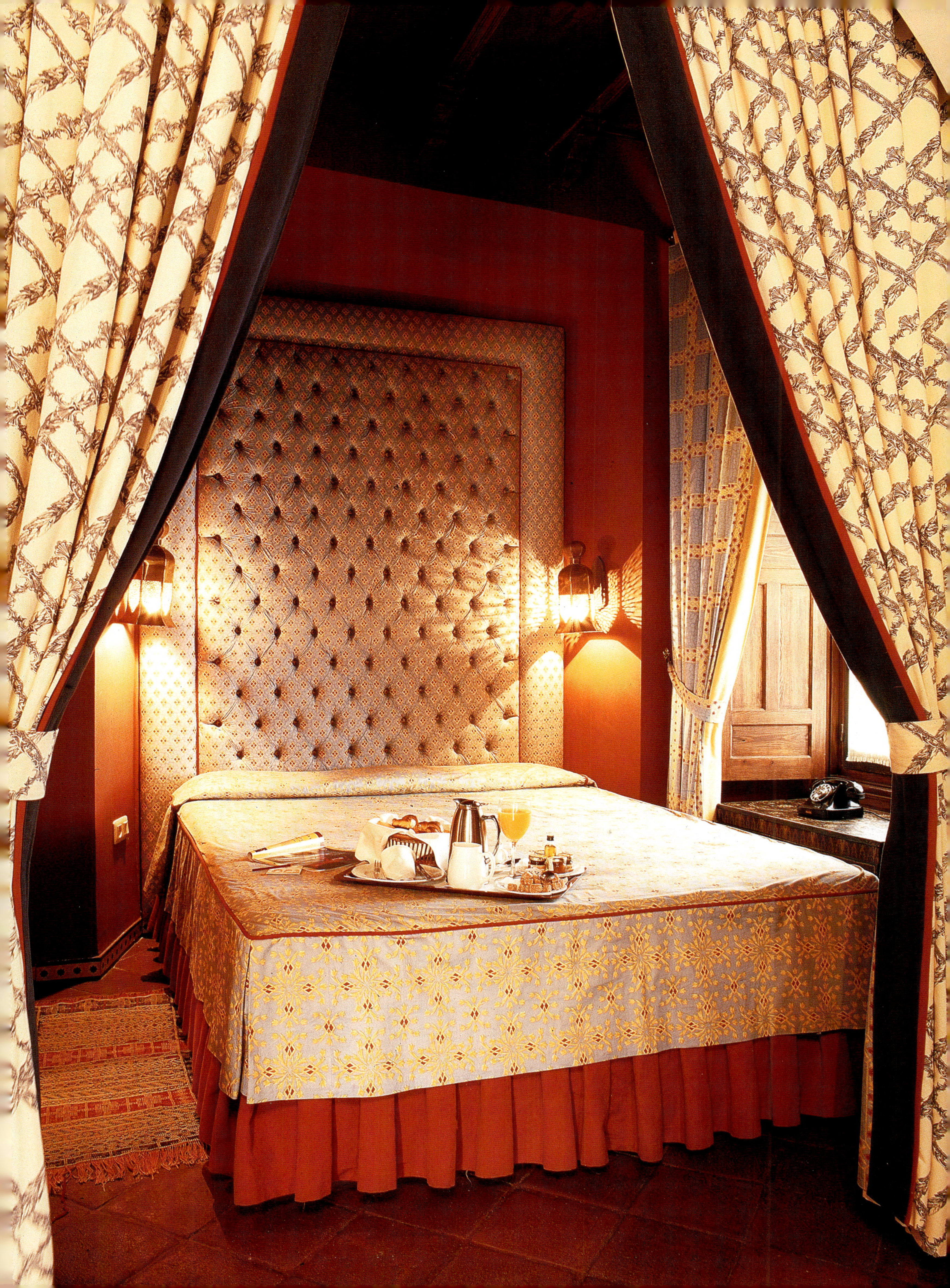

Hacienda Na Xamena

Back in the sixties, Ibiza was a quiet and contented rural island, a get-away-from-it-all paradise, visited by only one ship a week, popular with poets and artists, who lived their dreams on a shoestring in little beachside cottages, sharing their simple daily lives with the local fishermen, drinking with them in the bars, often becoming their friends and visiting them in their rustic homes.

It is all so different now. But, back then, a Belgian architect, Daniel Lipszyc, and his wife fell in love with the true and natural Ibiza, and bought some land up in the thickly-wooded north-eastern corner of the island, right on the cliffs, the wildest and most inaccessible area of all.

And here it was, in true pioneer style, that they set about fulfilling their dream of creating a lovely hideaway, where David could give free rein to his architectural fancy. In the early days, donkeys hauled in essentials on their sturdy backs. Roads had to be built, services installed, a whole infrastructure set up.

Daniel gave himself a particular brief: to interfere with the beauties of nature as little as he could. Everything was done to create harmony between the unspoiled countryside and the necessary man-made structures. Patios, arches, galleries - all painted dazzlingly white - were designed with an organic look that is very satisfying and full of charm.

The hotel opened its doors in 1971 and has gone from strength to strength, without ever compromising those early principles. Today, any guide book will tell you the Hacienda na Xamena is Ibiza's top hotel - the only five-star establishment on the island. They speak of its discreet and exclusive luxury, fine service and magnificent views.

Every room has a private balcony and a sea view - which is nothing less than extraordinary in the early evening, as the orange sun settles on the horizon and sets the far, glittering waves alight. Some rooms even have a jacuzzi outdoors: you can relax grandly in the bubbles, and will feel for all the world as if you own that gorgeous sunset.

There are no less than three swimming-pools, one indoors and heated, for those rare cooler days. There's a sauna, a massage and hydro-therapy suite, tennis courts, and several boutiqes. The youthful and energetic can hire a mountain-bike and go exploring through the pine forest, and there are organised hikes into the wilderness, in search of unusual flora and fauna.

For the guest who takes his eating seriously, the Hacienda has a choice of three restaurants: the Arabic-inspired El Sueño de Estrellas, romantic and refined; Las Cascadas, which offers a typically Mediterranean cuisine, with plenty of fresh fish and seafood, and the outdoor Grill Deck, just the place for lunch… choose yourself a lobster from the vivarium and they will prepare it while you sit in the sun with a drink, enjoying views across the spray-flecked ocean spread out below you.

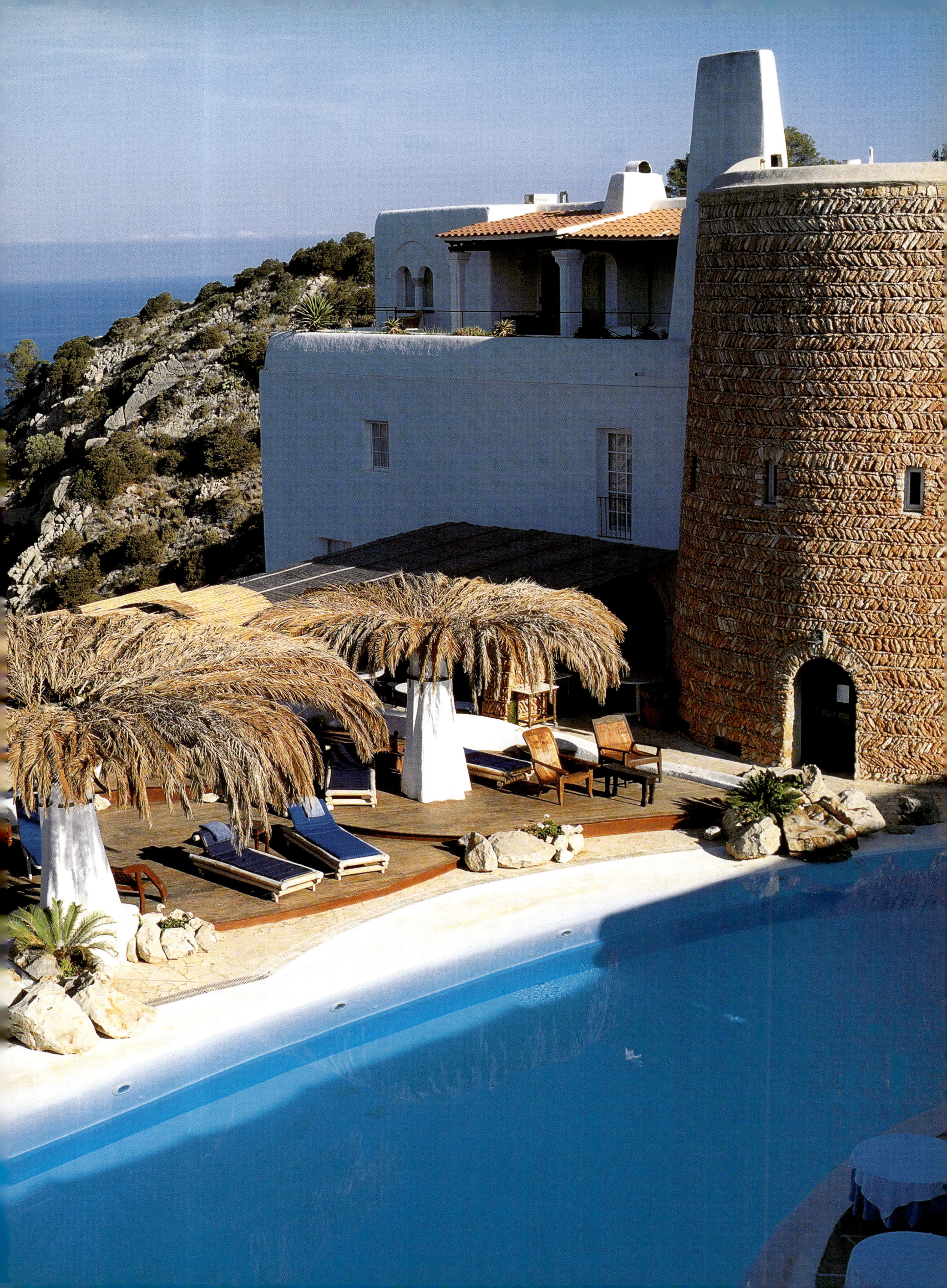

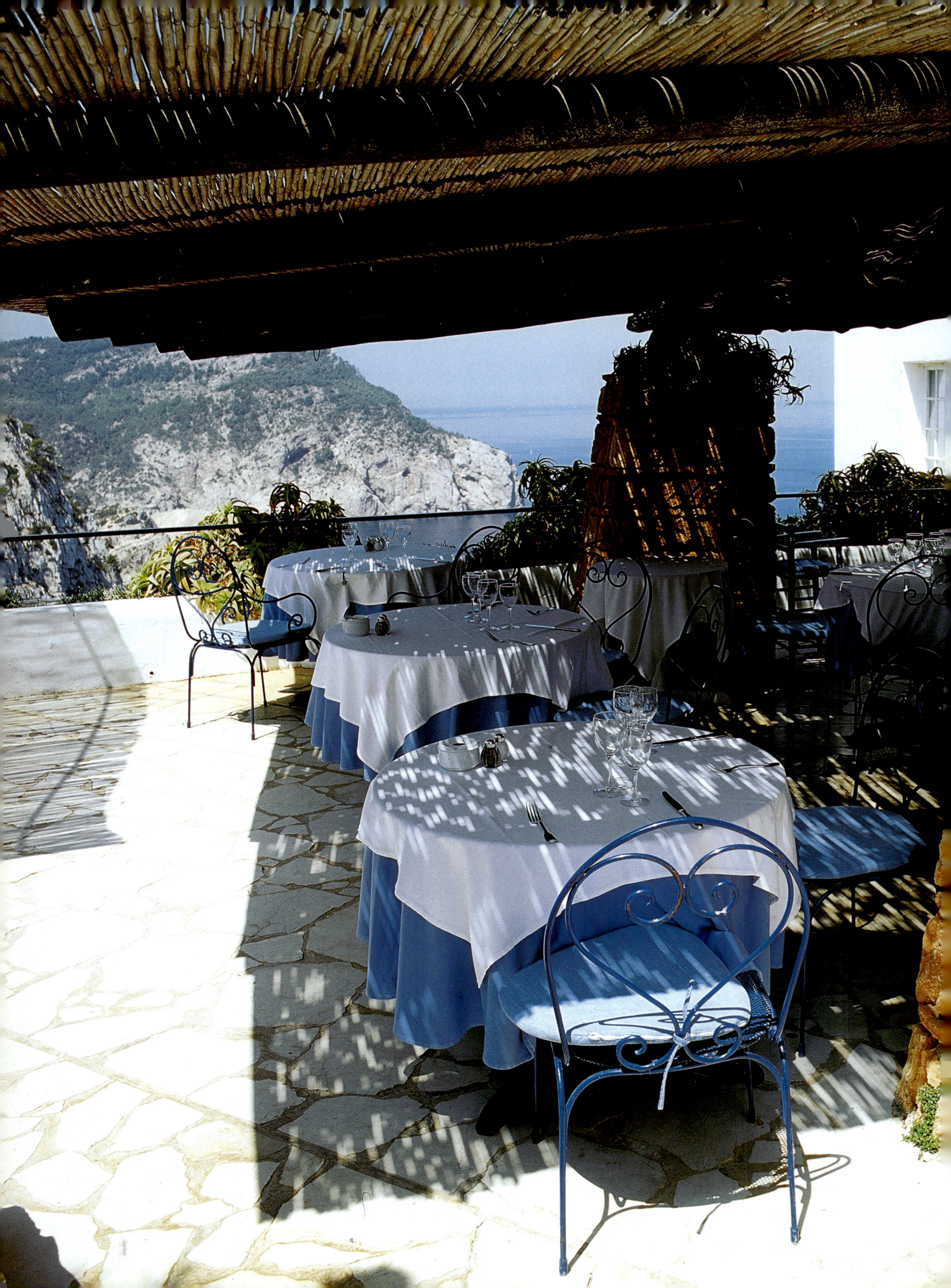

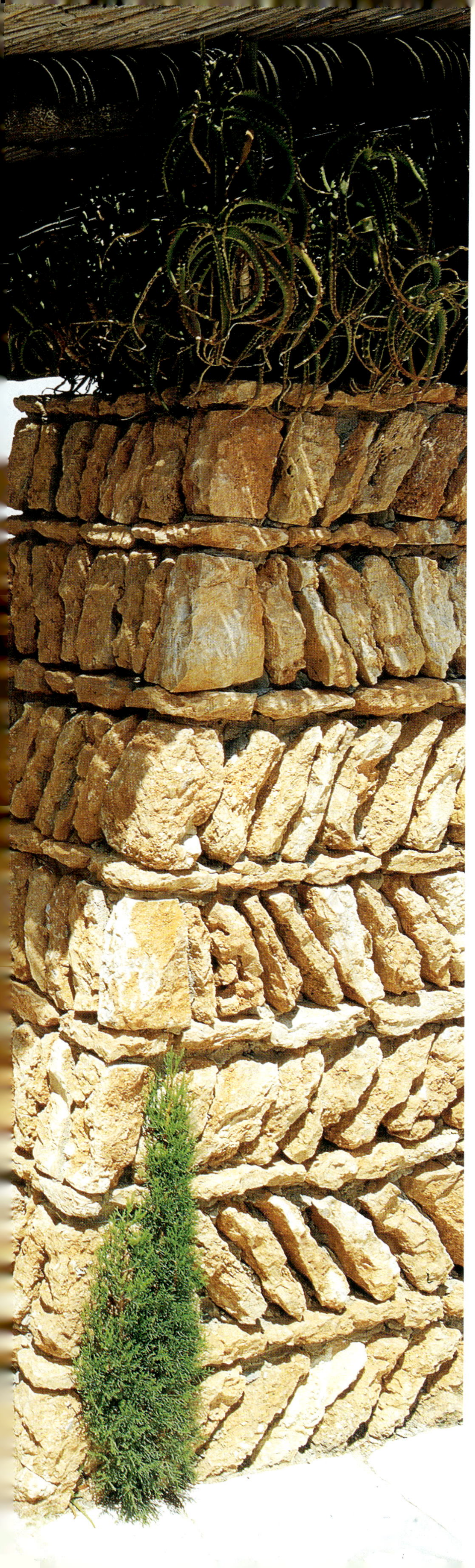
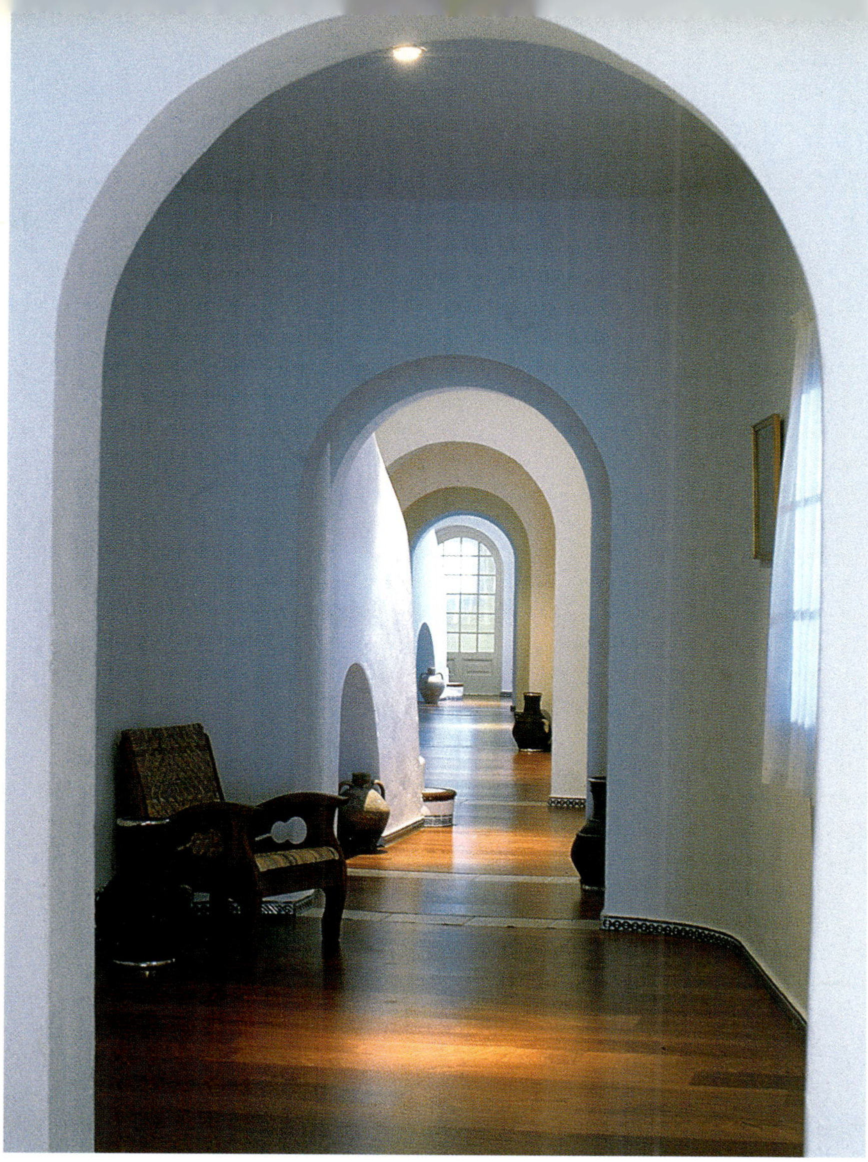
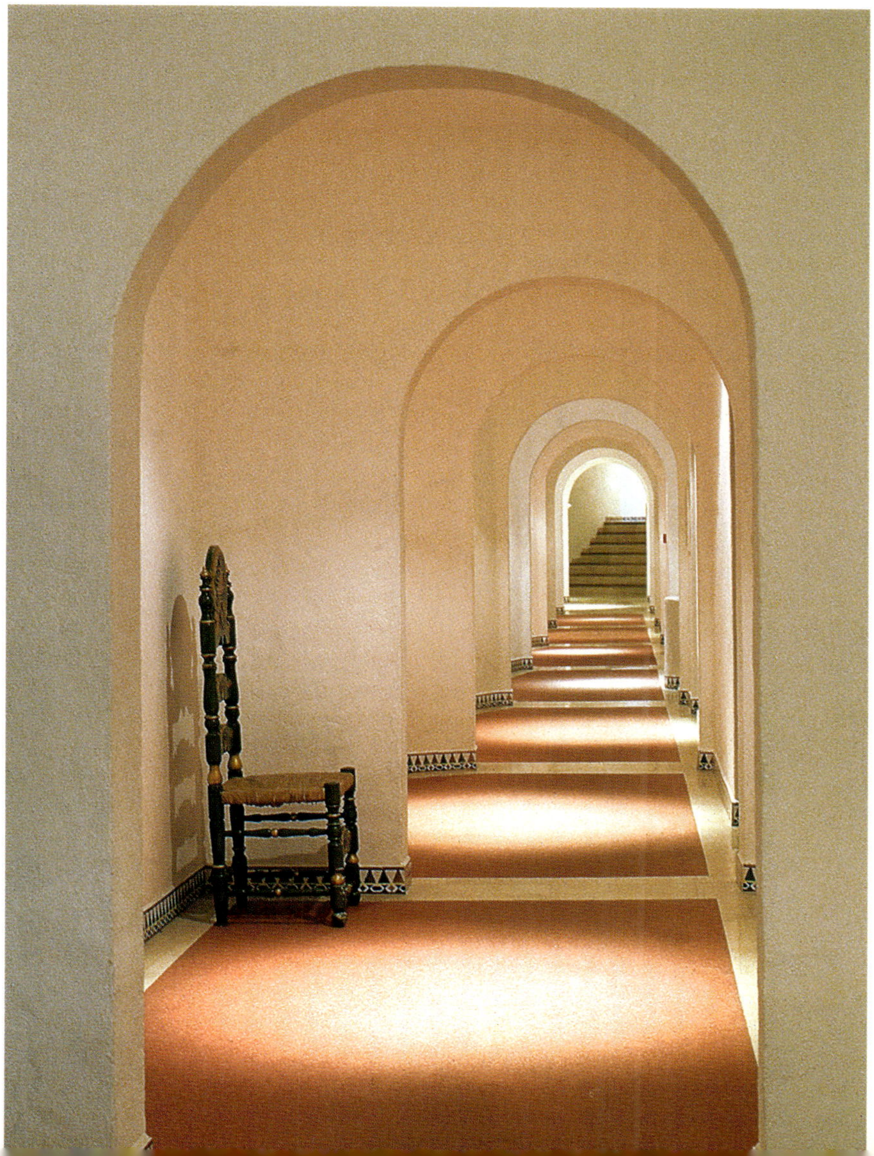

This hotel was created by Belgian architect Daniël Lipszyc; to this day, it has remained totally unique in Ibiza.

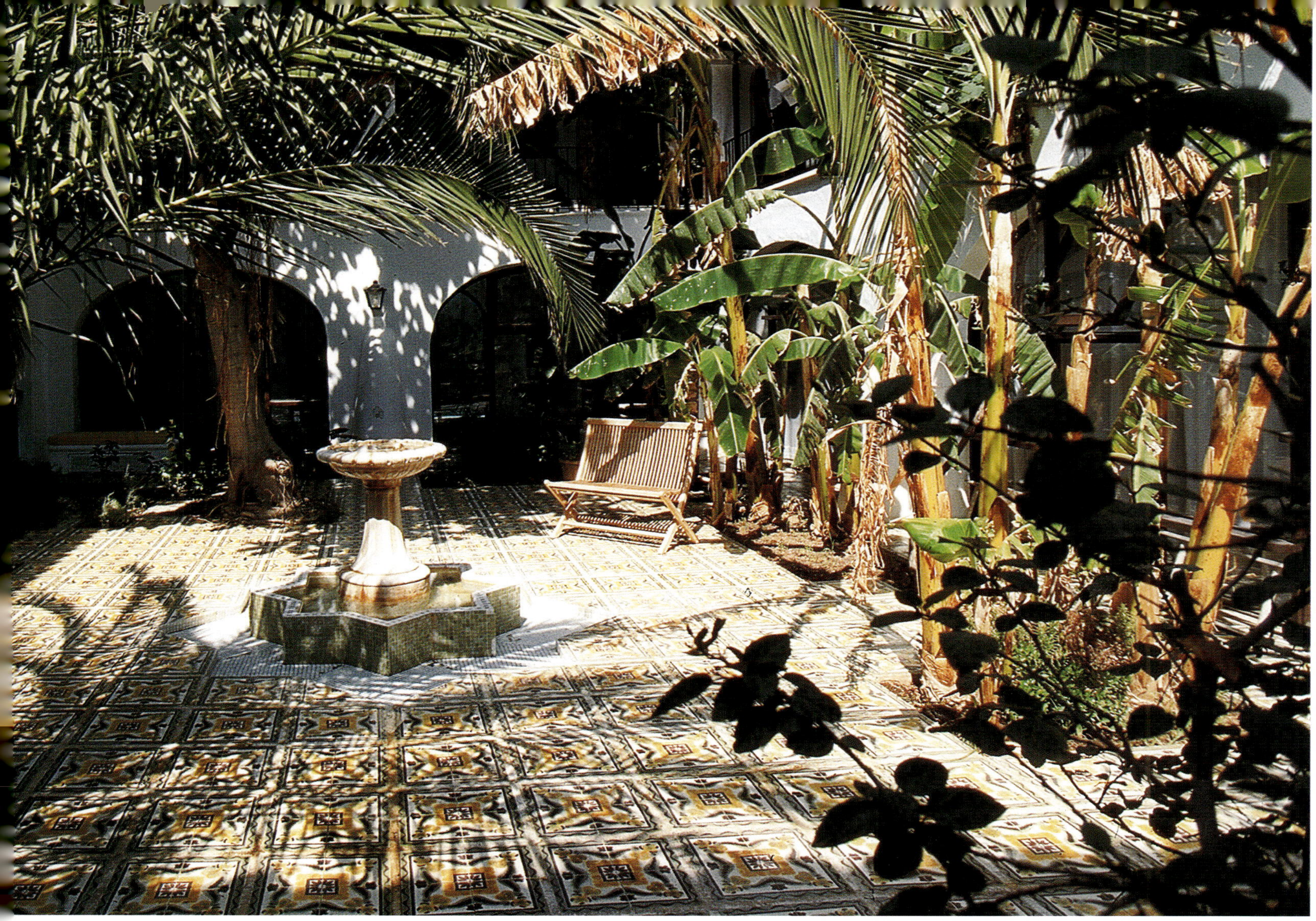

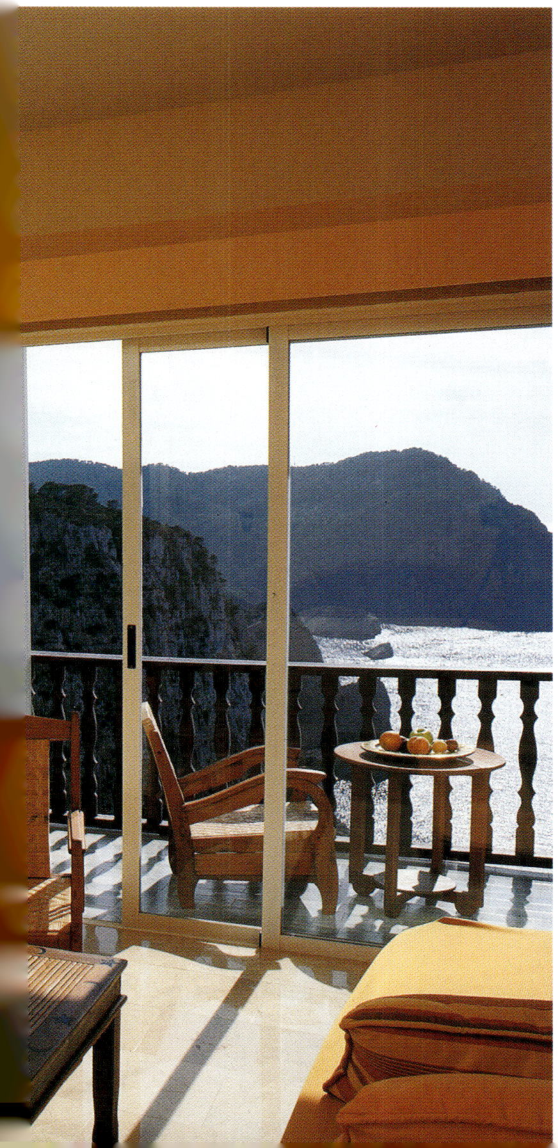

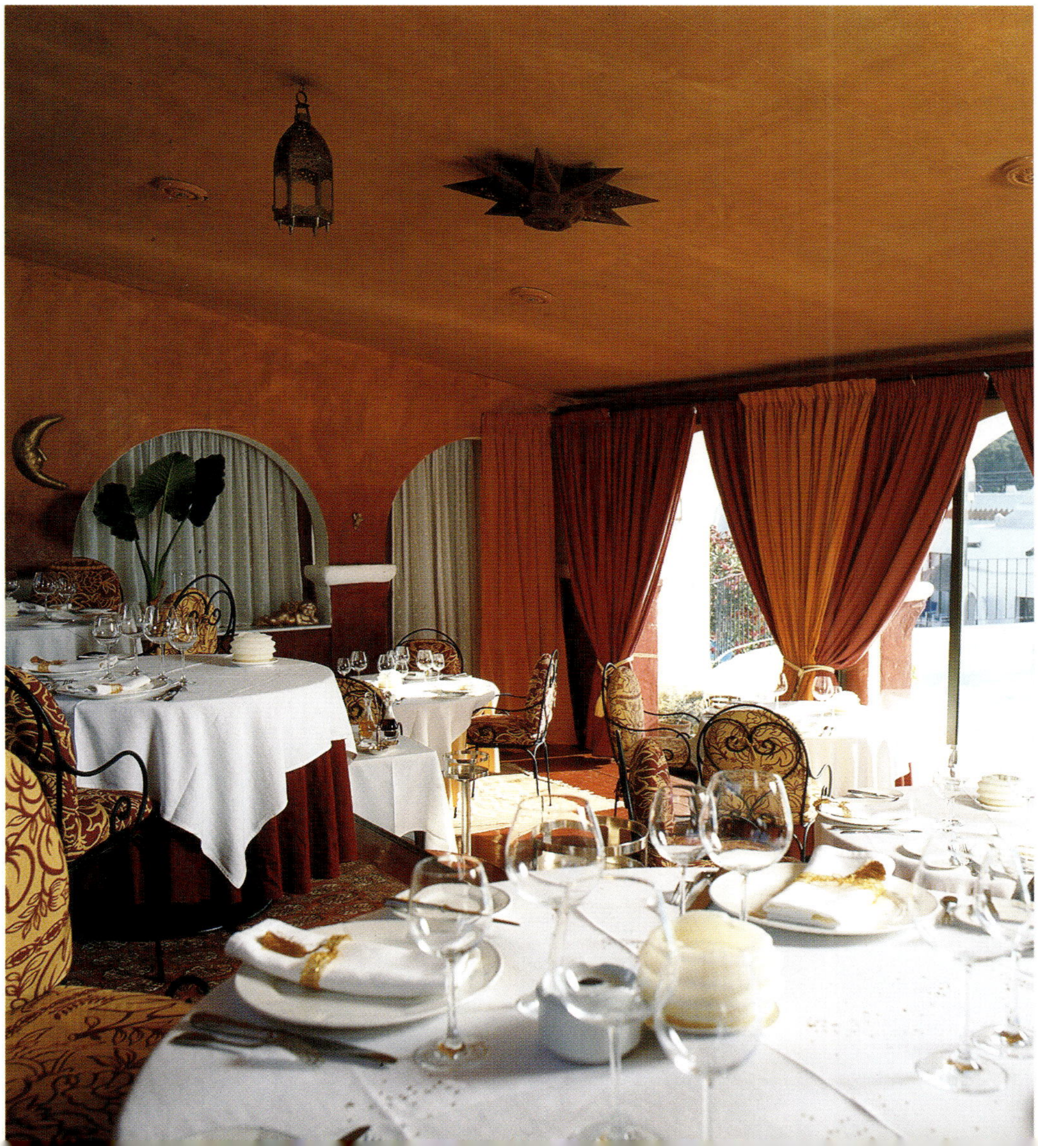

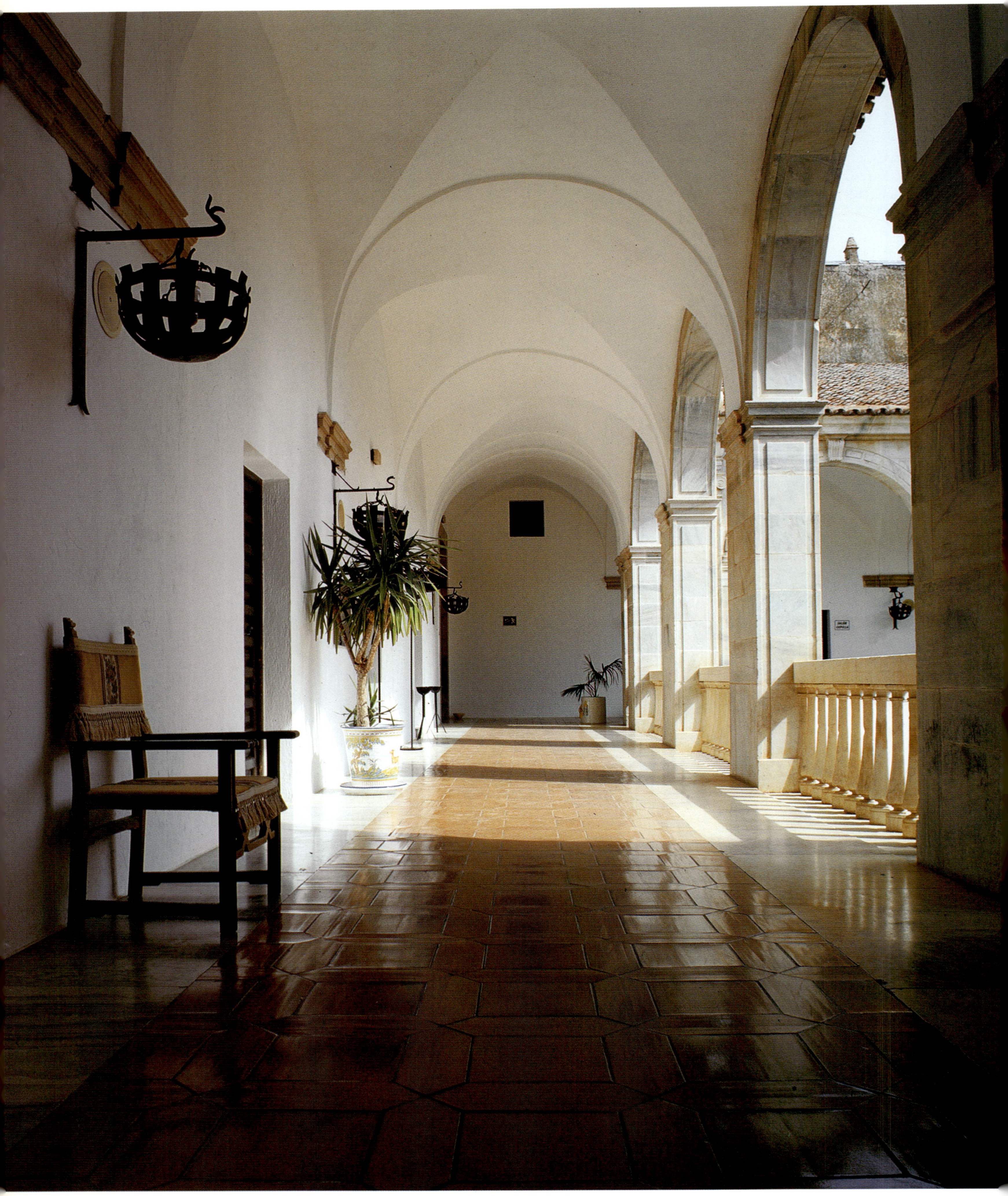

Parador de Zafra

This stylish castle with its wonderful furnishings can be found in the beautiful town of Zafra, well-known for its many white-washed buildings.

In 1437, Fernando III drove the Arabs out of their fortifications here, and D. Lorenzo Suárez immediately started building a new castle on top of the ruins of the old Islamic fort.

The castle became the residence of the Dukes of Feria and, in turn, many other grandees from the annals of Spanish history. From the start, the owners spent a great deal of time and money embellishing the castle, and the most expensive of materials were used. Prime examples of their penchant for elegance and luxury are the Guilded Bedroom with its impressive ceiling - an amazing 'sky' was sculpted from wood - and the sculpted and painted dome of the chapel.

Juan de Herrara, who also renovated the monastery at El Escoral, oversaw some early restoration and improvements of the castle. He divided the central courtyard into two galleries, each with three arches, and, as in the Renaissance, clad the whole in white marble. The result is a patio of wondrous beauty, which diffuses the light in a wonderful manner.

Outside, there are eight impressive towers and at the rear of the castle stands the robust Torre del Homaneje, a harmonious construction of slate and brick. A gigantic coat-of-arms takes pride of place on the spectacular façade. Inside, there is a monumental staircase, the very one Cortés descended immediately before he left on his epic voyage to Mexico.

The large, stunningly white dining room is the perfect environment to enjoy the wonderful delights of the regional cuisine. Many of the dishes are based on pork, but there is endless choice for everyone: lamb stew, Iberean pork with Ibores cheese and a speciality: 'fried breadcrumbs' from Extremadura. For dessert, 'rapapálos' with milk and cinnamon or the hotel's own patisserie. The exclusive wine list is equally tempting…

From the hotel, which can be found in the historic centre of Zafra, you can walk through the streets, where Muslims and Christians managed to live in perfect harmony, even after the Reconquista. The mixed culture which results from this, has left its traces in the old city centre, and attracts many lovers of art and antiquities. An altar piece by Zurbarán and a chapel devoted to Churriguera are precious examples of monuments you should seek out.

The surroundings are scattered with little villages, all worth a visit: rural Salvatierra de los Barros, walled Jerez de los Caballeros with its beautiful castle and rich past, and Almendralejo, birth place of poet Espronceda. After a day exploring this stunning area, the Parador in Zafra is a welcoming home from home to return to, as evening falls.

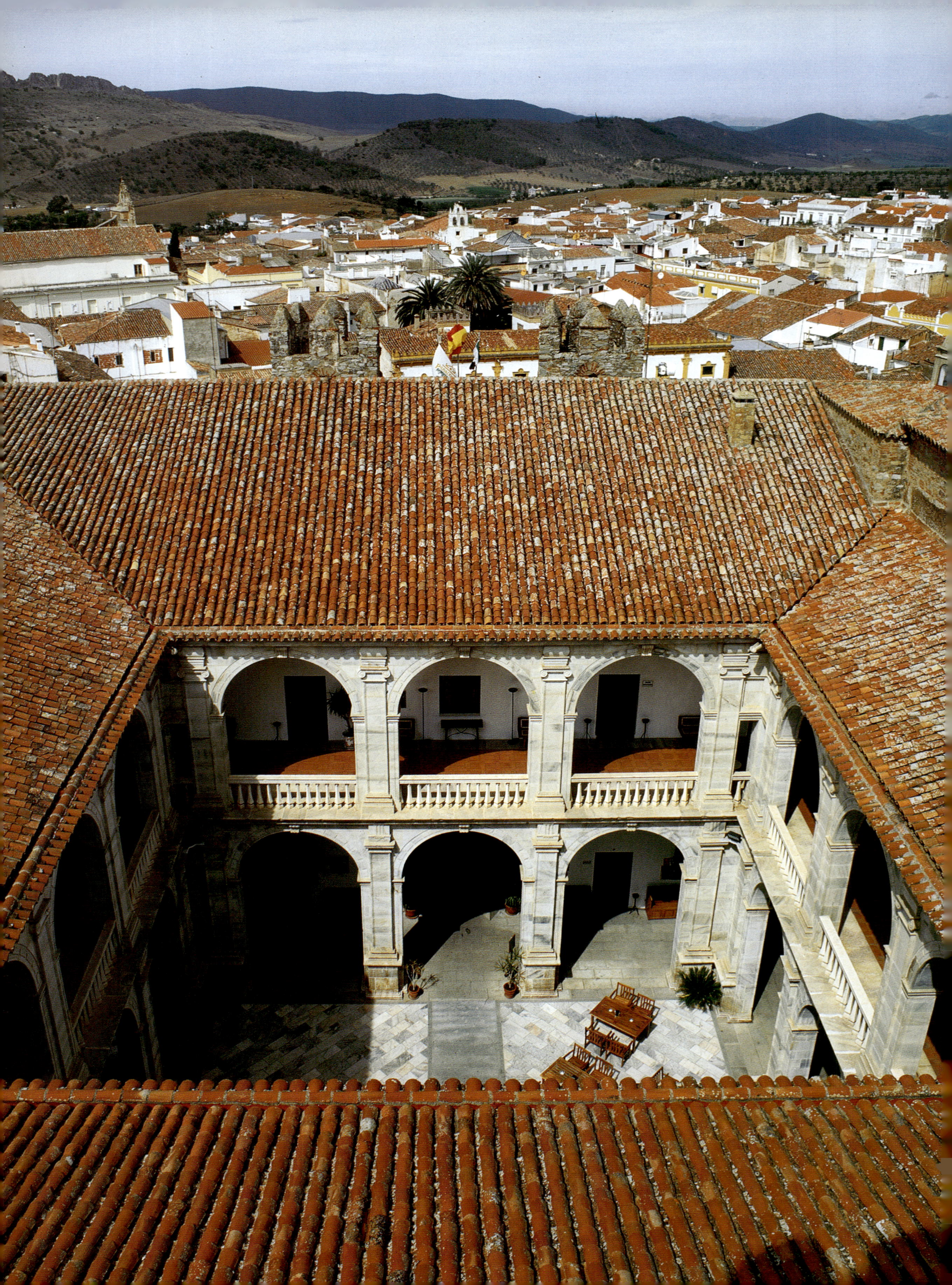

71

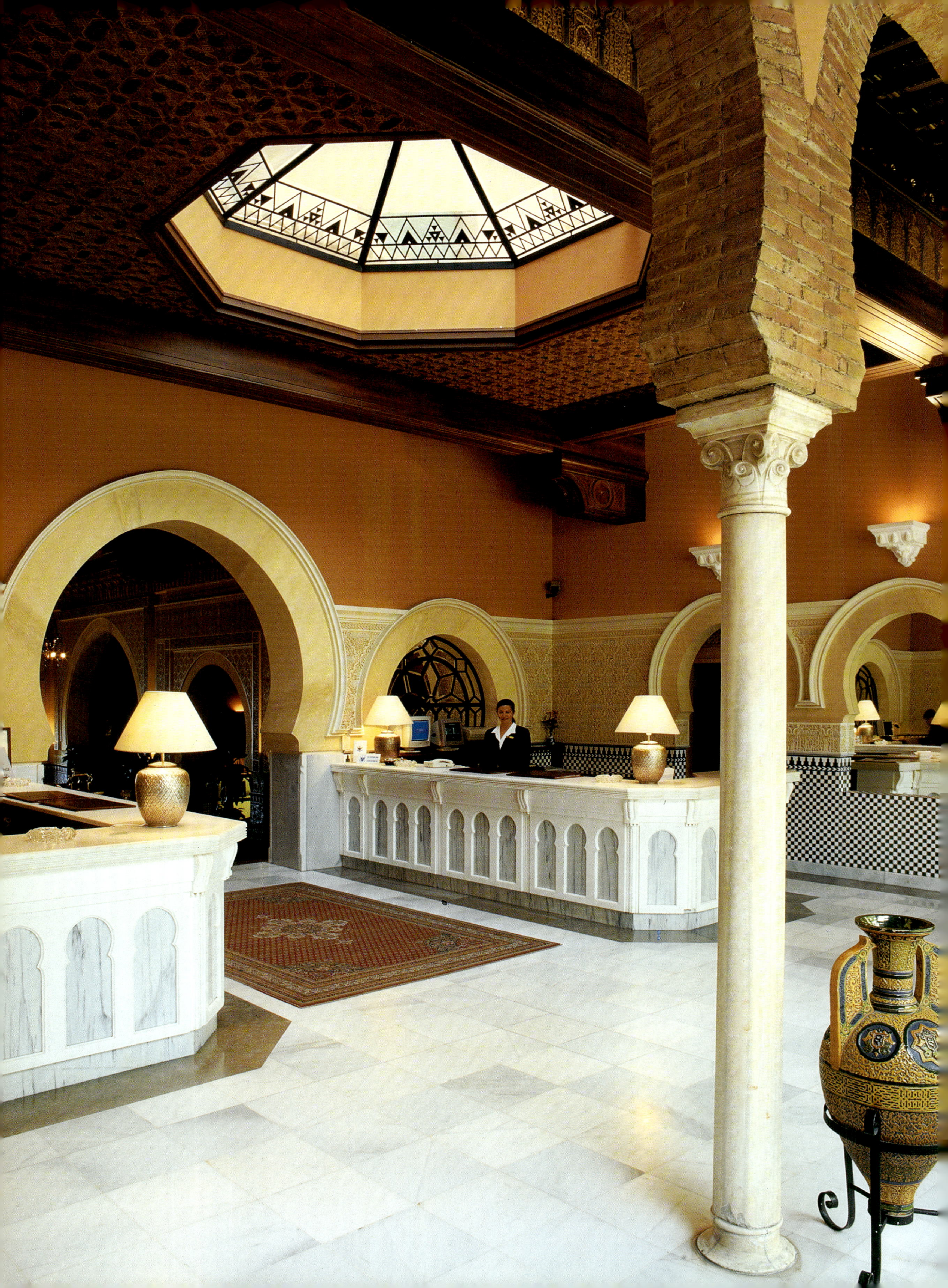

Alhambra Palace

Mention Paris, and the Eiffel Tower springs instantly to mind, New York, it would be the Statue of Liberty. Every great city has its famous signature. So it is with Granada.

Jutting into its very heart is a great rock promontory, red in colour, and poised upon it, like a dream almost, is the ineffable Alhambra, the fabulous palace of the Moors, ringed by almost two miles of walls and adorned with no less than 30 defensive towers.

Inside was a privileged world of heated rooms, elegant columns reflected in still pools, slim cypresses, burbling streams, little shady enclosed gardens, one after another, made for contemplation, sweet poetry and high romance; majestic groves of orange trees, too, where emirs and sultans, emperors even, might stroll at ease.

It predates another great Islamic edifice, the Taj Mahal in India, and it's said that Shah Jahan took a few ideas for himself from the Alhambra.

An easy stroll from this elegant and mighty fortress is a hotel, itself of considerable eminence. The Alhambra Palace Hotel was, indeed, as its name suggests, a palace once, and still today the names of kings and nobles can be found in the visitors' book.

Pause before it, and look up… All its original grandeur remains intact. A castellated tower stands guard one side of the façade, an ancient and pretty balcony softens the solid castle-like walls that rise up, tall and patriarchal, towards blue skies.

Back in 1910, the palace was first made into a hotel of grandeur and beauty. Artisans of reknown were called in from Seville and from Cordoba to assist in the extensive renovations. The building, the architects insisted, had to be integrated sympathetically into its surroundings.

At first it was named the Hotel Casino Alhambra Palace, for indeed it housed a casino of repute. During the Spanish Civil War, in 1936, it was commandeered as a mlilitary hospital.

When it finally reopened once more, in 1943, the 'Casino' was dropped from its name. Today, there are 135 rooms and 13 suites, all beautifully furnished, very individual, and supremely comfortable, with lovely bathrooms, air-conditioning, satellite television, personal safes, a mini-bar and direct phone line.

Business clientele are made especially welcome. There are meeting rooms, halls for banquets and for concerts, as well as boutiques offering that special exclusive gift to carry home, a cosy lounge and intimate bar. The cuisine is inventive and yet traditional.

The main attraction in Granada is the Alhambra, of course - it is unmissable. But do get to the gates early, and experience the gardens first, before you have to share them with everyone.

But there is lots more in Granada to see: La Madrasa, the old Arabic University, and the cathedral, and the buildings that were once the Hospital Real, and now house the University. And afterwards, return to your air-conditioned room at the Alhambra Palace Hotel, pour yourself a glass of wine and toast… not the haughty grand vizier of Moorish times, but his lowliest mason, placing yet one more stone into the Alhambra's timeless walls.

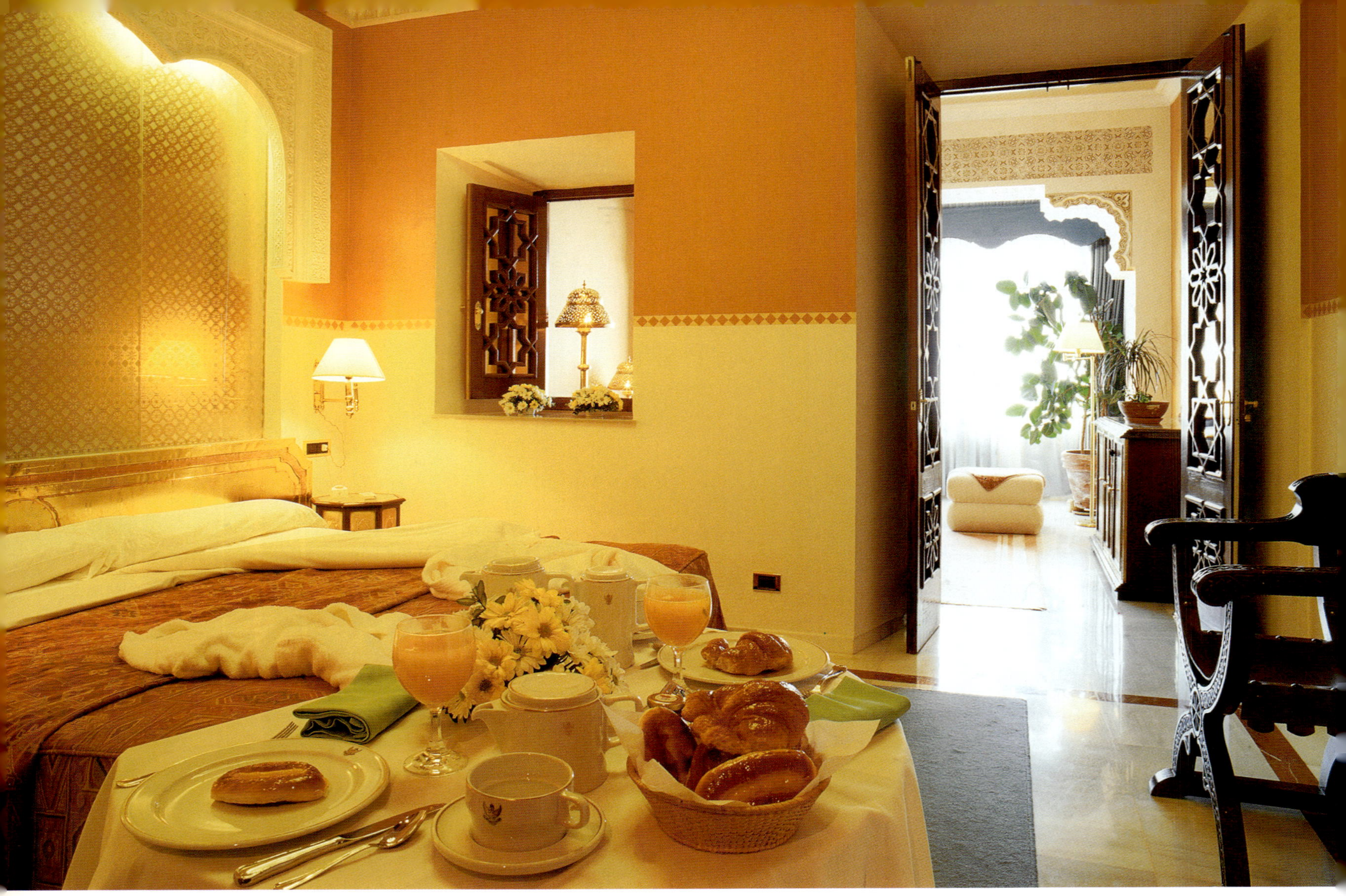

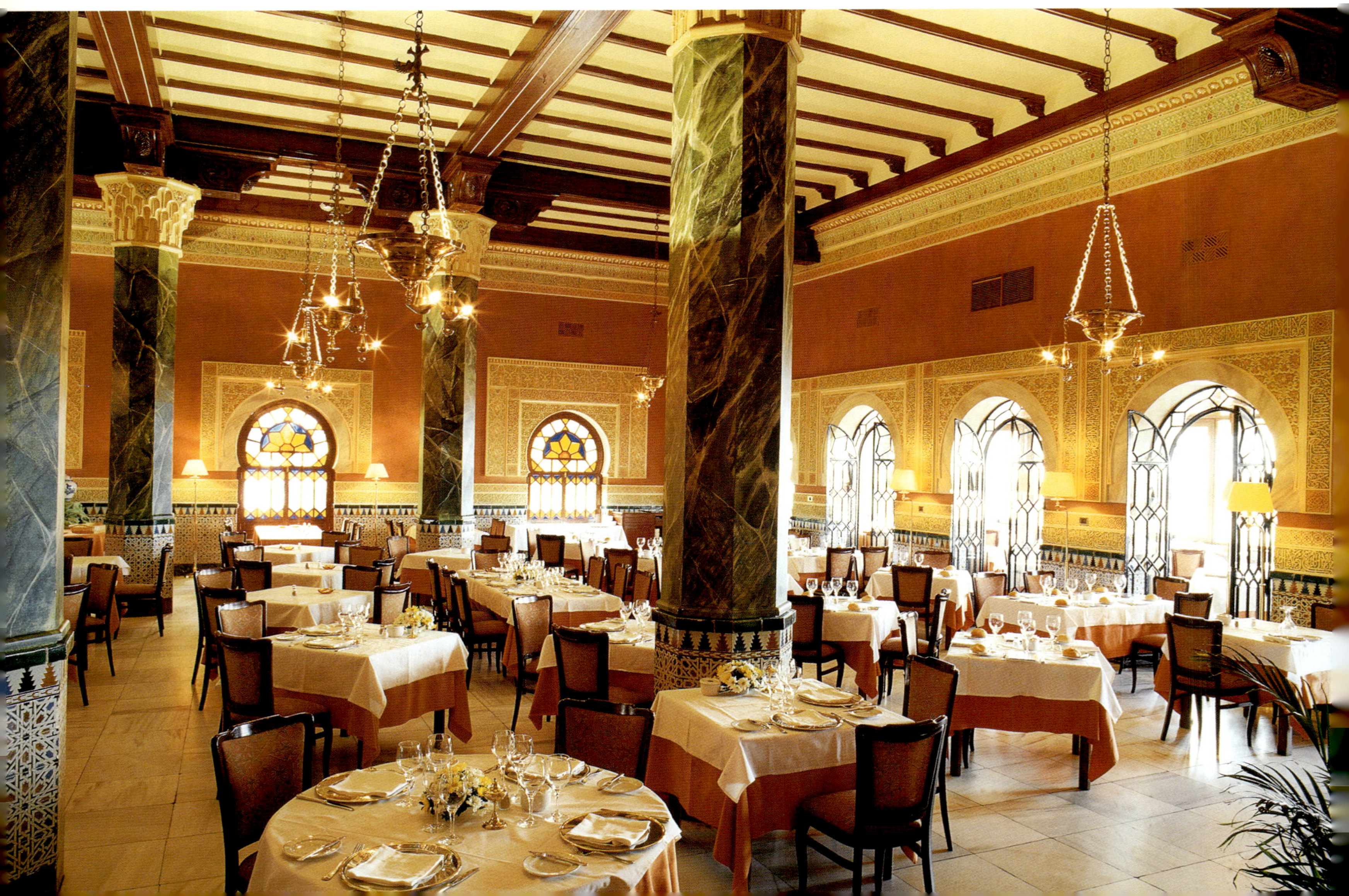

In 1910 this Moorish-style palace became
a luxury hotel.

Above: The terraces of the Alhambra Palace offering a breathtaking view of Granada.

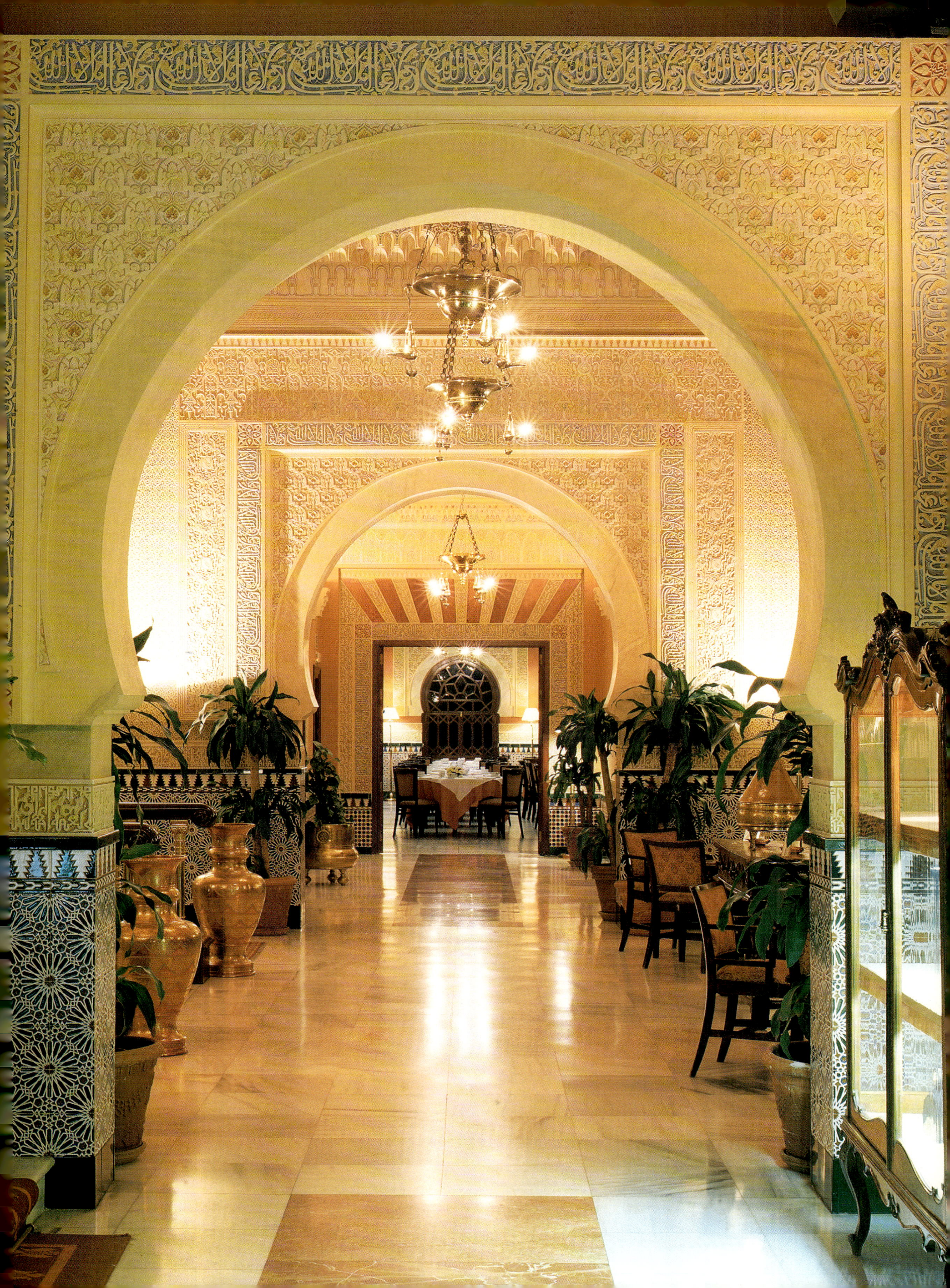

La Residencia

The picturesque village of Deià on Mallorca slumbered peacefully for year after year on the rocky coast of the Mediterranean island, under the dramatic Tramuntana mountains. Villagers were fishermen and farmers, ekeing out a living from the sea, from their olive trees and citrus groves on the steep and stony terraces behind the cottages.

The simple beauties of the island, and this secret place in particular, were discovered by English writer Robert Graves. He was already famous and seeking a refuge from his many admireres, a place where he could continue his studies and writing unmolested.

In time, poets and artists formed a community around him and Deià became something of a far-flung centre of the arts. Mallorca was eventually discovered by tourists, lured by hot sun and blue waters, but Deià has been fortunate: in spite of its dramatic and beautiful situation, it has escaped the grasp of mass tourism.

La Residencia, fashioned from two original manor houses, with some stylish and sympathetic recent additions, can be found in Robert Graves' beloved village and retains all of the original authenticity and tranquillity the writer himself embraced. There is still a thriving artistic influence here, a collection of fine modern paintings on the walls, and a Steinway piano - dating from 1887 and first played by the Spanish composer Albéniz - in one of the lounges.

La Residencia has achieved renown not only by way of its stunning geographical location, but because of its luxurious and captivating appointments and the fine food offered by chef Philippe Lasargue in the hotel's celebrated El Olivo restaurant.

The artists drawn to Deià today include rock stars such as Sting, Bruce Springsteen, Van Morrison and Annie Lennox, and movie stars like Tom Hanks, Goldie Hawn and Michael Douglas. Even the King and Queen of Spain have graced La Residencia's portals.

But you will love the hotel, not for its famous visitors and equally famous owner, Richard Branson, but for the warmth and intimacy with which it embraces everyone who comes here. Every day you will find a lovely bouquet of fresh flowers in your room, and a colourful and tempting bowl of fruit. The hotel has its own tennis courts, gymnasium, private beach, sauna and beauty parlour, but if all this - and 30 acres of landscaped gardens, dotted with tall and graceful palm trees and olive trees, is not enough, the adventurous can set off for

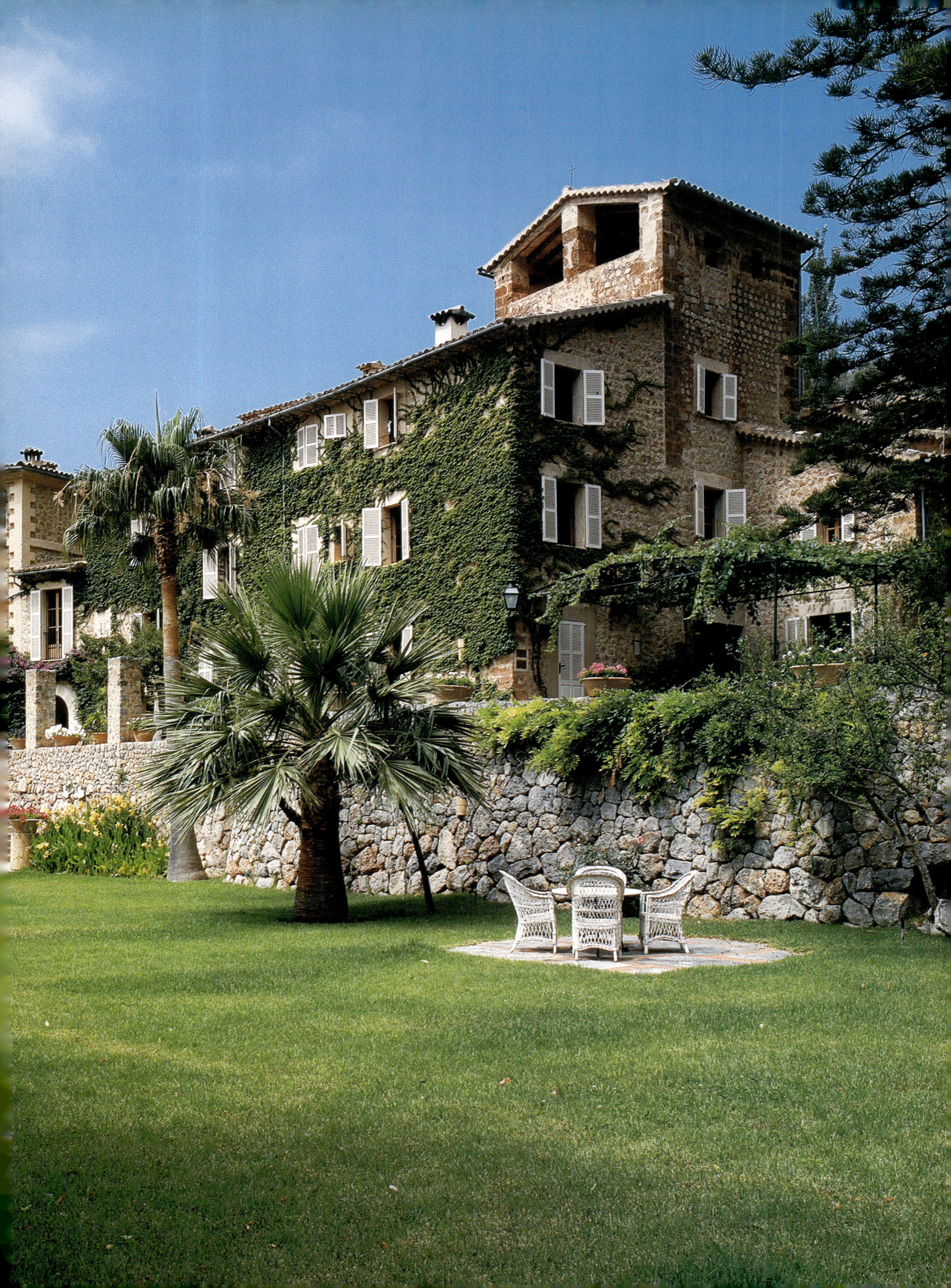

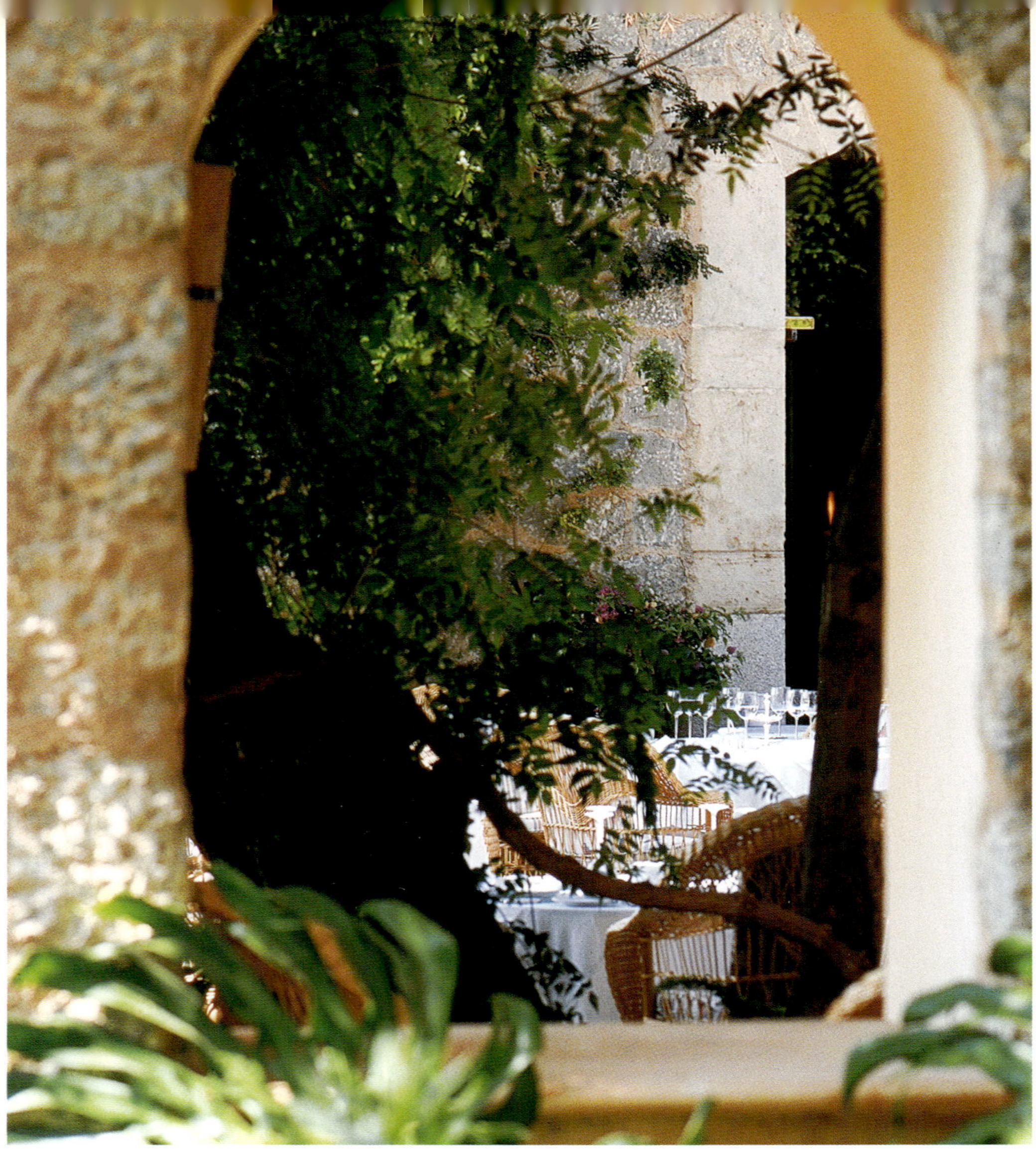

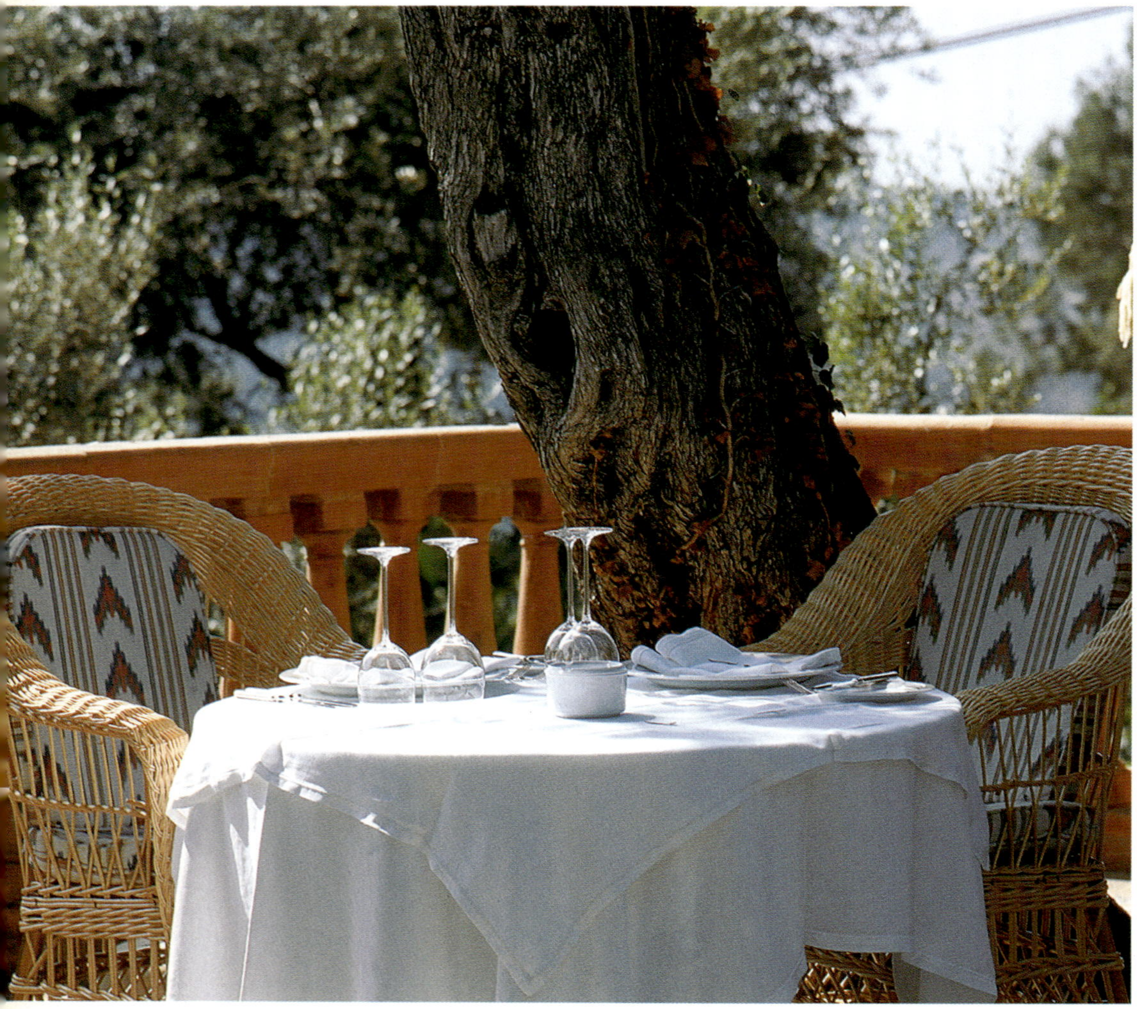

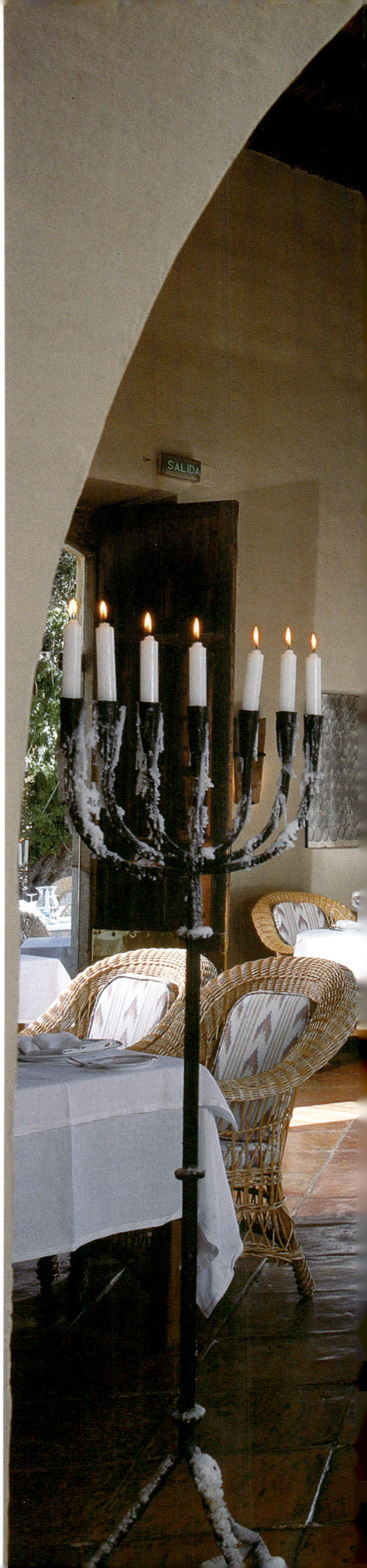
SALIDA

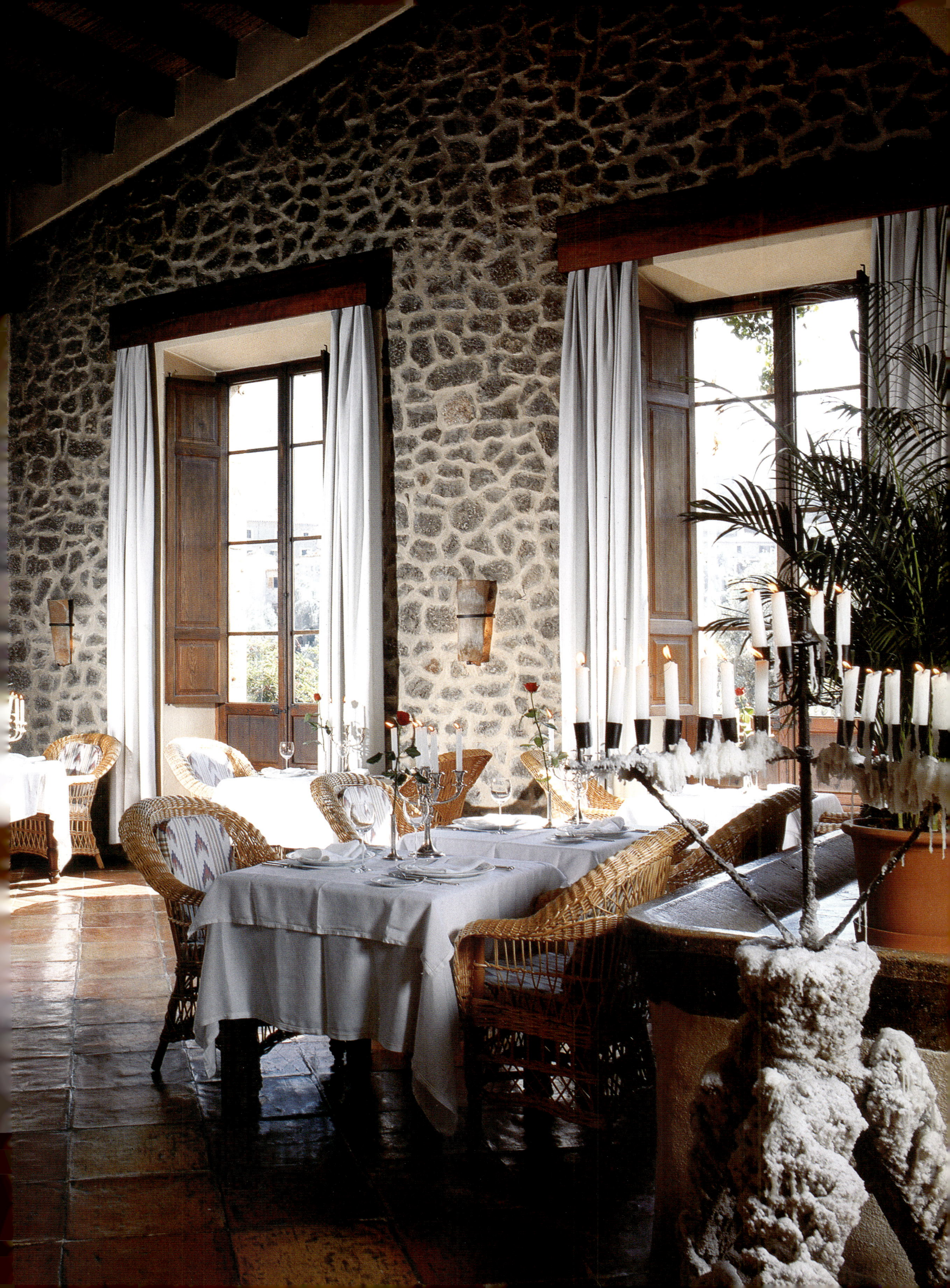

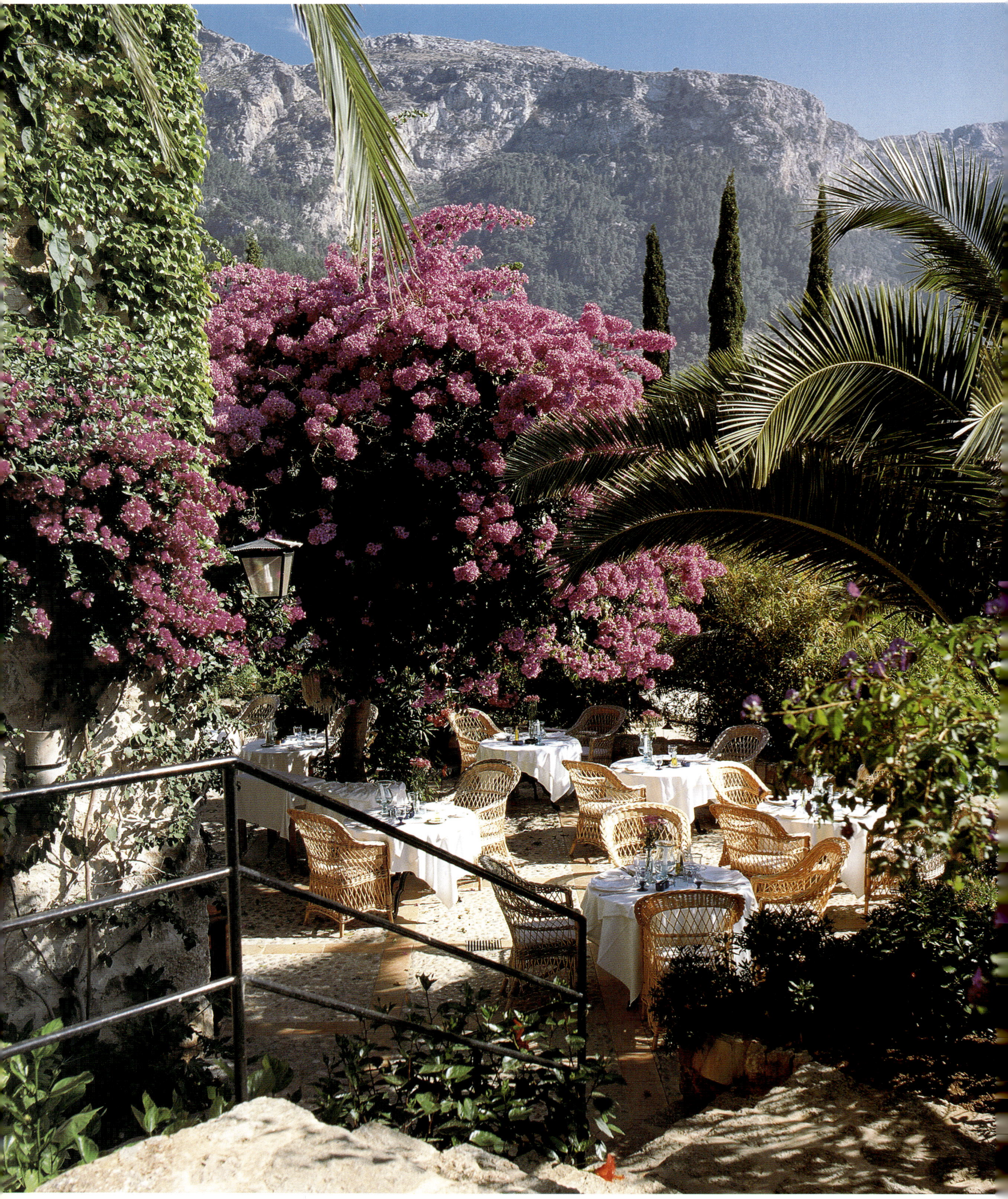

the mountains, or go scuba diving, play golf and go sea fishing.
At the end of a full day you can return to your suite at La Residencia and settle contentedly, like any visiting star, into its comfortable and attentive bosom.

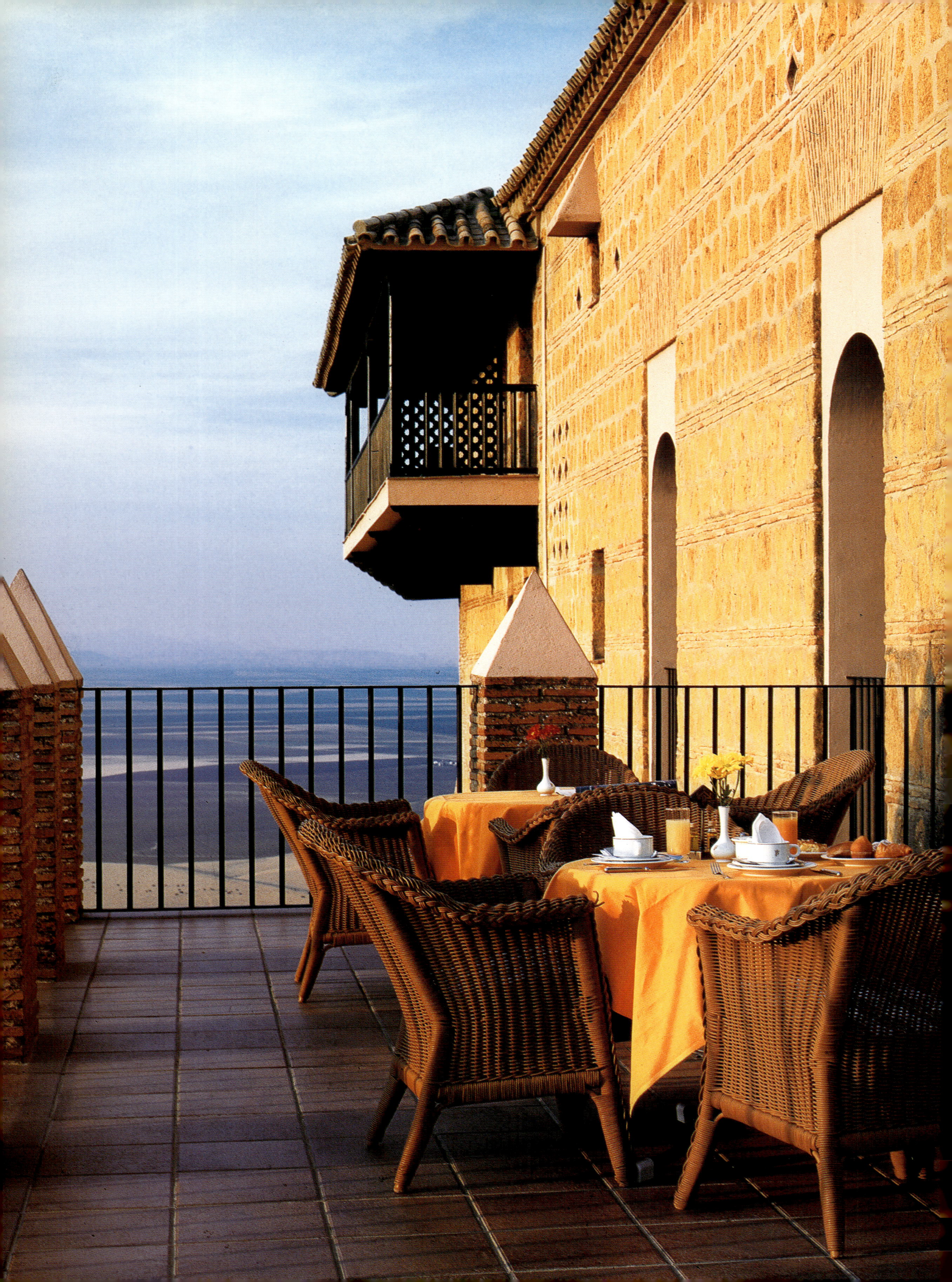

Parador de Carmona

The man who built this wonderful castle was widely known as a tragic king who had had many risqué adventures. The 14th century King Pedro I, called cruel by some and justice itself by others, was stabbed to death during a power struggle with his bastard brother Enrique of Trastamara. But long before this, Pedro had come to Carmona, where he discovered an old, inhospitable-looking Roman castle, and fell in love with it. He left the refurbishment of the building to the architects and artisans who were also responsible for the metamorphosis of the Seville Palace. Their numerous improvements and embellishments transformed the castle into a miracle of medieval architecture. Even now, it retains Gothic and Islamic elements that take guests straight back to a glorious past. After Pedro I, the luxurious castle became a temporary residence for the Reyes Católicos during their siege of Granada.

The elegant, light rooms in the castle, with their breathtaking views over the Carmona valley, invite you to sit by the window for hours and just dream of the past.

And what better way to conclude an unforgettable day than a gourmet dinner in the hotel's exquisite restaurant, no doubt one of the finest of all the Parador restaurants? Its menu includes a wide variety of dishes, all of them prepared with the wonderful fresh produce of the area and cooked impeccably.

When you have daydreamed enough, the town of Carmona itself is worth a visit. It is full of ancient convents, monasteries, Baroque palaces and impressive mansions. A little further afield are other fascinating towns such as Itálica, Marchena, Ecija, Morón de la Frontera, Utrera and Osuna. Even the historic city of Seville, only 26 kilometers away, is close enough for a trip out.

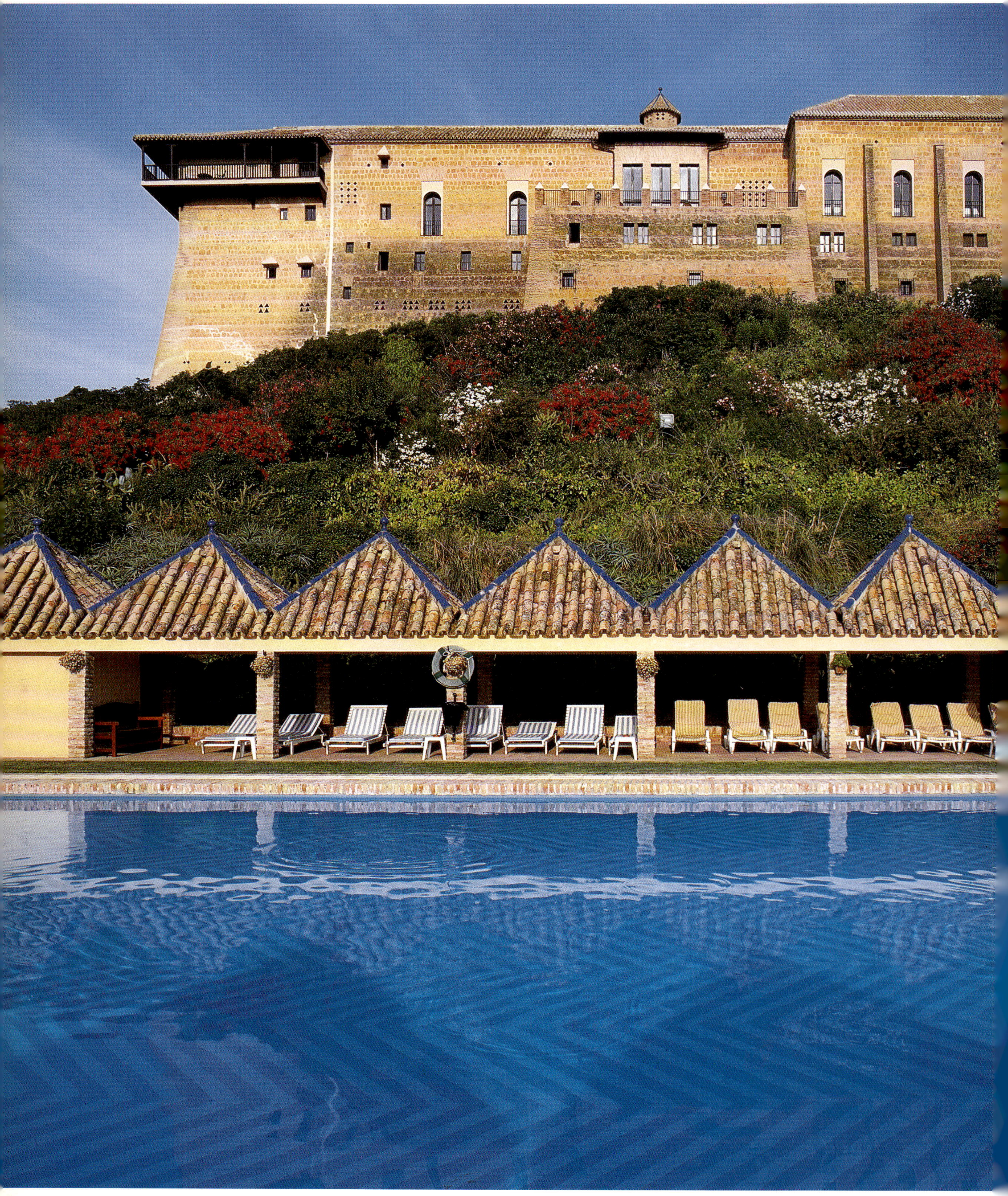

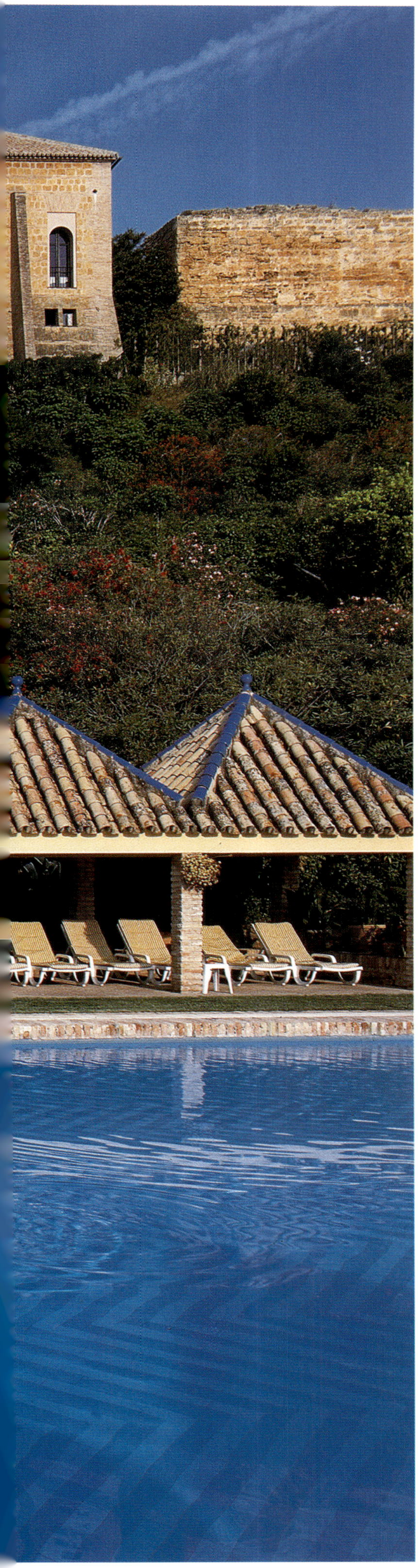
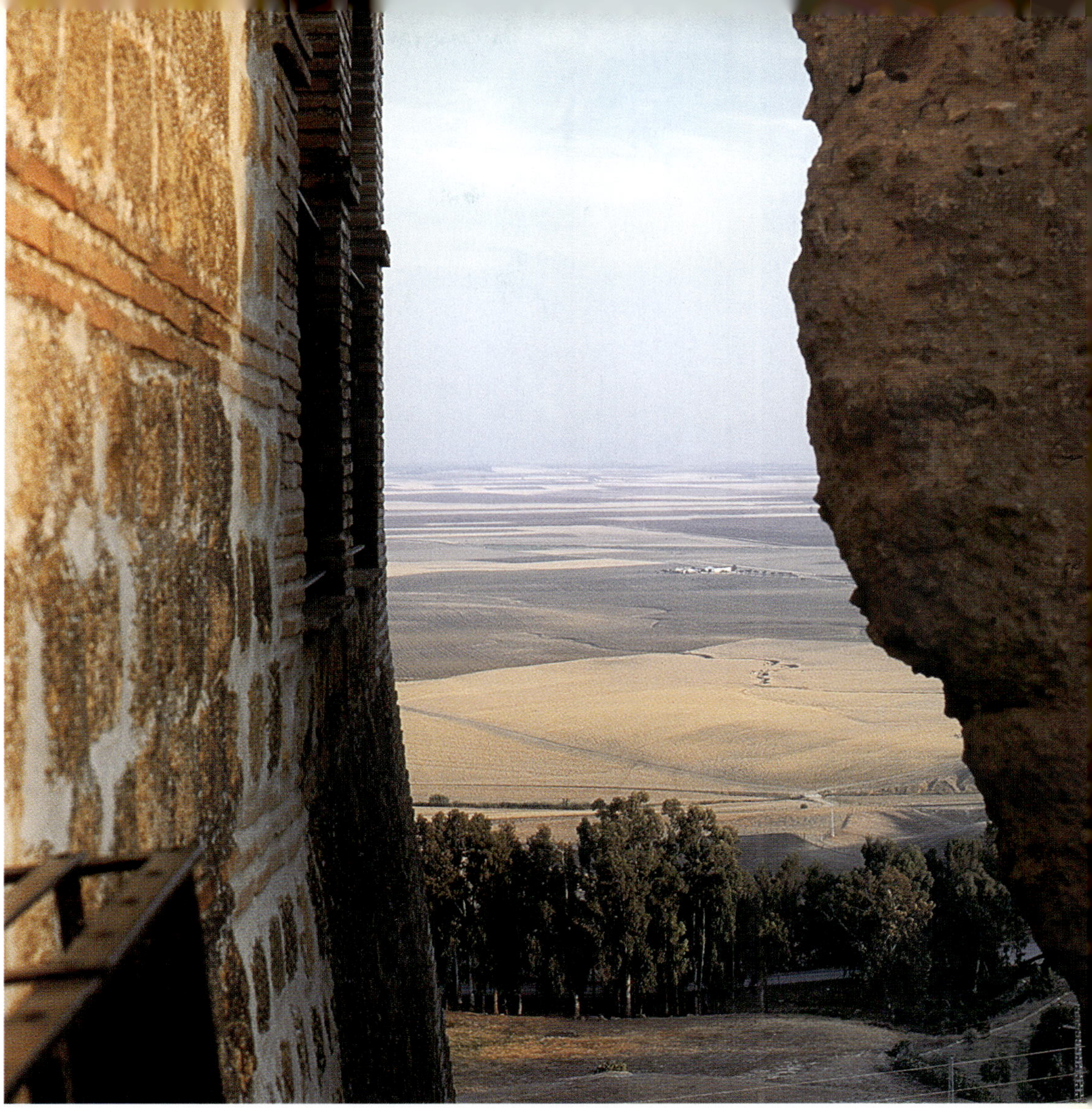
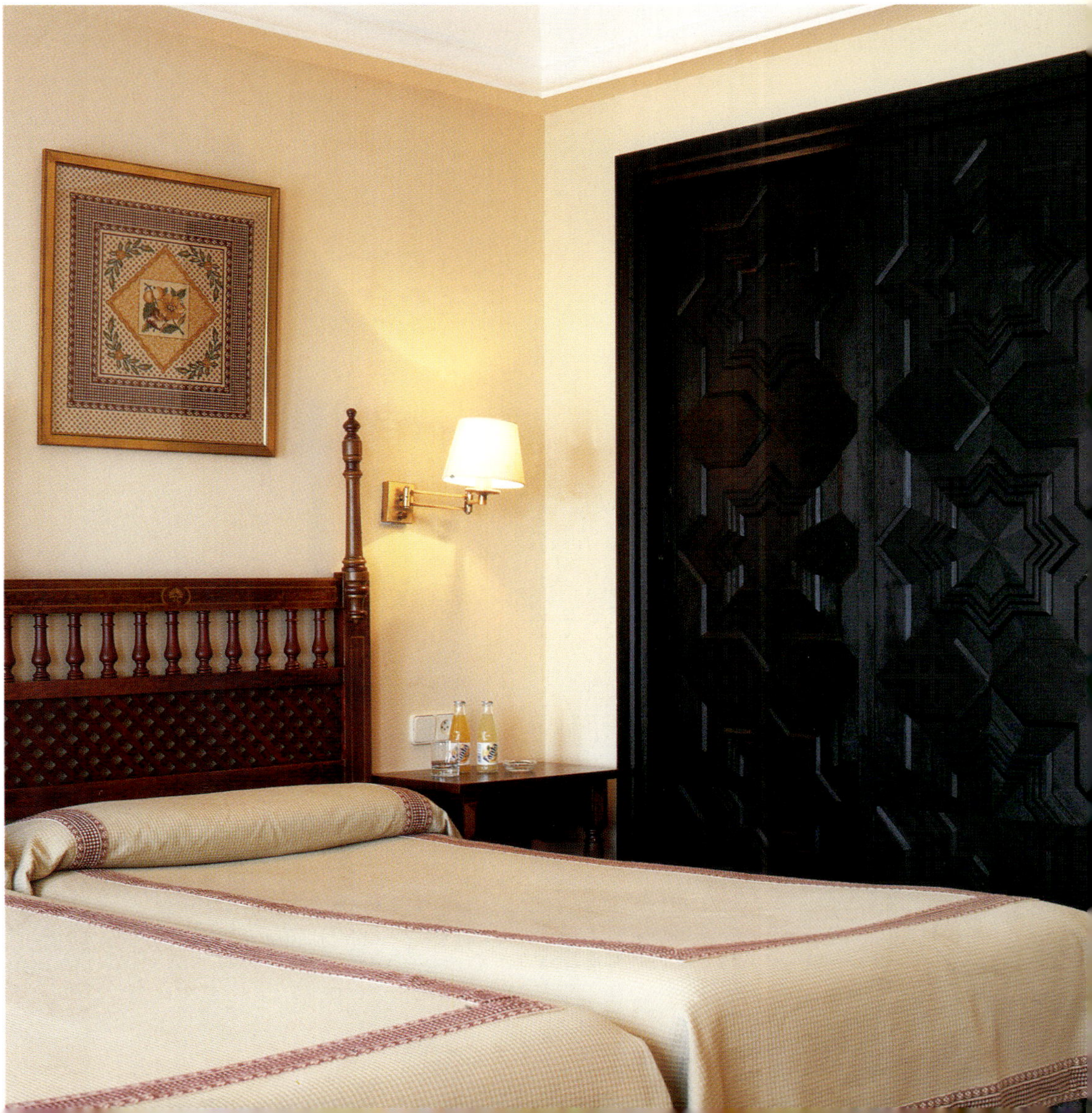

88

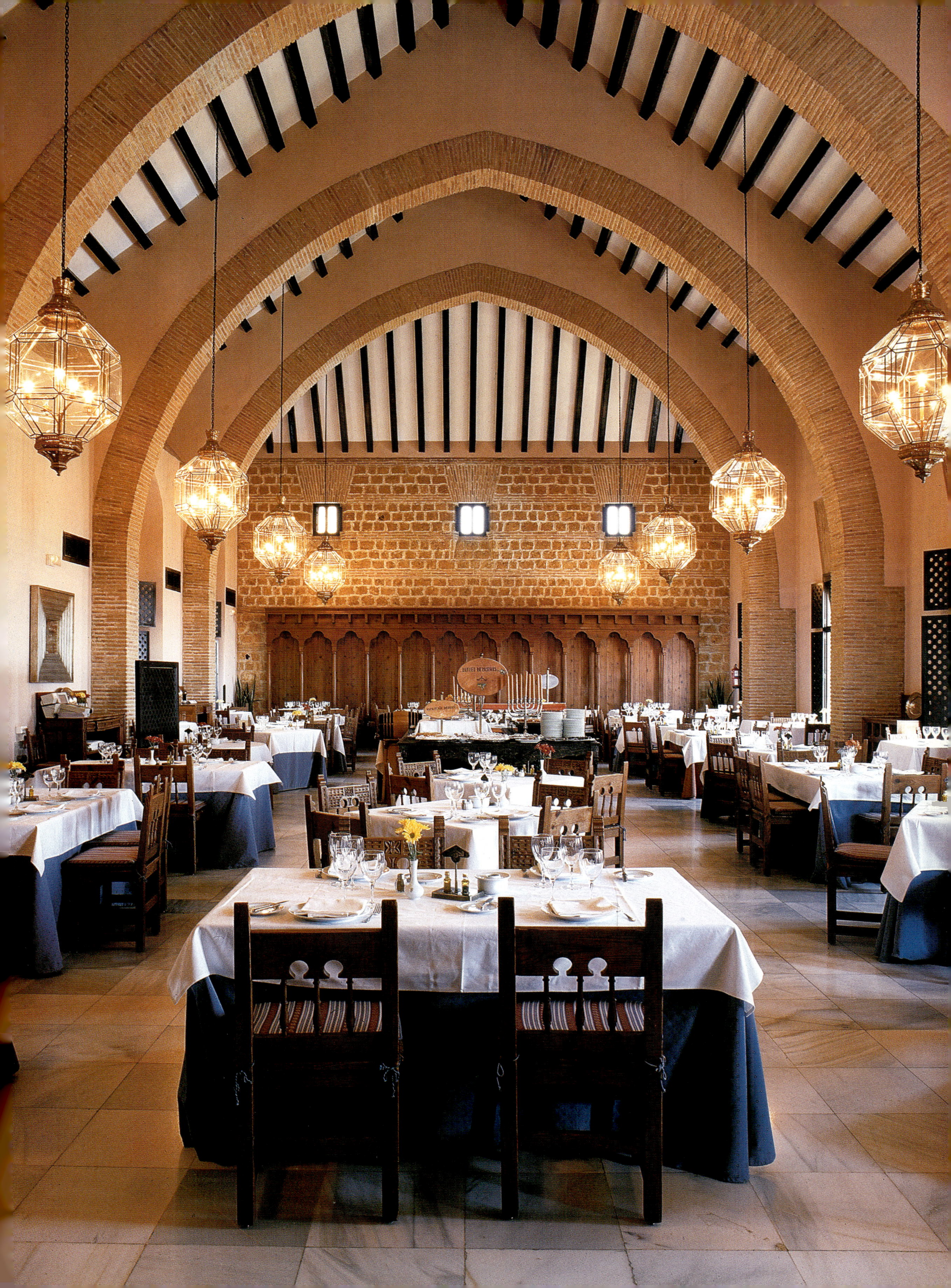
BUFFET DE POSTRES

Claris

The spirit of the Hotel Claris looks both ways, out into the future, which it finds has an elegant and alluring sparkle, and back toward the ancient past, for the inspiration of its antiquarian art, of which the hotel's managing director Jordi Clos has been an enthusiastic and highly knowledgable collector.

The Claris, which opened its doors as recently as 1992, is the newest of five major hotels in Barcelona owned by the Derby group, a real triumph of modern atchitecture set in one of the most enviable and central locations in the city.

The beautiful Plaza de Catalunyas, laid out in the 19th century, is just around the corner and the famous street Las Ramblas is equally close. For many, Barcelona is Antonio Gaudi, the very reason they have come... and guests of the Claris are fortunate again: Gaudi's Holy Family Temple, the Sagrada Familia, and two other of his stunning and controversial buildings, Casa Batlló and La Pedrera, are all within an easy walk.

Ildefons Cerdà was another famous figure of the modernist art nouveau movement in Spanish architecture and the side streets around the centre, of the Paseo de Gracia especially, offer examples of his and Gaudi's work. But you need only step just yards out of the Claris to see spectacular art. Jordi Clos has generously put 72 items from ancient Egypt on display in the hotel's own museum. They include a sarcophagus and a mummified falcon. 333 other works of art - a 1,600-year old head of a Hindu goddess is one - are disposed all about the hotel, both in the public areas and in the guest rooms themselves.

There are acres of fine redwood parquet and lovely wood-panelled walls in the Claris, art deco furnishings in the gorgeous and welcoming lobby, and in the 100 sound-proofed rooms and 20 junior suites, you'll find every 21st century convenience and luxury: marble bathrooms, top-of-the-range-toiletries, satellite television, air-conditioning and fax and modem facilities.

The swimming pool has been placed in the sunniest spot of all... out on the rooftop. Lovely old kilims - I told you the past and the future co-exist -are spread on the floors of most rooms.

But none of all this will satisfy natural hunger - and with so much to see around the capital guests will certainly have appetites to care for. It goes without saying, the Claris will do them proud. There are two restaurants to choose from - and three in the summer months, when a terrace eaterie, the Barbacoa Claris, opens to take advantage of those long, warm evenings.

The main restaurant specialises in tasty Catalonian cuisine, exquisitely prepared and presented. The Beluga Restaurant is a small intimate retreat for up to 18 diners, that, as its name suggests, serves caviar in many guises as its principal speciality.

It's my guess you'll remember your favoured stay at the Hotel Claris as vividly as any of Gaudi's curiosities.

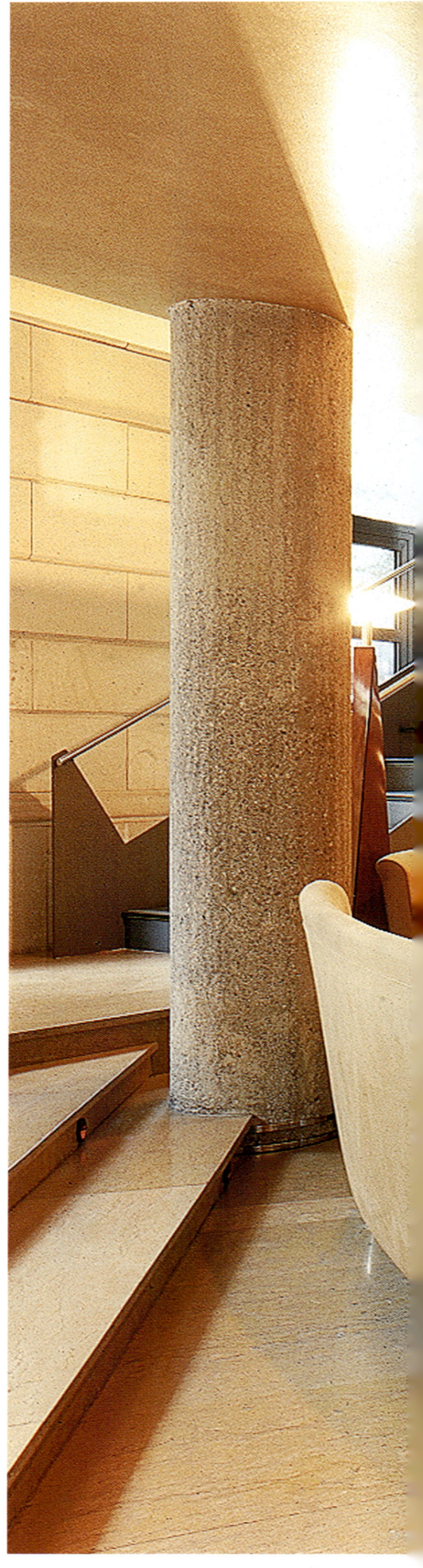

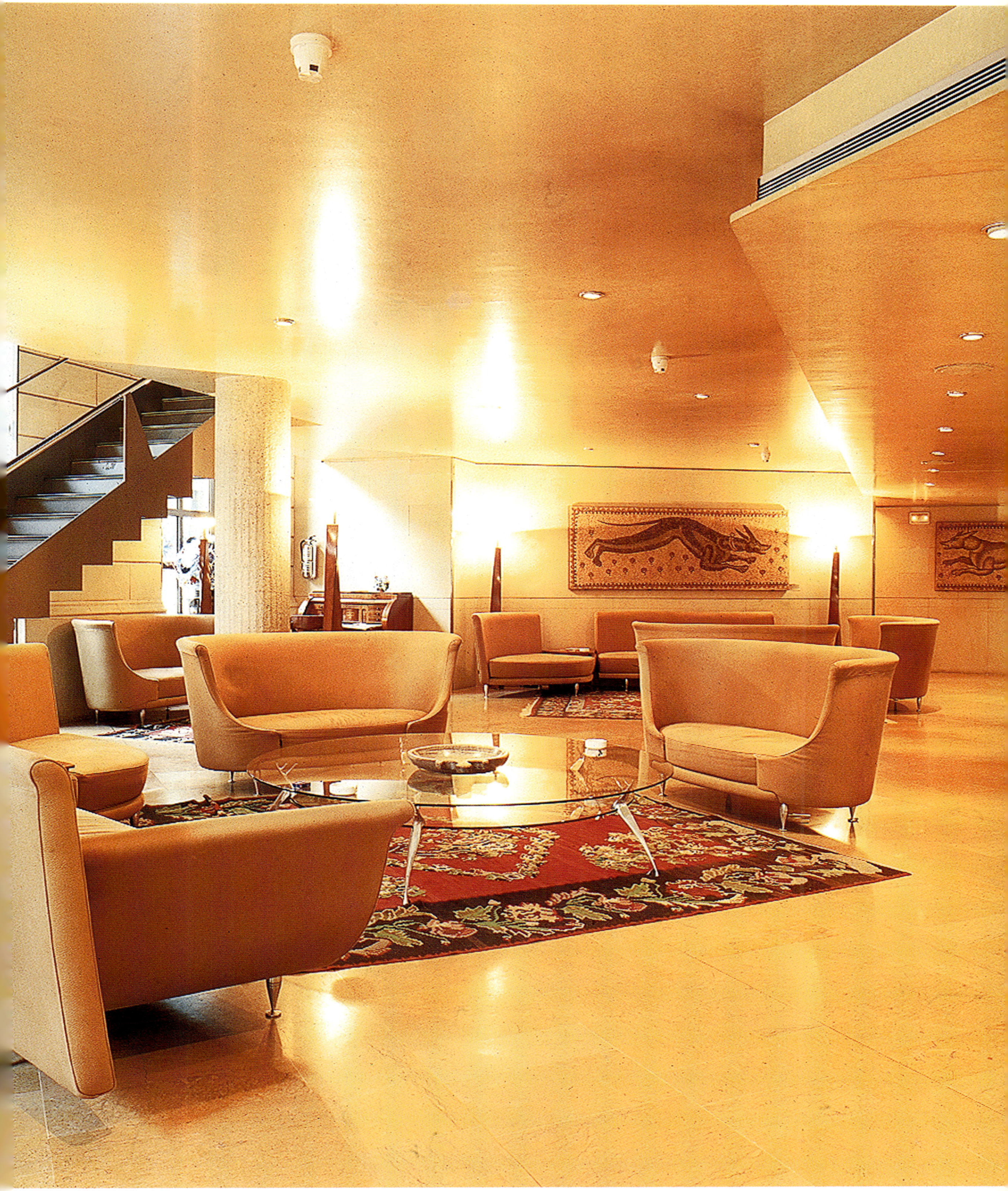

Hotel Claris: a triumph of modern architecture, filled to the brim with antique art.

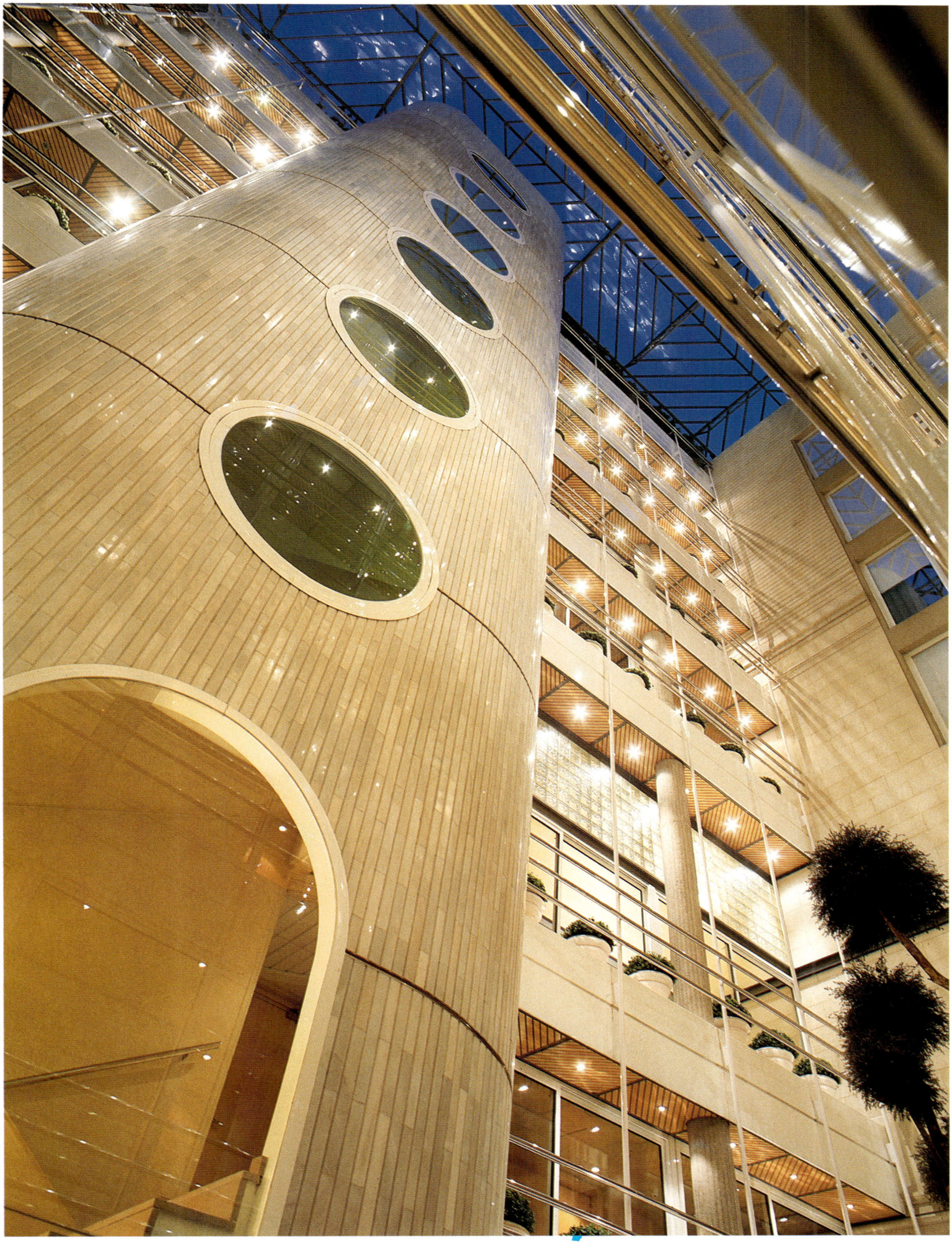

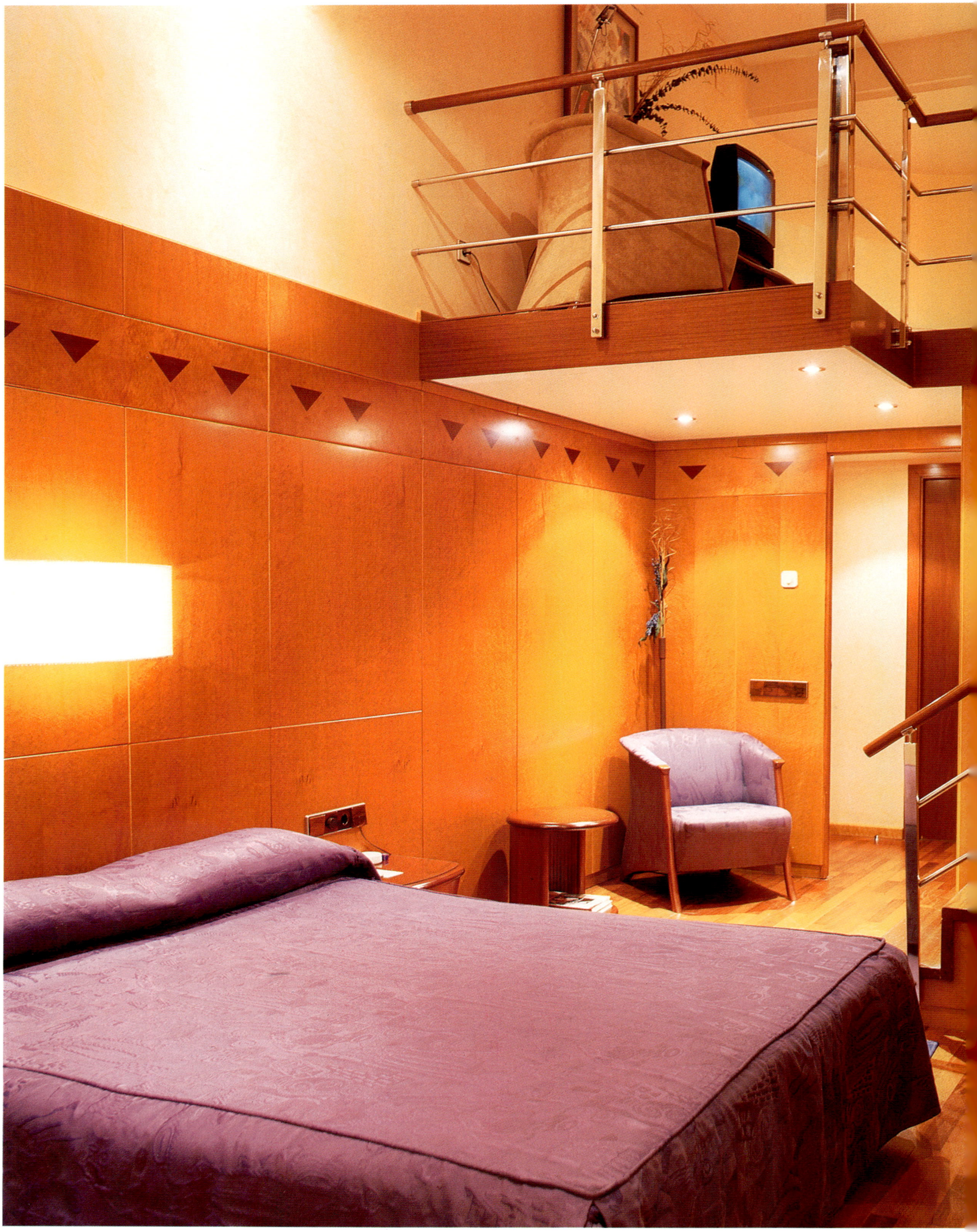

95

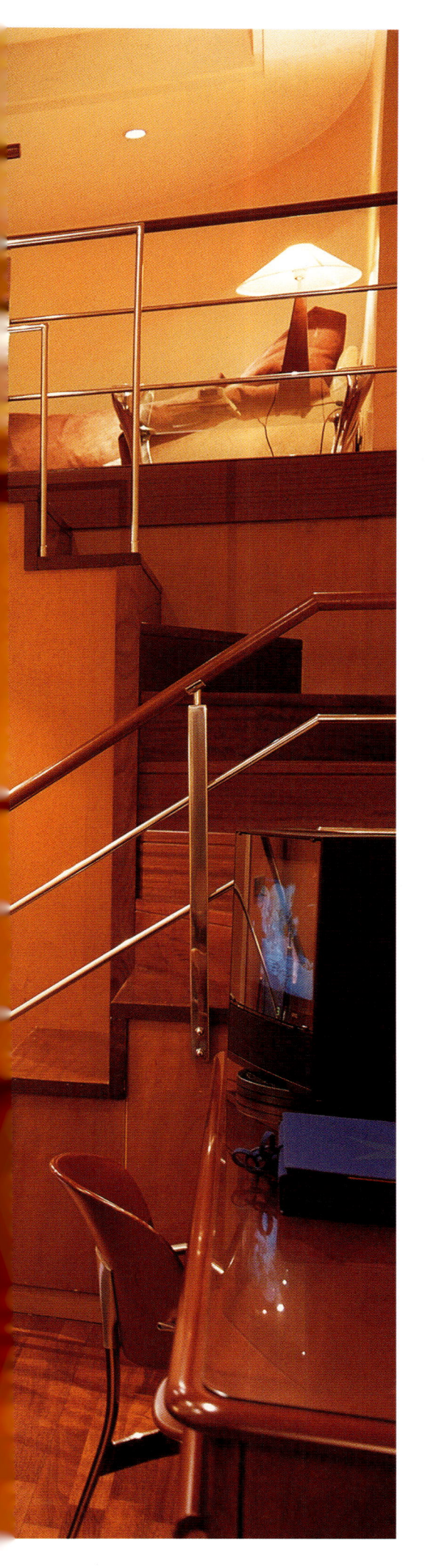

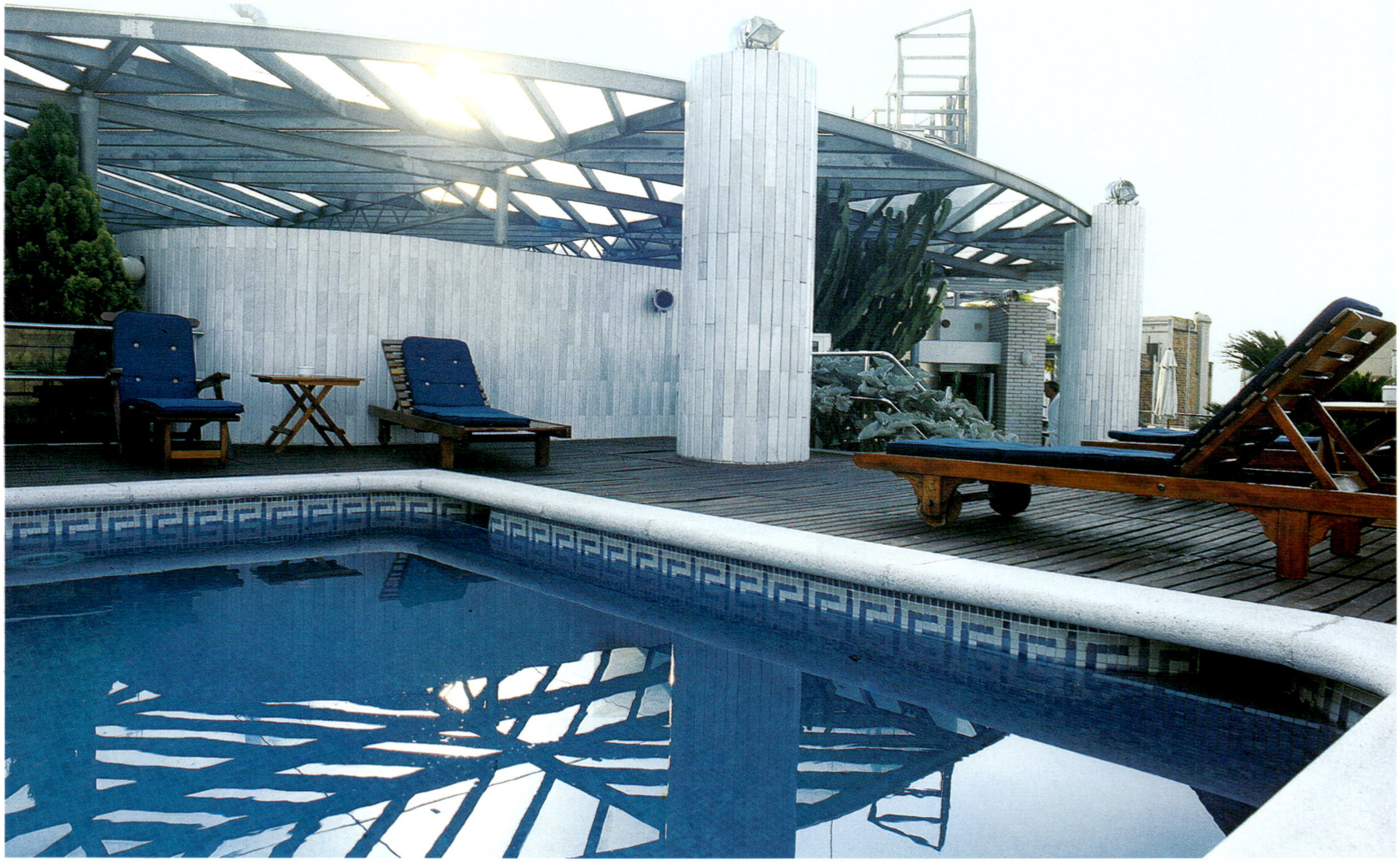

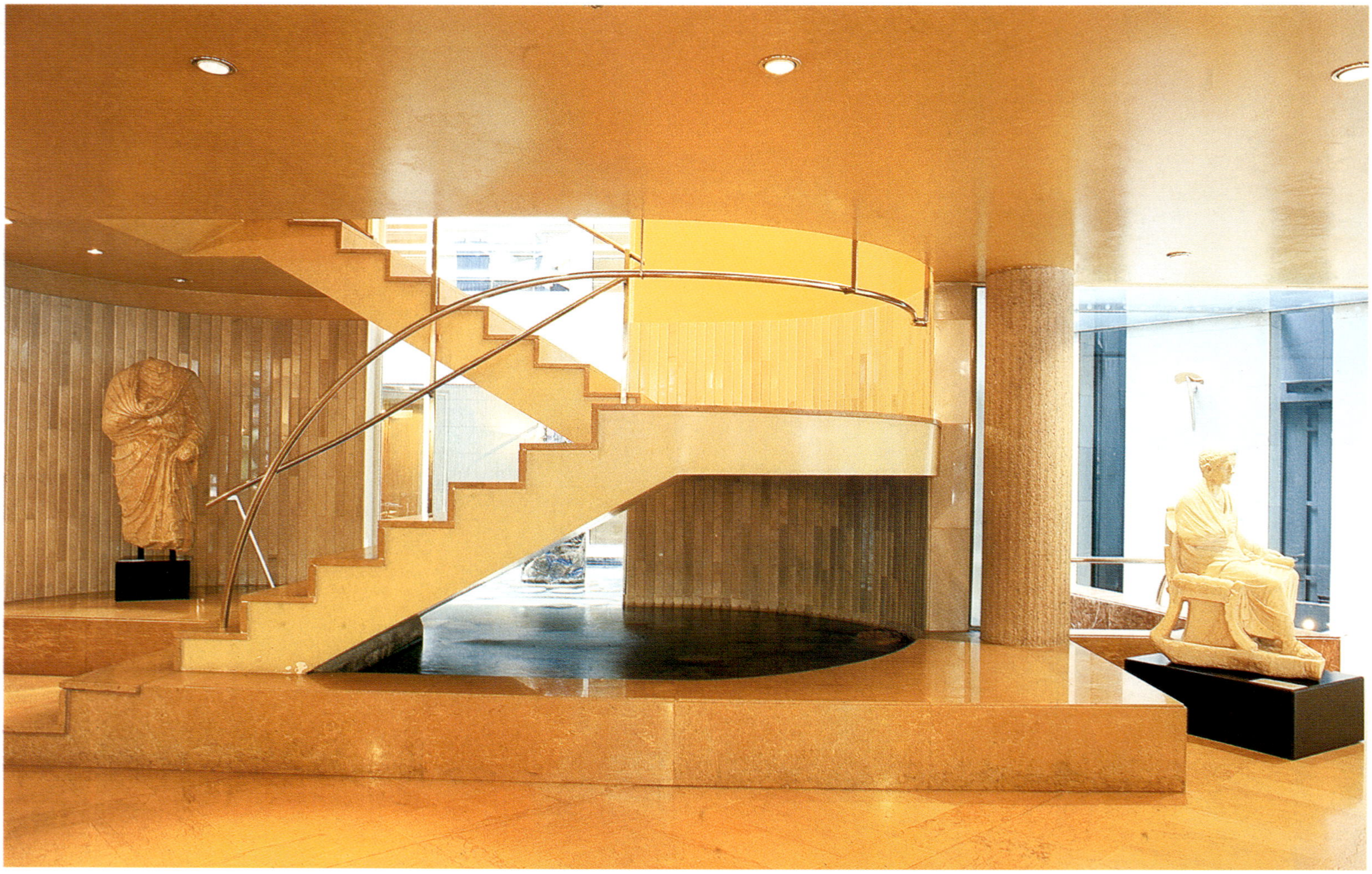

97

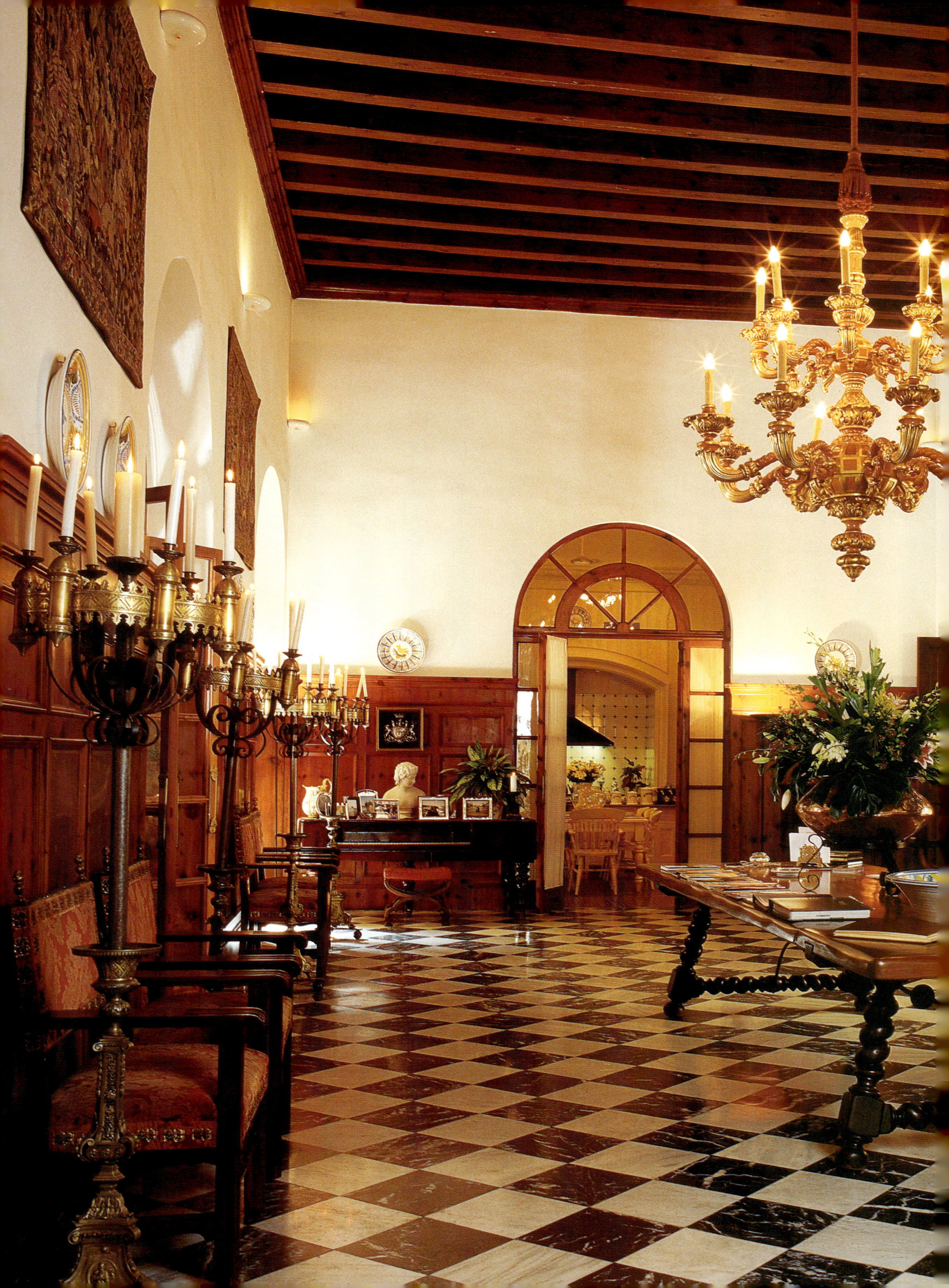

Palacio Ca Sa Galesa

Palma is a beautiful and ancient port town and the capital of Mallorca. In summer, Palma and, indeed, the whole island, is a popular tourist destination. And so it is all the more happy to report that a little jewel of a five-star hotel has opened right in the centre of Palma, that offers all the peace and quiet and the restrained elegance the discerning travller might be seeking.

The Hotel Palacio Ca Sa Galesa may be something of a mouthful, but in translation it is, simply and rather modestly, 'the Welsh woman's residence', a nod in the direction of the origin of the original owners.

The mansion was built for a rich bourgeois merchant back in 1571, and has only recently been fully restored to a standard that would fill its original owner with envy. To begin with, there is a charming and very original courtyard, reached through a venerable stone archway, whose ironwork gates have been thrown open in friendly welcome, yet nevertheless mark a boundary between the hustle and bustle of Palma and the quietude of this enchanting retreat.

A few feet from your parked car and you'll be stepping across the threshold, savouring your first taste of the hotel's homely peacefulness. There are just seven rooms and five suites, which makes you feel as if you were a guest in a private house.

Your hosts are great lovers of classical music and each room has been dedicated to a particular composer, and every one of them is decorated differently. The Sibelius room is predominantly blue and offers a cosy and traditional Mallorcan-style bathroom. Vivaldi is something of a Venetian romance and in the lovely bathroom you'll find an old-fashioned bathtub standing on clawed feet. The Blue Rhapsody suite opens out onto the hotel's private gardens.

Everywhere on the walls are old family pictures, and in the lounge there is a welcoming open hearth, where on cooler evenings a cheerful log fire burns. Sitting here, you will soon fall into friendly conversation with other guests fortunate enough to have discovered this delightful small hotel.

There is no restaurant, but because Ca Sa Galesa is so centrally placed you will find any number of choice restaurants within a few steps of the hotel - just ask, and you will be given some excellent advice as to where to go.

In the morning you can enjoy a wonderful breakfast buffet with hot dishes. In the afternoon, in the brightly decorated kitchen, inspired by the painter Claude Monet, you can taste all kinds of tea from the London department store Harrods.

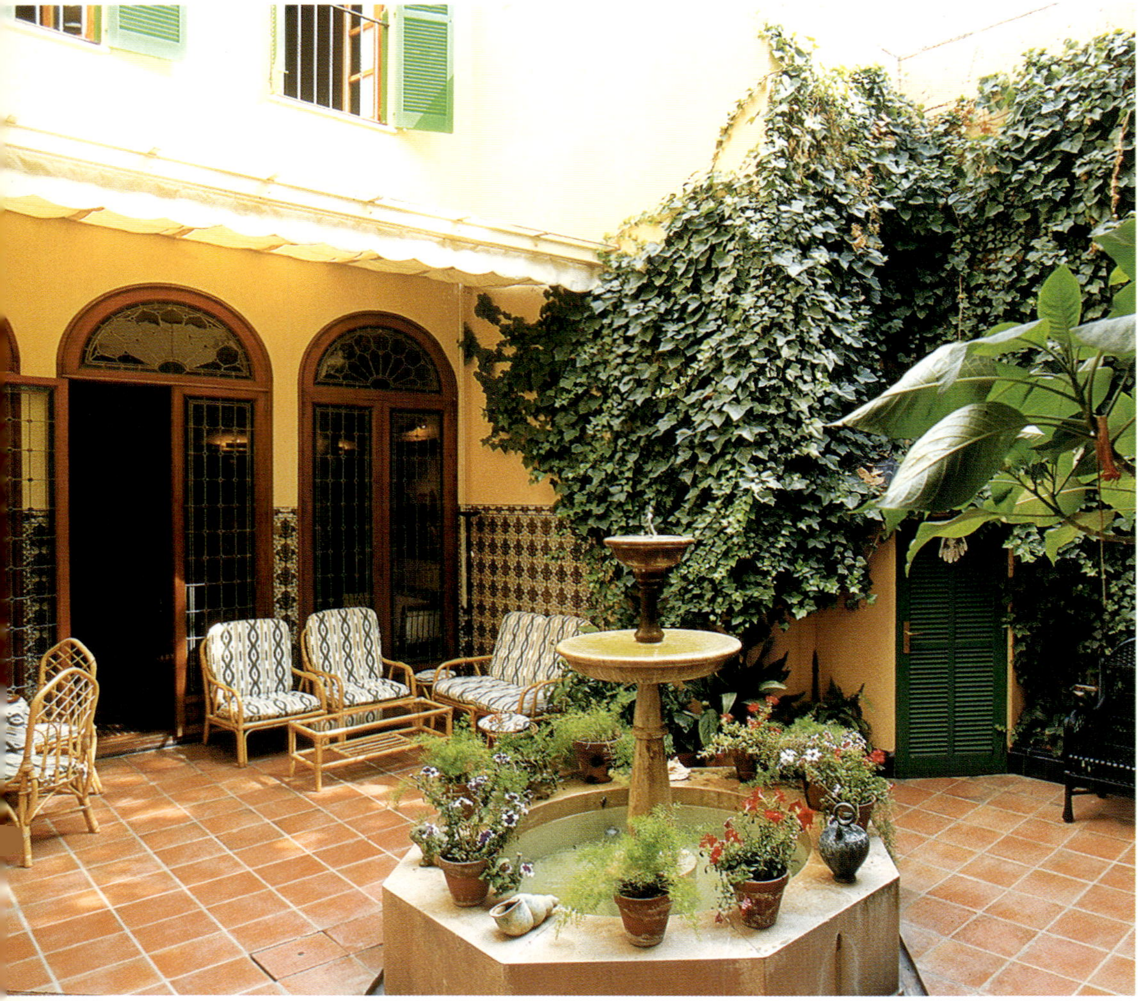

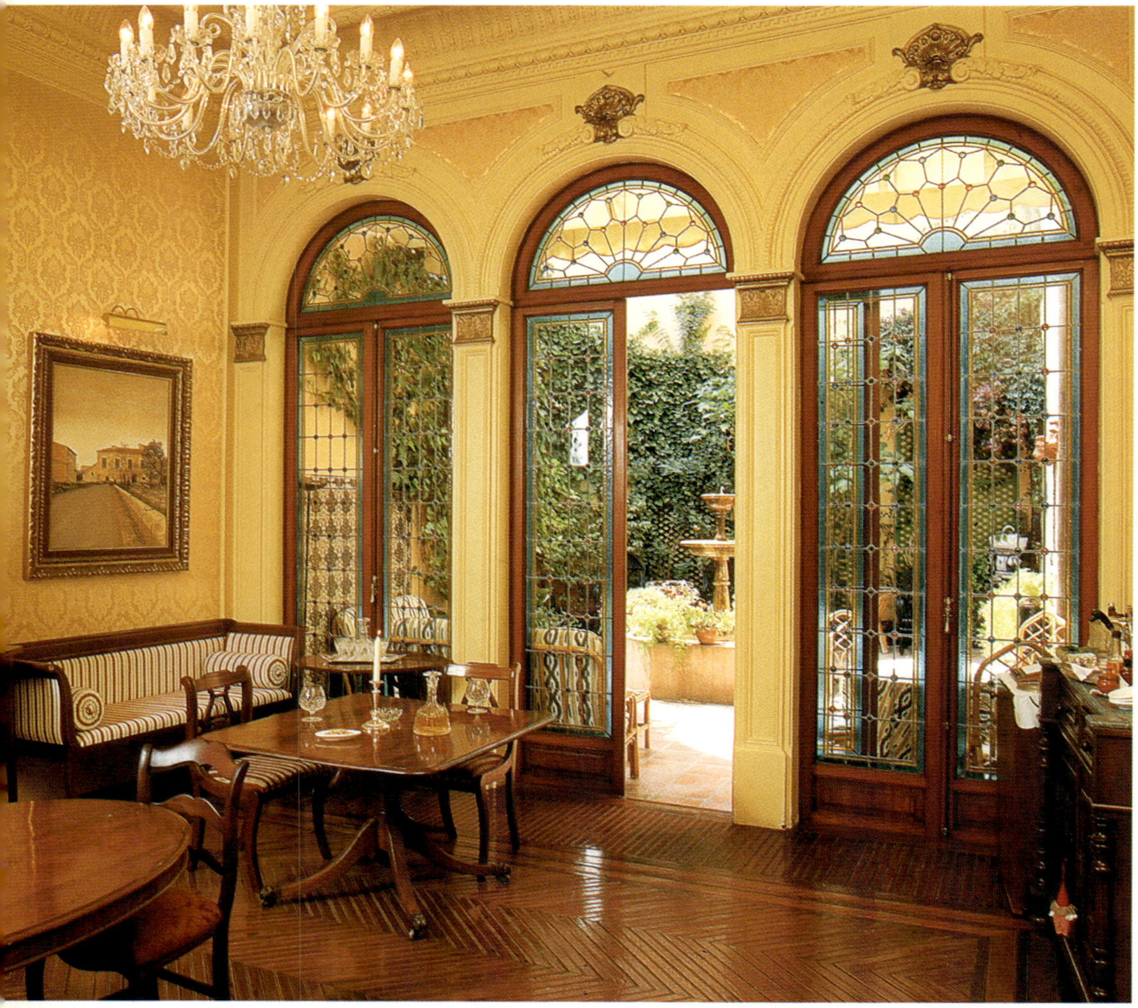

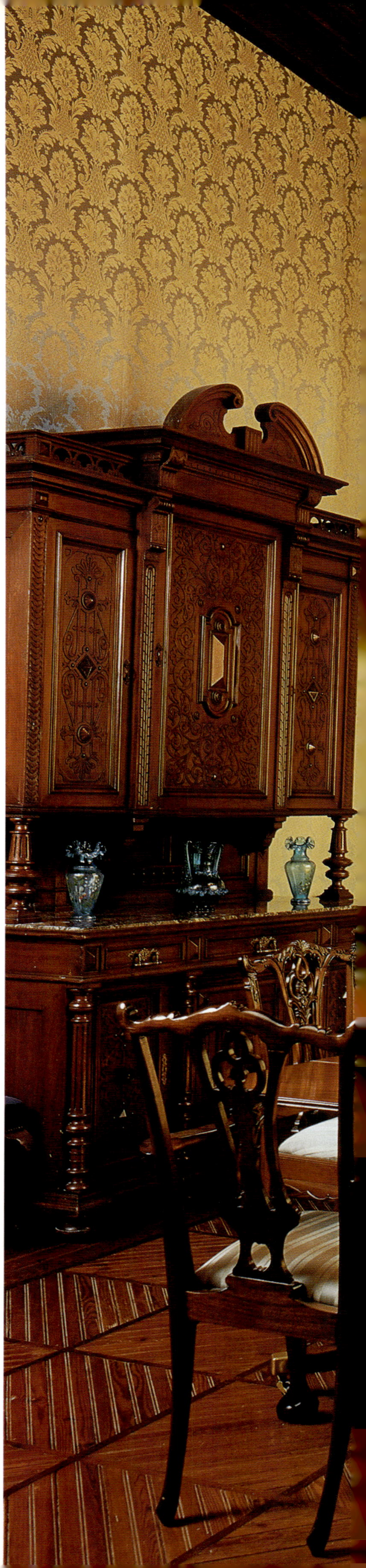

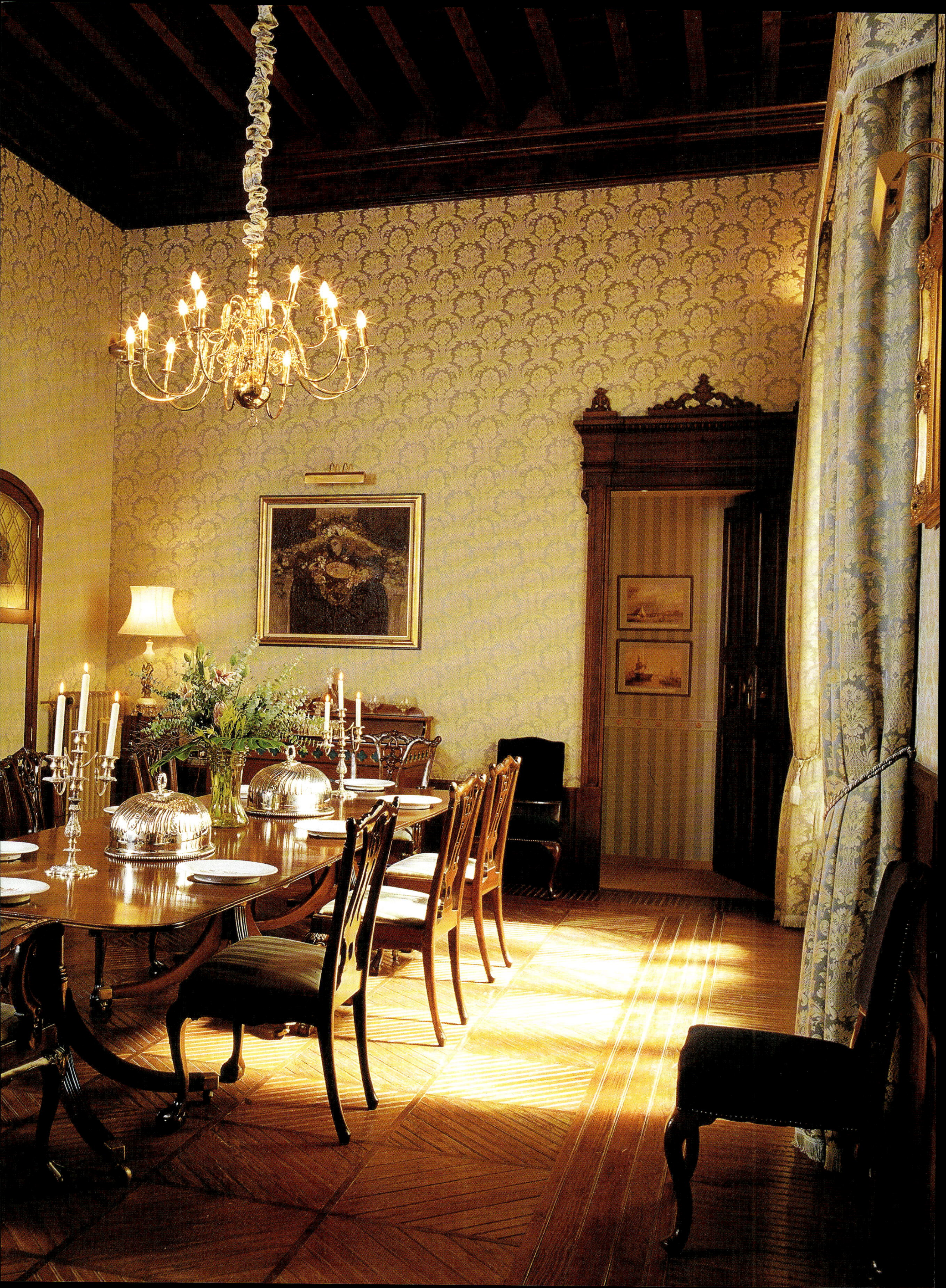

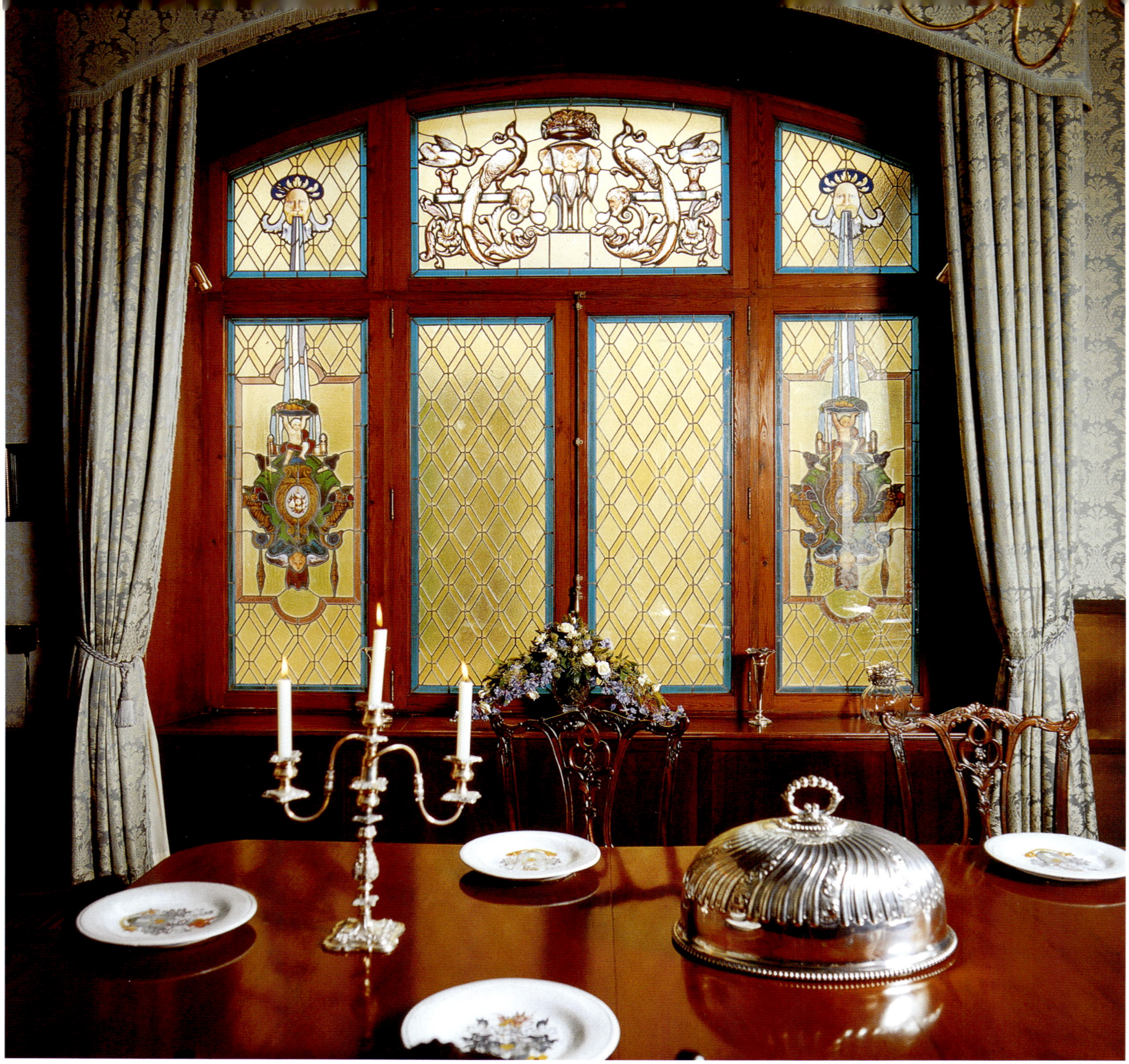

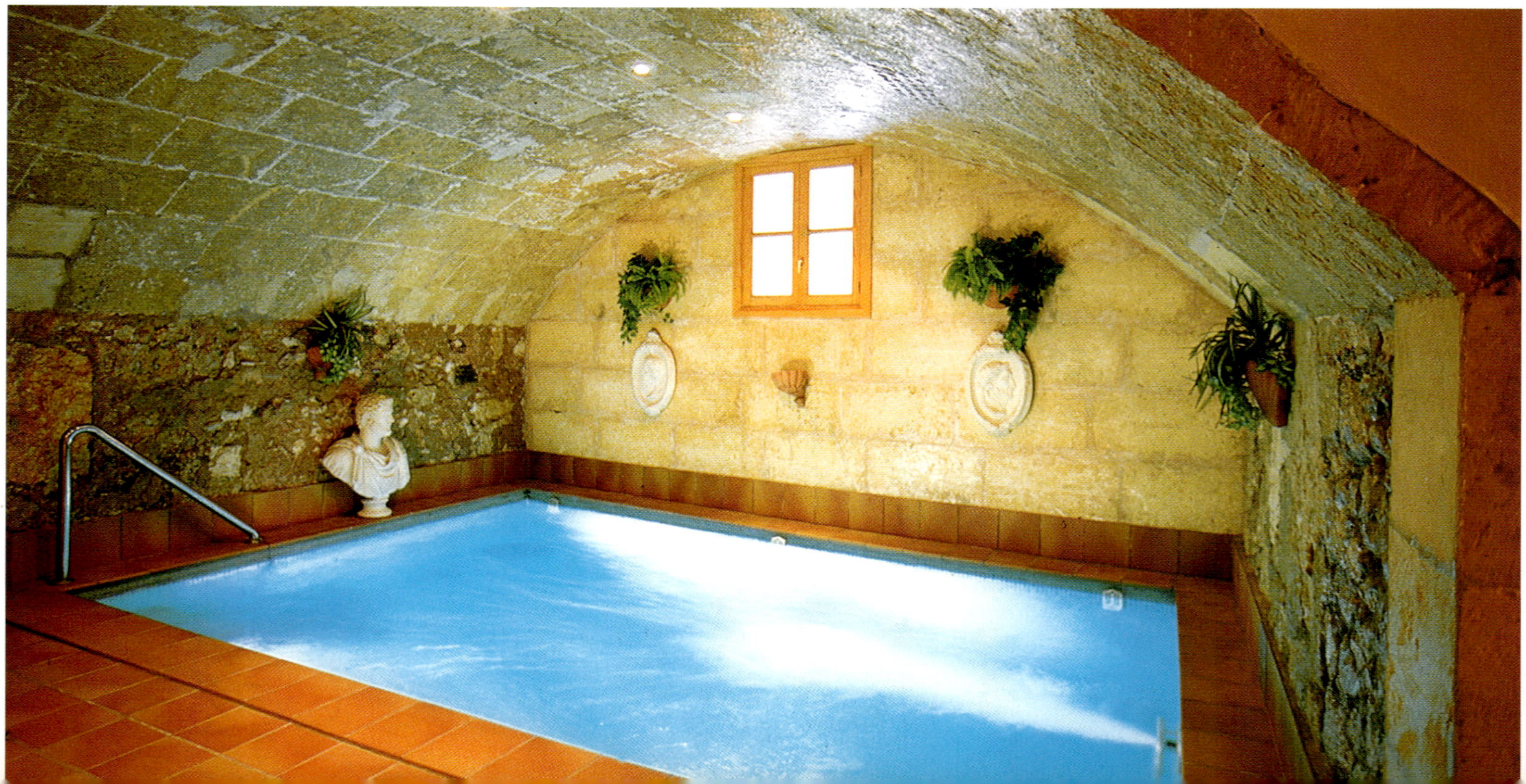

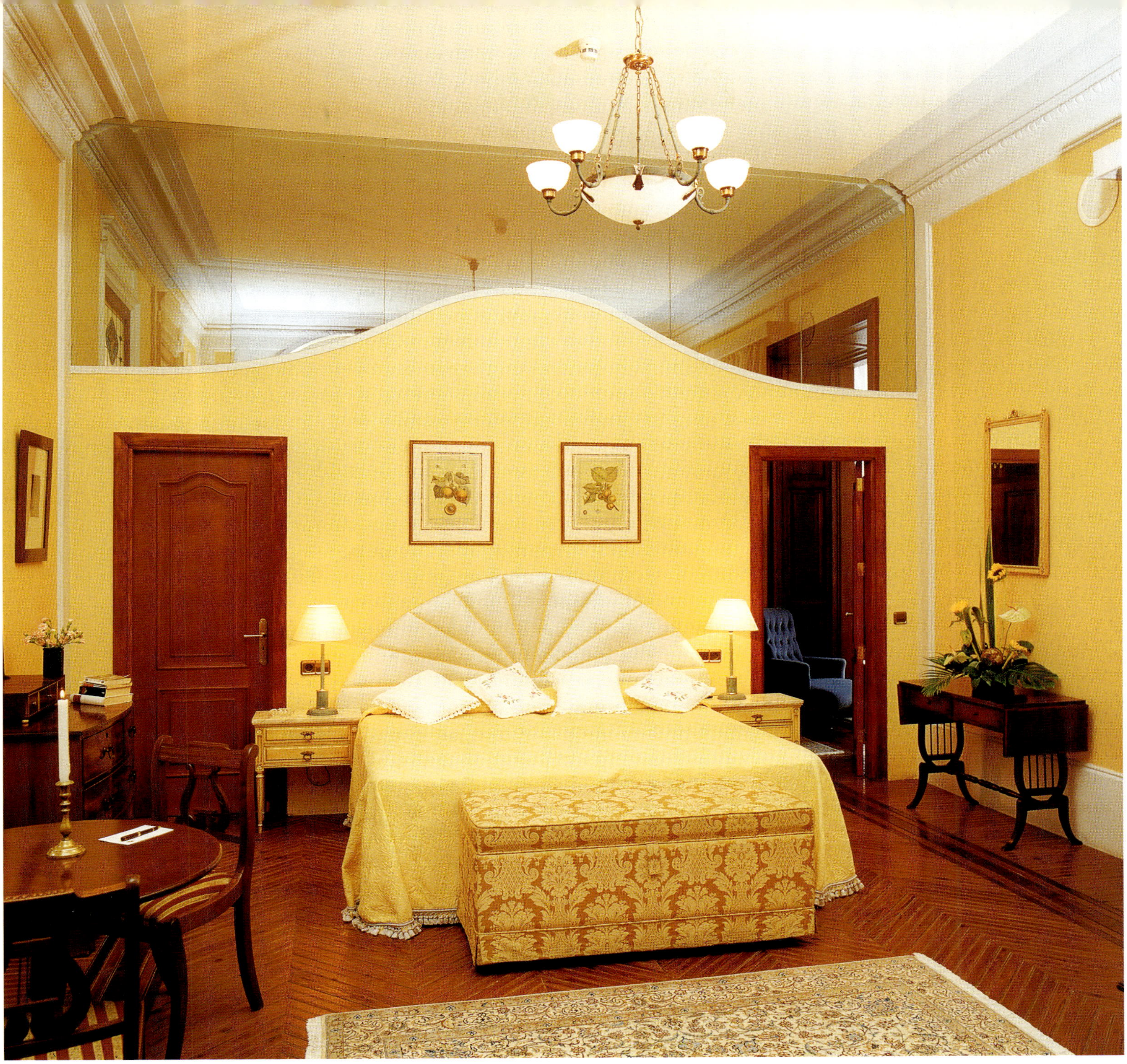

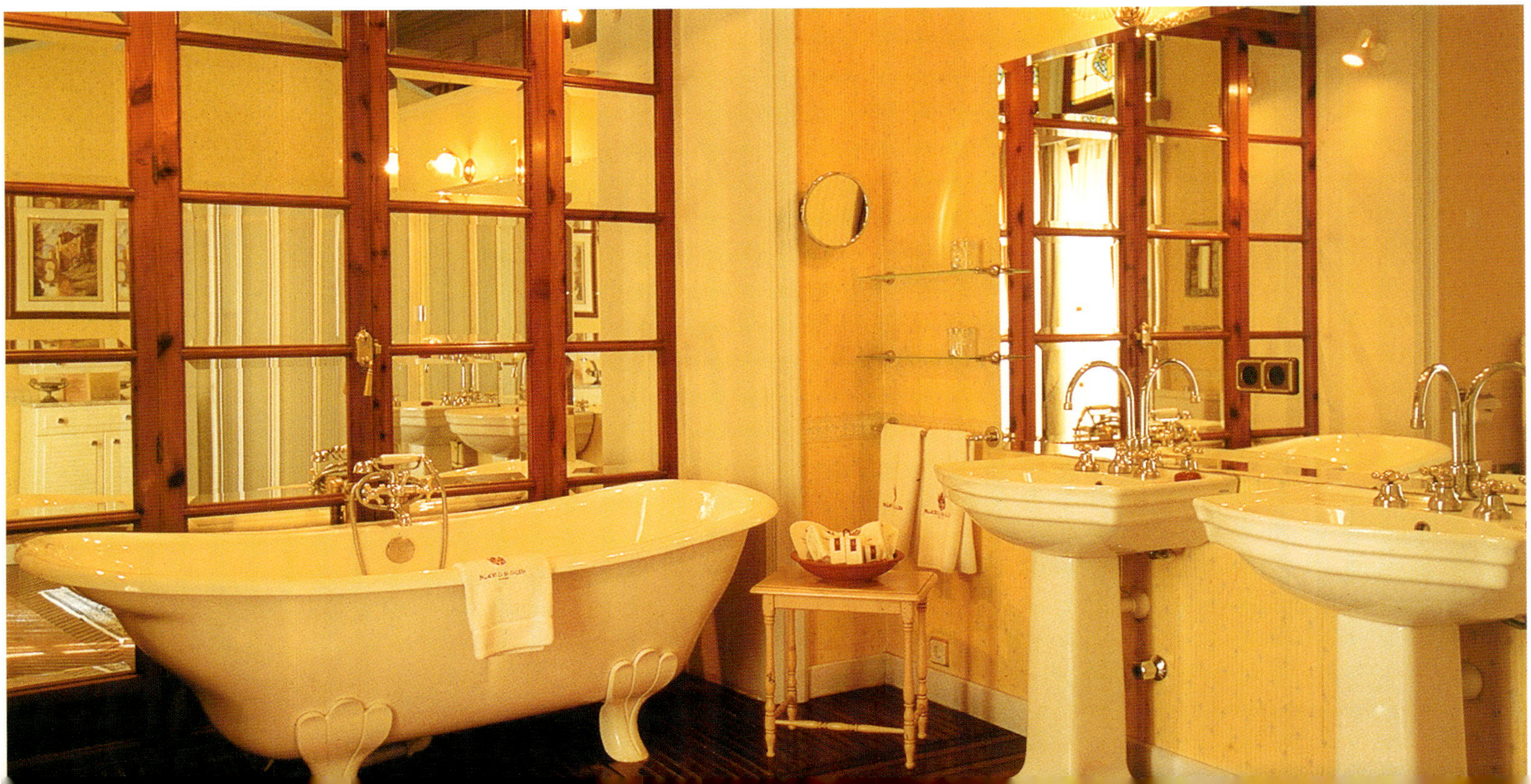

Parador de Jarandilla de la Vera

When King Charles I of Spain chose this magnificent castle, he certainly knew what he was doing. He wanted to spend the last years of his life here, and stayed from 1565 to 1567, until he finally retired to the monastery of Yuste. His personal advisors had recommended the idyllic rural area of La Vera, and this residence in particular, to relax his body and soul. Charles fell in love with the place, which even inspired him to say: "It is heaven on earth. It is where I want to be buried and where I want to start my journey to heaven."

The castle still contains many interesting reminders of the famous King, who was emperor, in his time of about half the known world. There is an impressive coat of arms that still adorns the façade, and the very same fireplace in his bedroom, which he had built to add a romantic touch. Numerous towers and the drawbridge show us the original shape of the castle. The counts of Oropesa and the marquesses of Jarandilla ordered the building of the original edifice in the 14th century, and so a majestic fort arose over the remains of what once was an ancient temple. The building was inspired by the contemporary Italian love of square shapes.

The impressive Parador has two rustic looking floors, built around a central courtyard embellished with a double gallery of columns. Densely-planted gardens, vines and cypresses lend a wonderful green touch to the surroundings.

Charles I was fascinated by the wonderful local cuisine. It was here that he tasted his first roast kid, stuffed Extremadura pig, wonderful cheeses from La Vera and the famous Piornal ham. His chefs were his favourites amongst the staff. Nowadays, a team of masterchefs cook dishes that satisfy even the most refined of palates.

Their local specialities are widely known: the special tomato soup, the roast pig and the excellent La Vera cheese pie.

Visitors to the area are soon charmed by the mild climate, the beautiful surroundings, the remote hermitages, royal castles and monasteries. The hotel can help you organise fascinating trips out into the countryside beyond its venerable walls, stopping off in the beguiling little villages scattered all through this area, even to the monastery of Yuste, only 10 kiometers away, where Emperor Charles spent his final years.

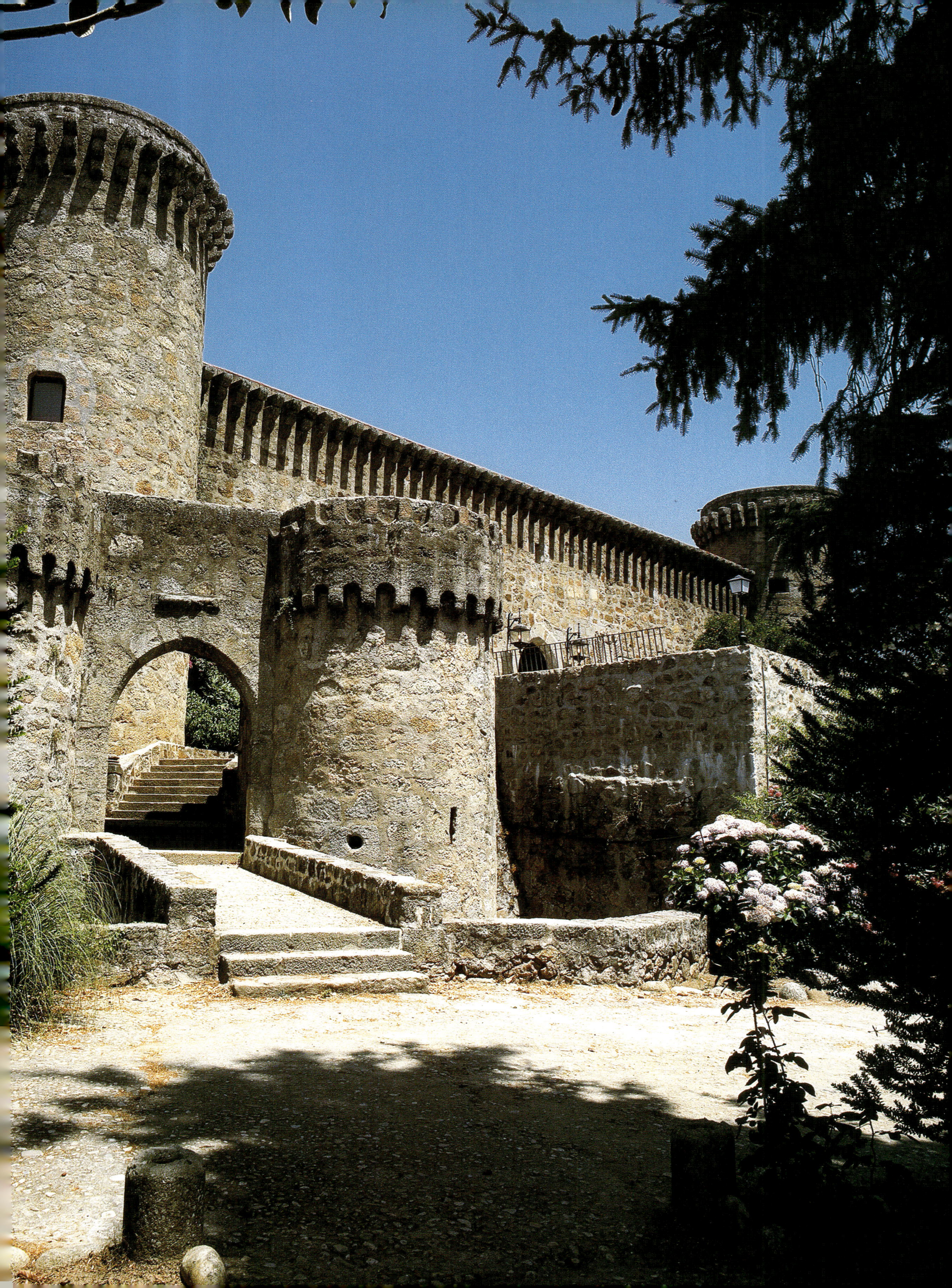

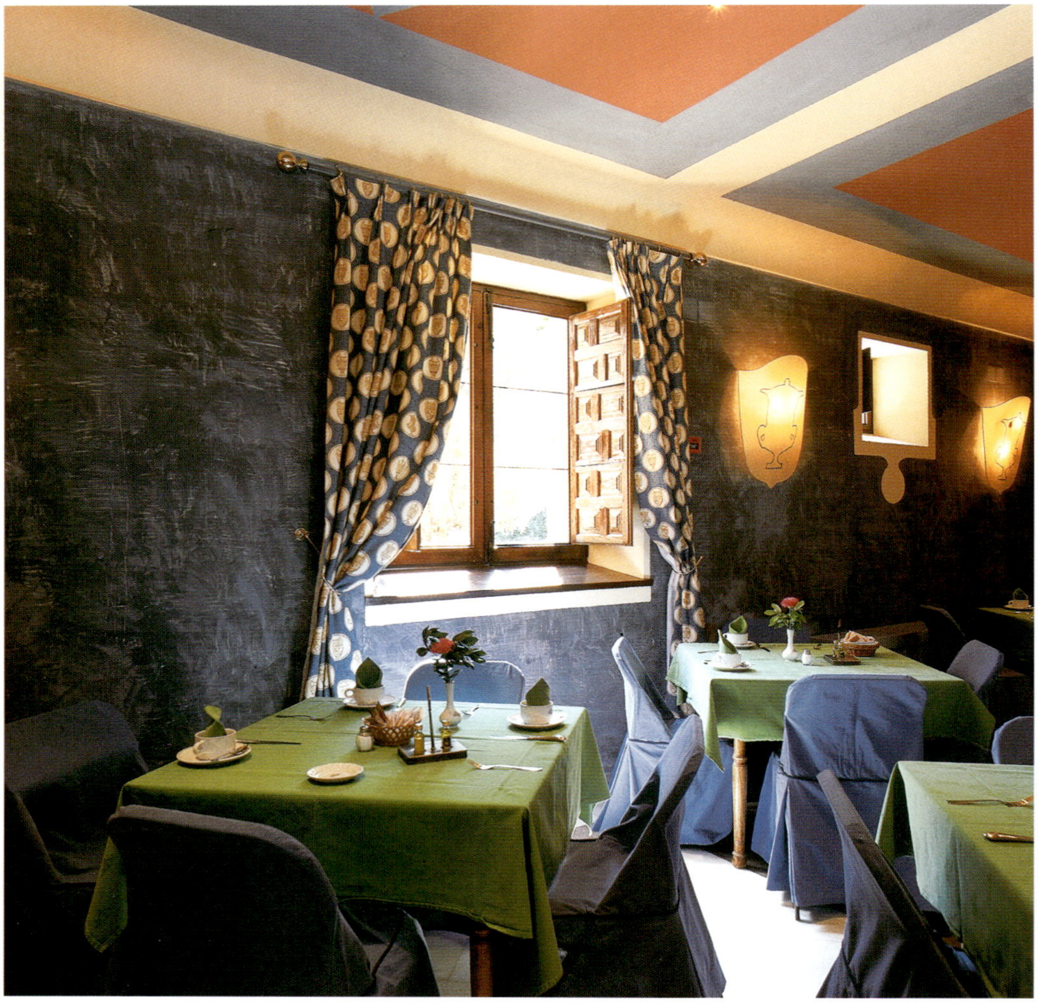

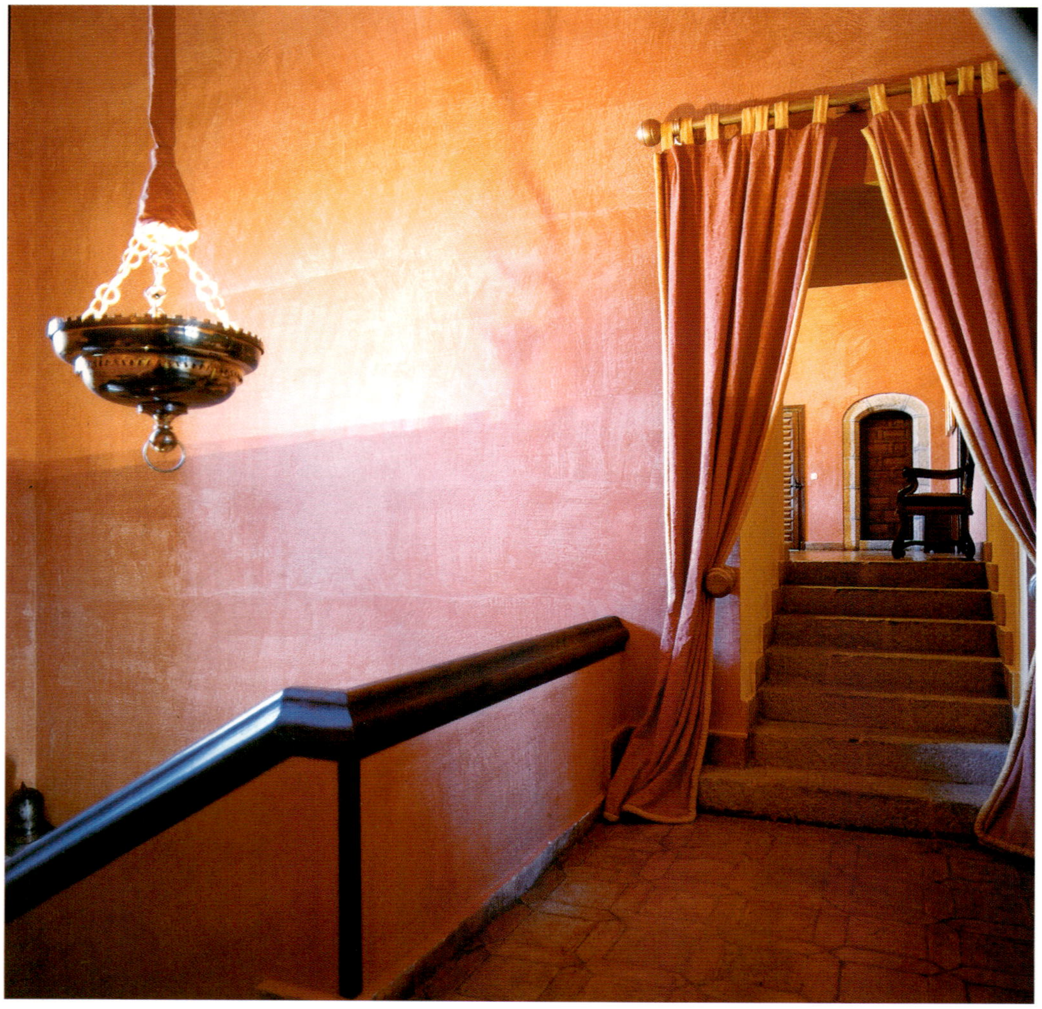

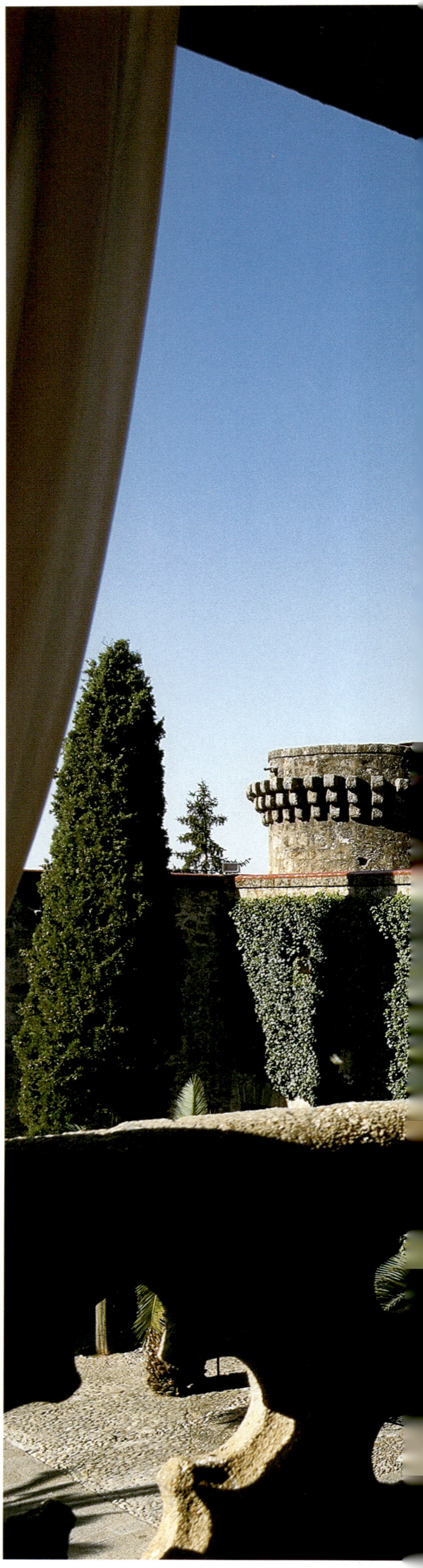

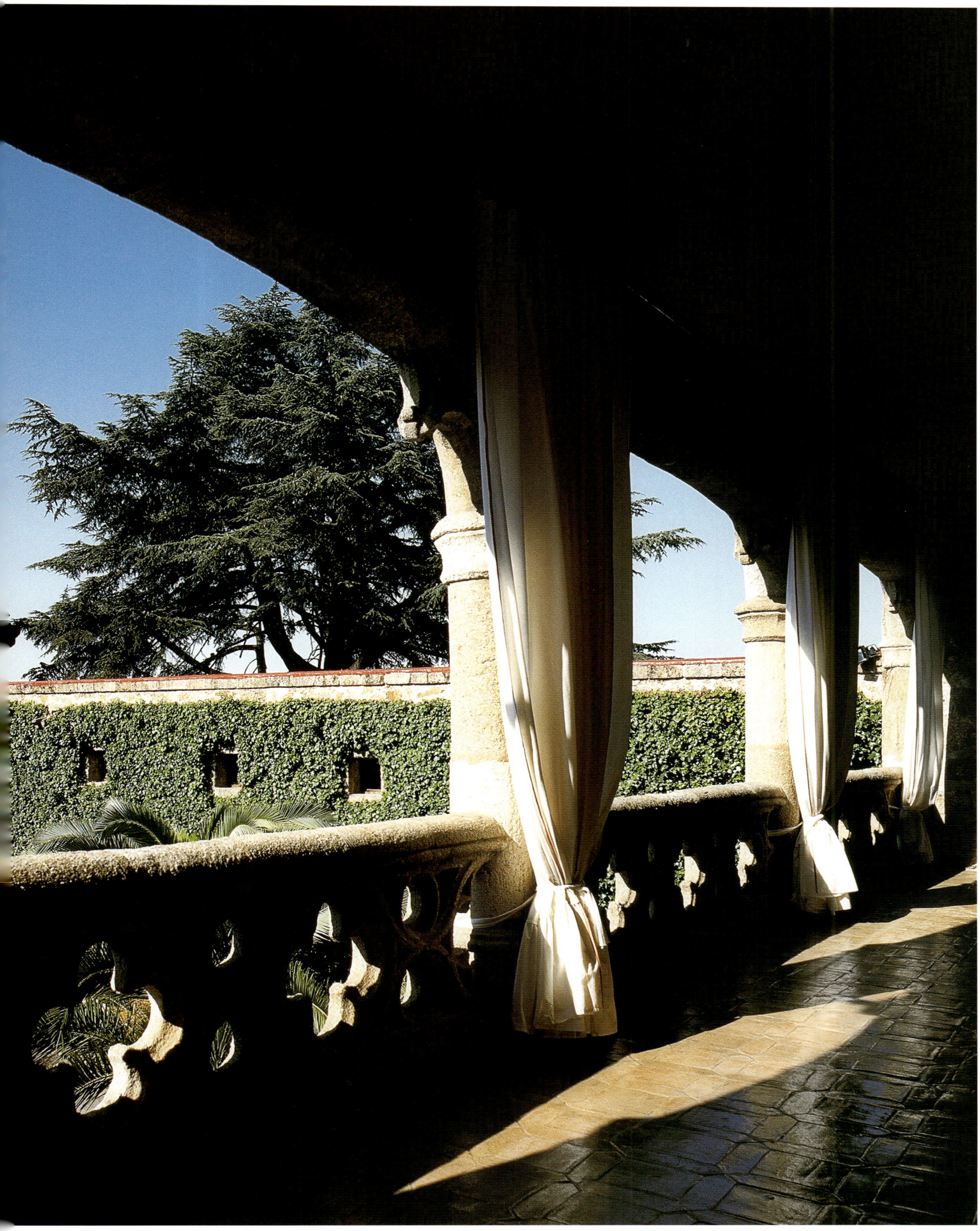

Hacienda Benazuza

My visit to Benazuza began early in the day. For once, I had not travelled far and I was full of curiosity about this very special place I had heard so much about, and in such glowing terms.

The history of Benazuza can be traced back to the 10th century, when it was founded by the Moors. Two hundred years later, Fernando III finally ousted the Muslims and gave the choice estate to his son Alfonso.

Today, almost a thousand years later, Benazuza has been restored and transformed into a wonderful hotel, full of light and space, offering at once every modern luxury and a pervasive sense of medieval quietude.

As I approached the entrance, a sonorous clock struck noon and a hot sun was beating down. A breeze rattled the palm fronds and their dark shadows danced along the bone-white walls.

But inside, it was refreshingly cool. The interior walls are painted in softly glowing dark lemons and terracottas. Shadowed patios give shelter from the heat of the day. Murmuring fountains, pools and rich ferns in large earthenware pots made me feel I had stepped into a safe and welcoming oasis, a Persian garden of delights.

Benazuza is close enough to the busy city of Seville to make it an ideal hideaway for anyone wishing to explore this poetic and vibrant city. I had already spent a fascinating two days there and was ready to relax for awhile, swim in the gorgeous pool, sip a glass or two of fine dark Jerez wine and contemplate the gourmet meal that awaited me as the evening closed in and waiters touched a flame to candles that flickered across the white linen of the Alqueria Restaurant.

There are 44 lavish, air-conditioned rooms and suites, equipped with every modern luxury - some with frescoes on the ceiling, minstrel galleries, jacuzzis or private patios.

When you've had your fill of museums and street cafés, the hotel can arrange for you to take part in an exciting traditional hunt in the wild countryside beyond its walls; the spectacular Doñana National Park is waiting to be explored; there are tennis courts in the grounds and fine golf courses not far away.

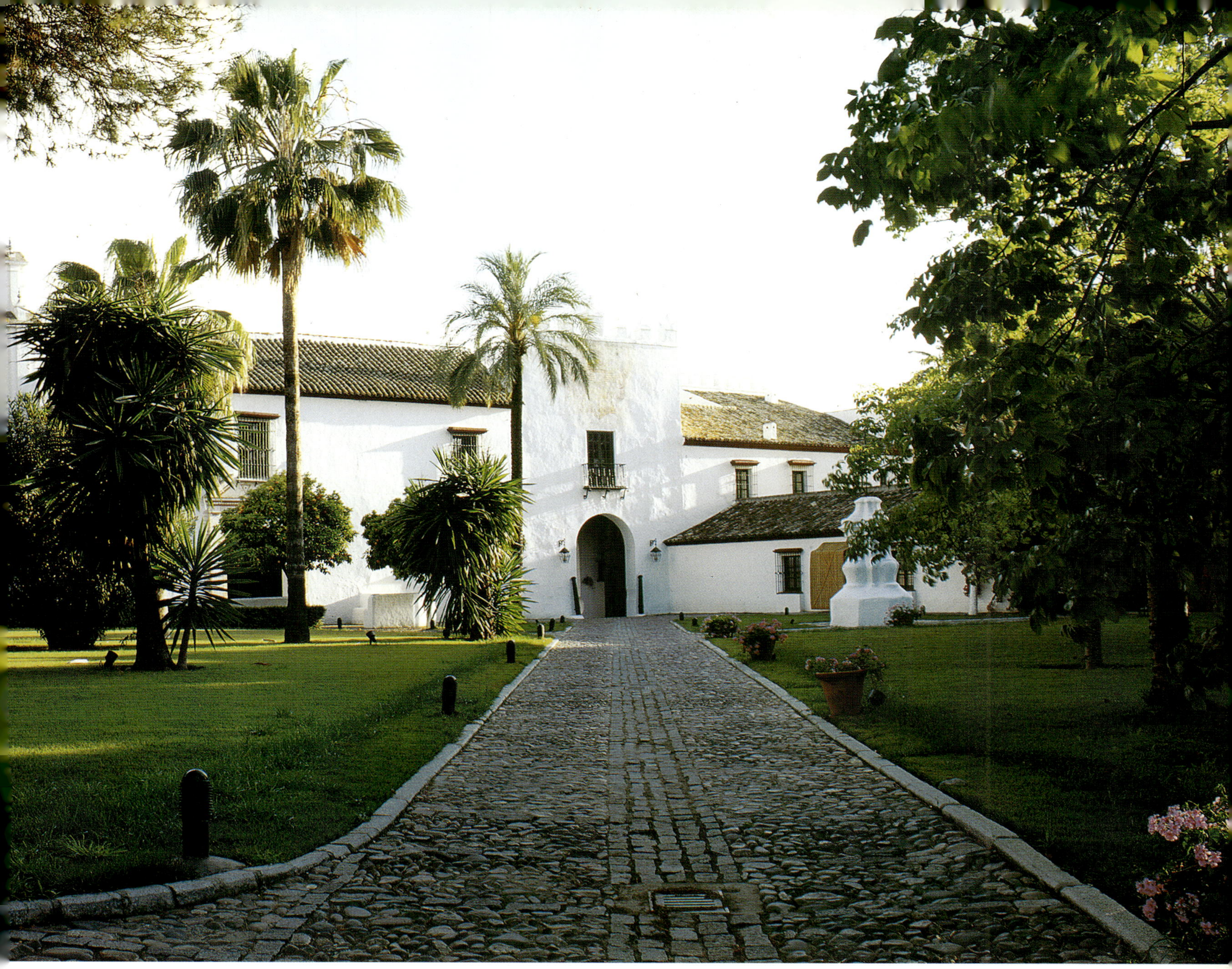

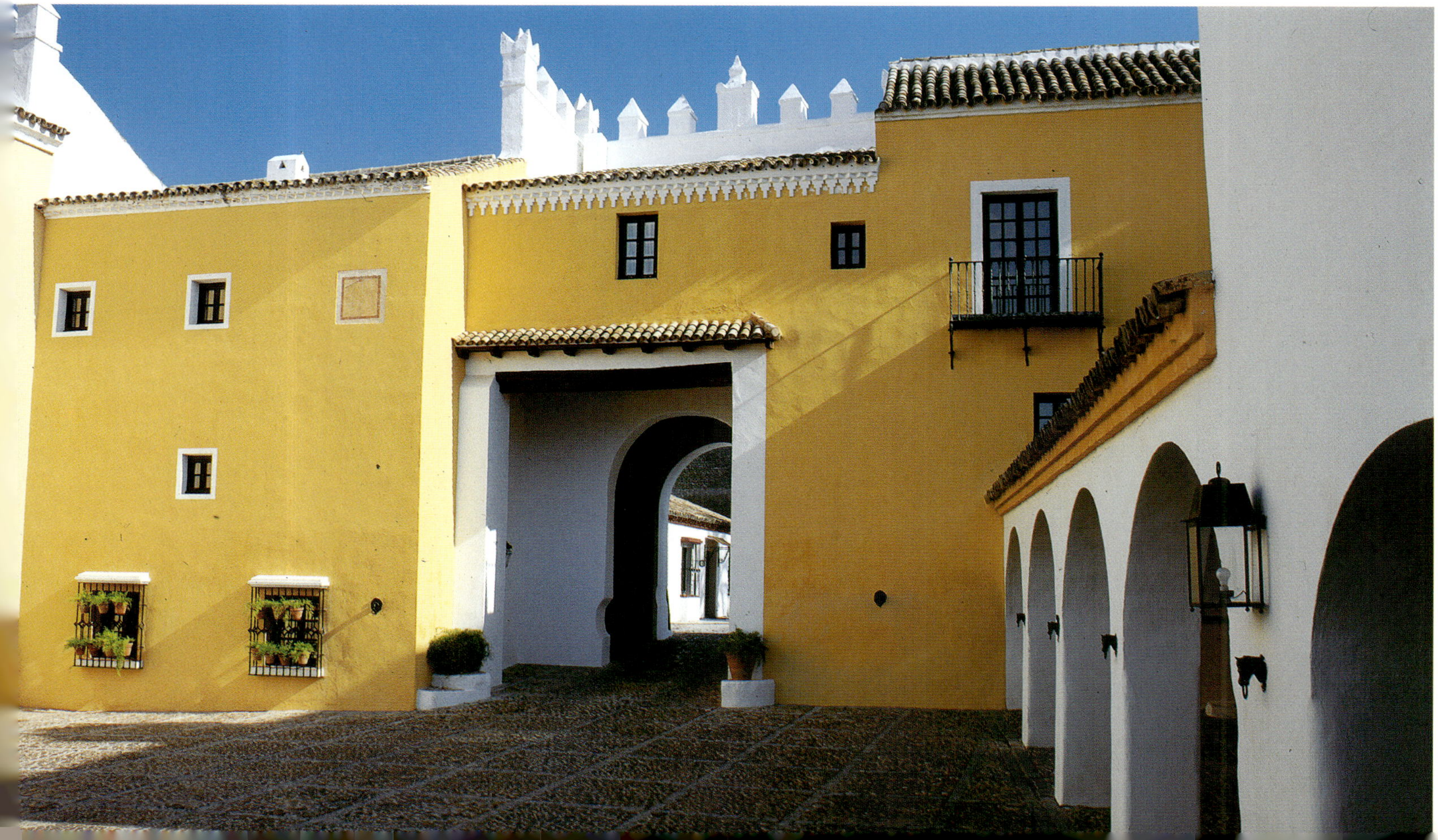

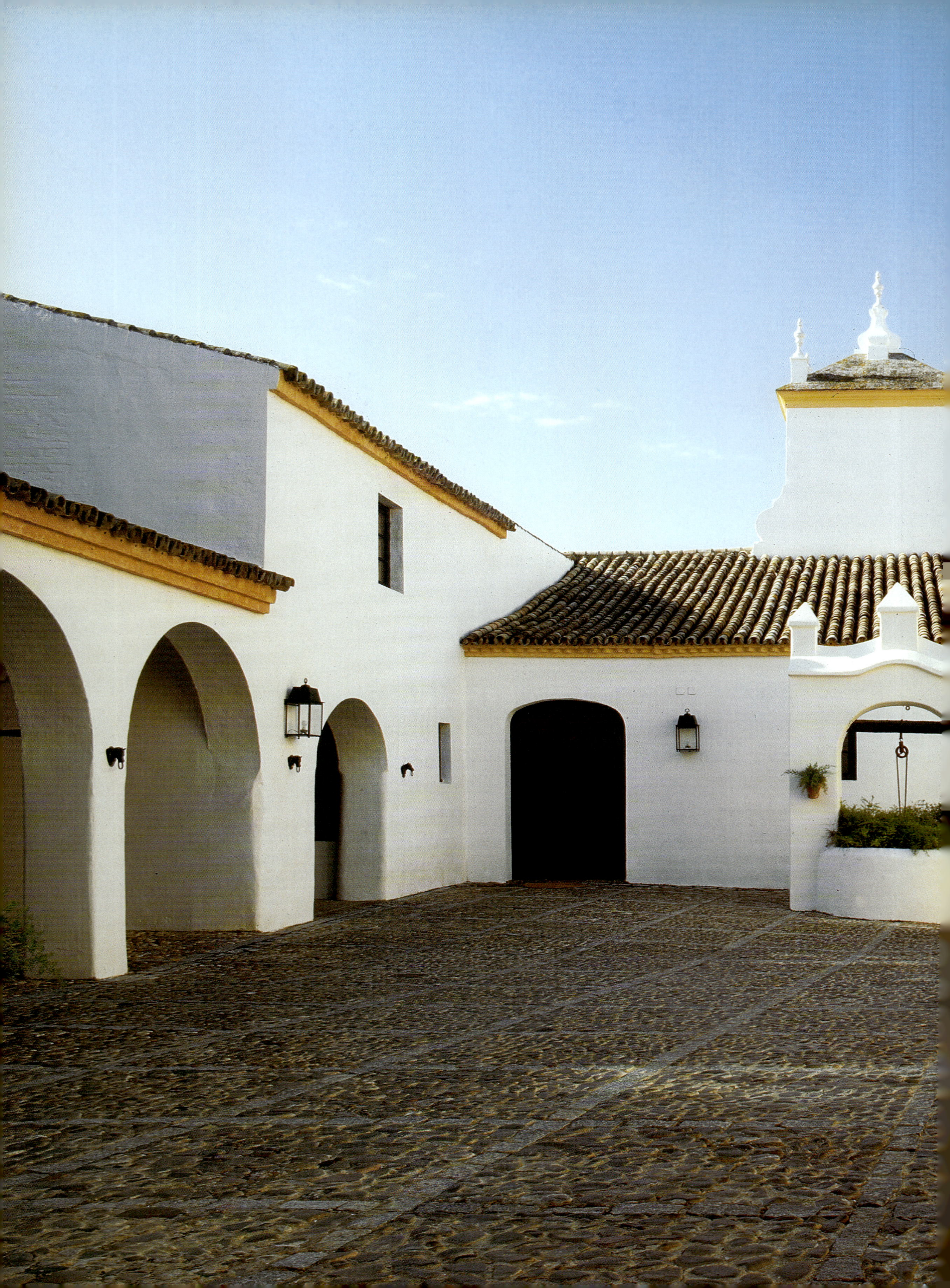

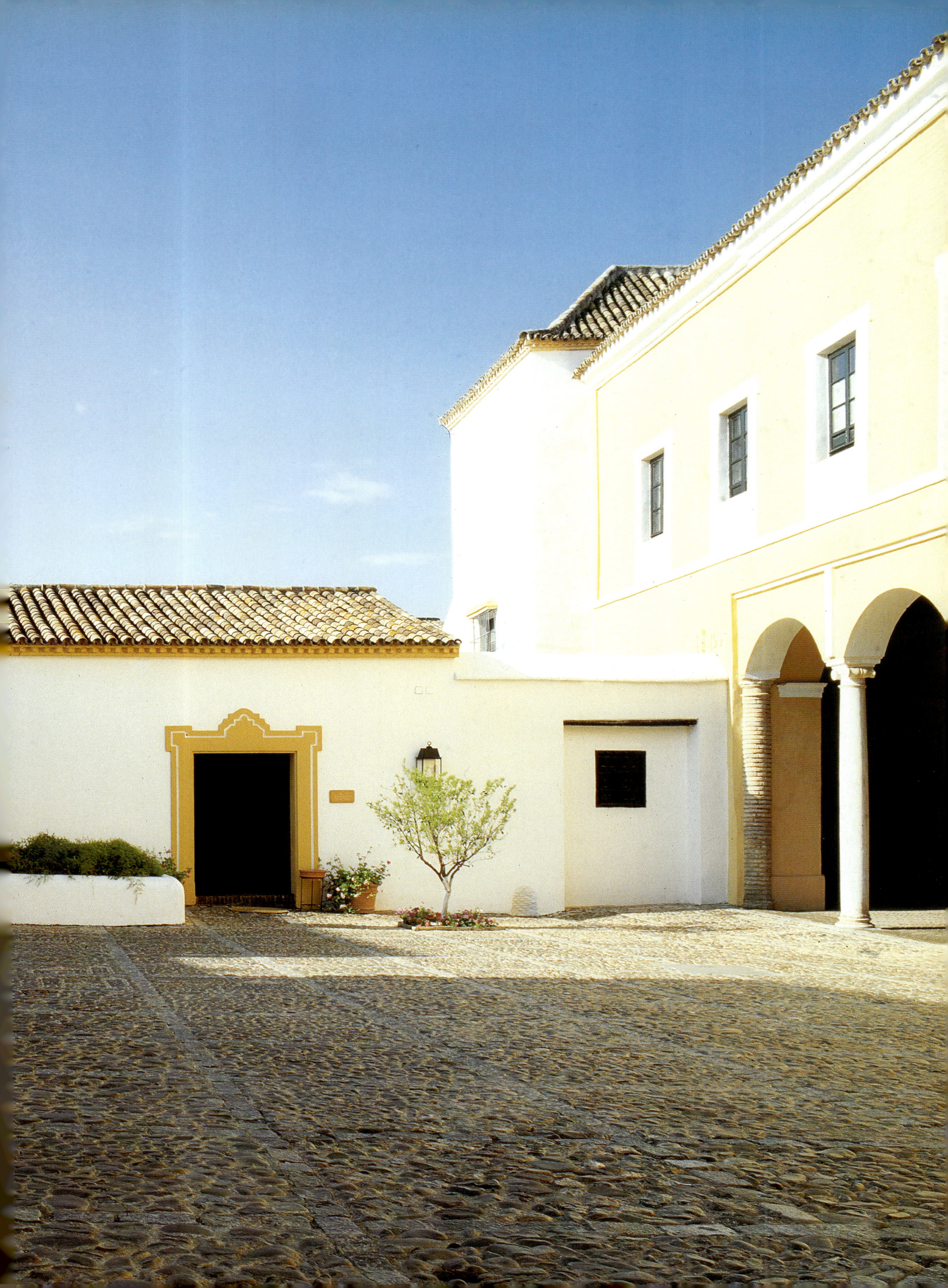

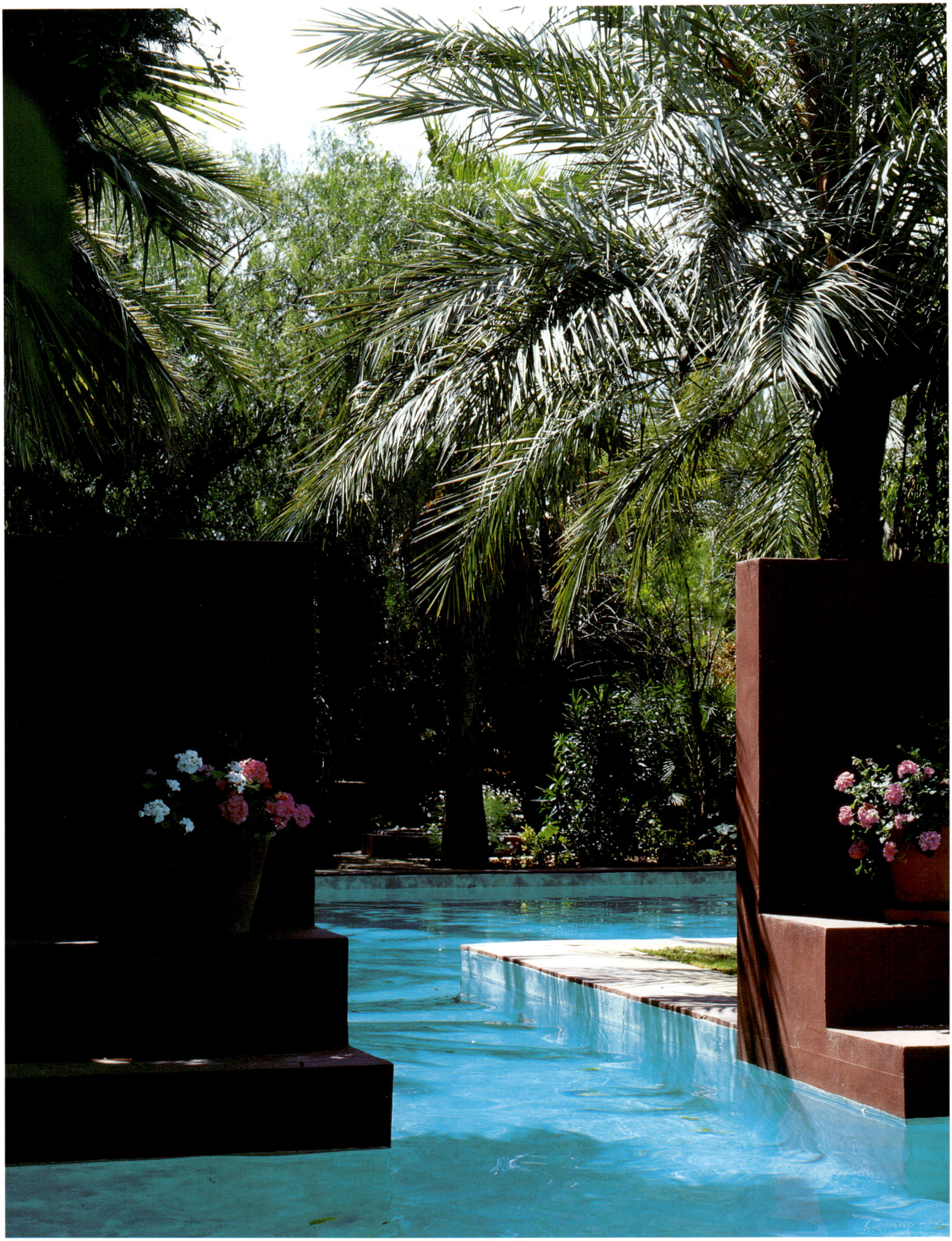

On my last morning, I strolled down to the breakfast restaurant for a long and leisurely breakfast, al large pot of coffee at my elbow. The barons of old who lived here at Benazuza might have led lives of considerable luxury, but they could not have been any more cossetted than a guest is today.

Refinement and a genuine Spanish atmosphere...

114

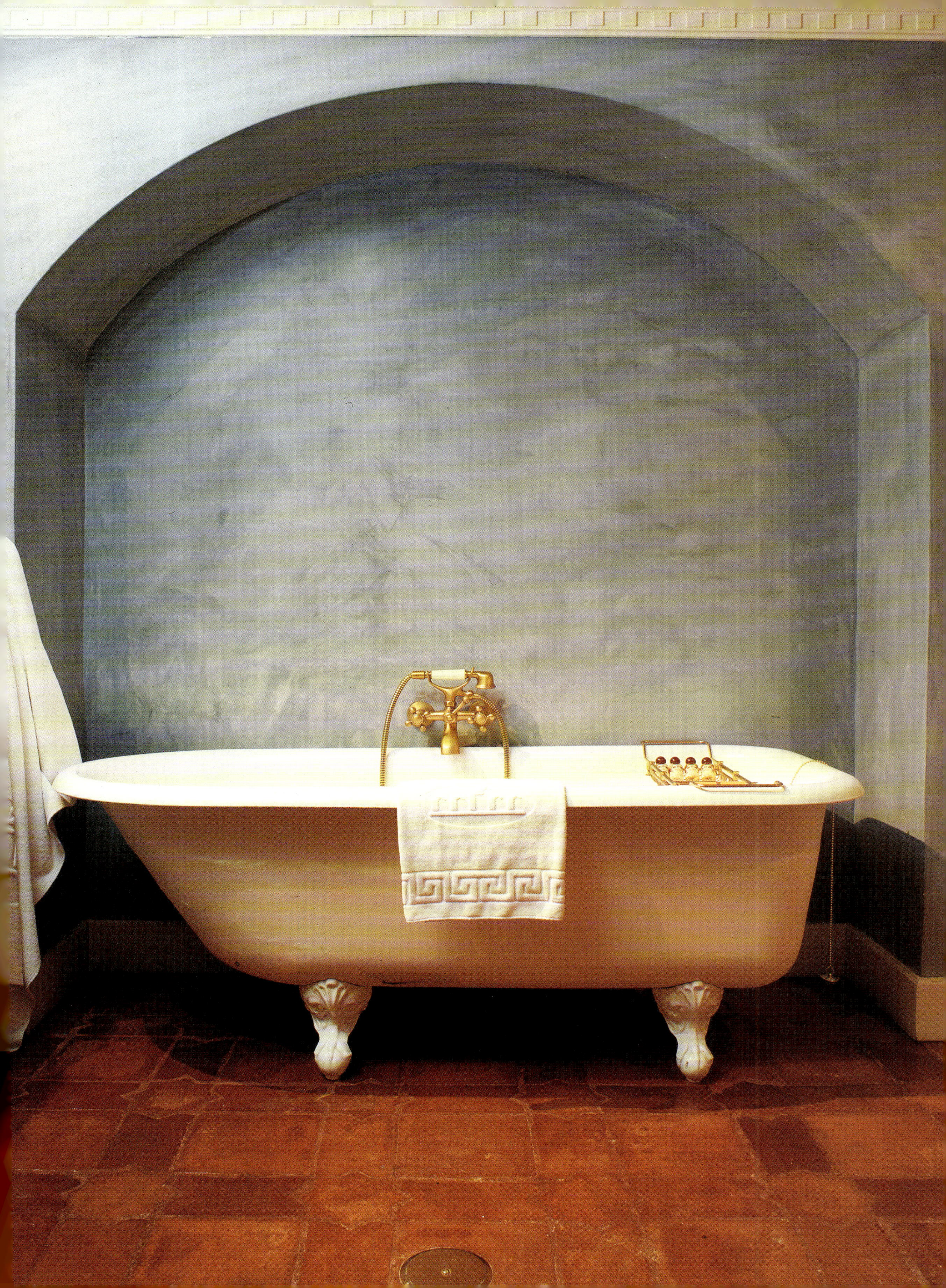

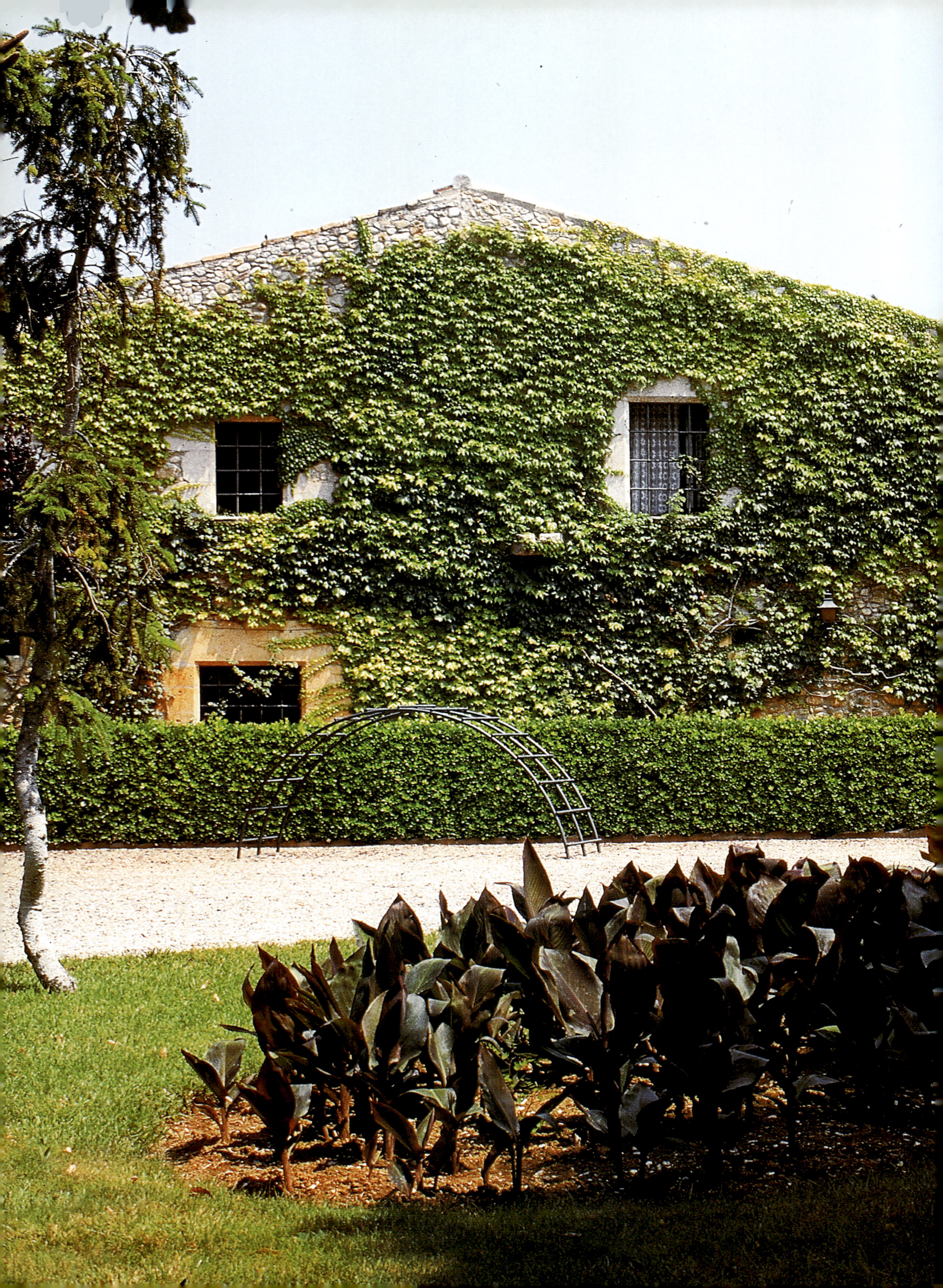

Mas Pau

Any seasonal and well-informed traveller entering Spain by the eastern seaboard, at Perpignan, will have but one destination in mind. Whether they intend to sit down to a good meal before they take a brisk stroll around the Salvador Dali Museum or, more sensibly in my view, if they are going to put their feet up in superior comfort for a night or two and eat something special as well, they will be heading for the Hotel Mas Pau, in Figueres.

Set back a few miles from the glistening Mediterranean, the Mas Pau is tranquil and serene, sophisticated and charming.

Long ago, in the 16th century, Mas Pau was an estate farmhouse presiding in a down-to-earth way over far acres of citrus groves, with a quiet mien and its back to the world. It is still a place to go when the hustle and bustle seems too much, but the farmhouse, over the passage of time, was extended and has now been restored with panache and a careful and sympathetic regard for history.

Most rooms are situated in an annexe that is totally modern but constructed seamlessly in the same spirit as the old farmhouse, now the main part of the hotel, housing their very well-known restaurant. There are several double rooms and a single suite, but they offer all the refinements you'd expect in any urbane grand hotel, and all face out onto the colourful and seductive gardens, with cosy and shaded terraces close by lined with trees in fat terracotta pots.

The meals are fabulous… and locals from miles around come to sample them, and return again and again. Mas Pau's chef, Xavier Sacrista, has the artistic and dramatic look of one of Dali's descendants, though he's not. His menu is cleverly divided between offerings in the vanguard of modern international cuisine and (my own preference) traditional Catalonian dishes, with a personal twist all the chef's own.

There is nothing surreal about Mas Pau, but down the way is a shrine to the Spaniard with the wonderful moustache, Salvador Dali. Don't hasten through the museum in Figueres, take your time and see the world, for just an hour or two, his way. It will be an exciting and quite unforgettable experience.

The very same could be said of Mas Pau. Don't hurry away… rest up, dream awhile and let the ancient magic of the place overtake you, at its own rural pace.

118

In the 16th century, Mas Pau was a farm. Even in those days, the citrus trees stretched as far as the eye could see.

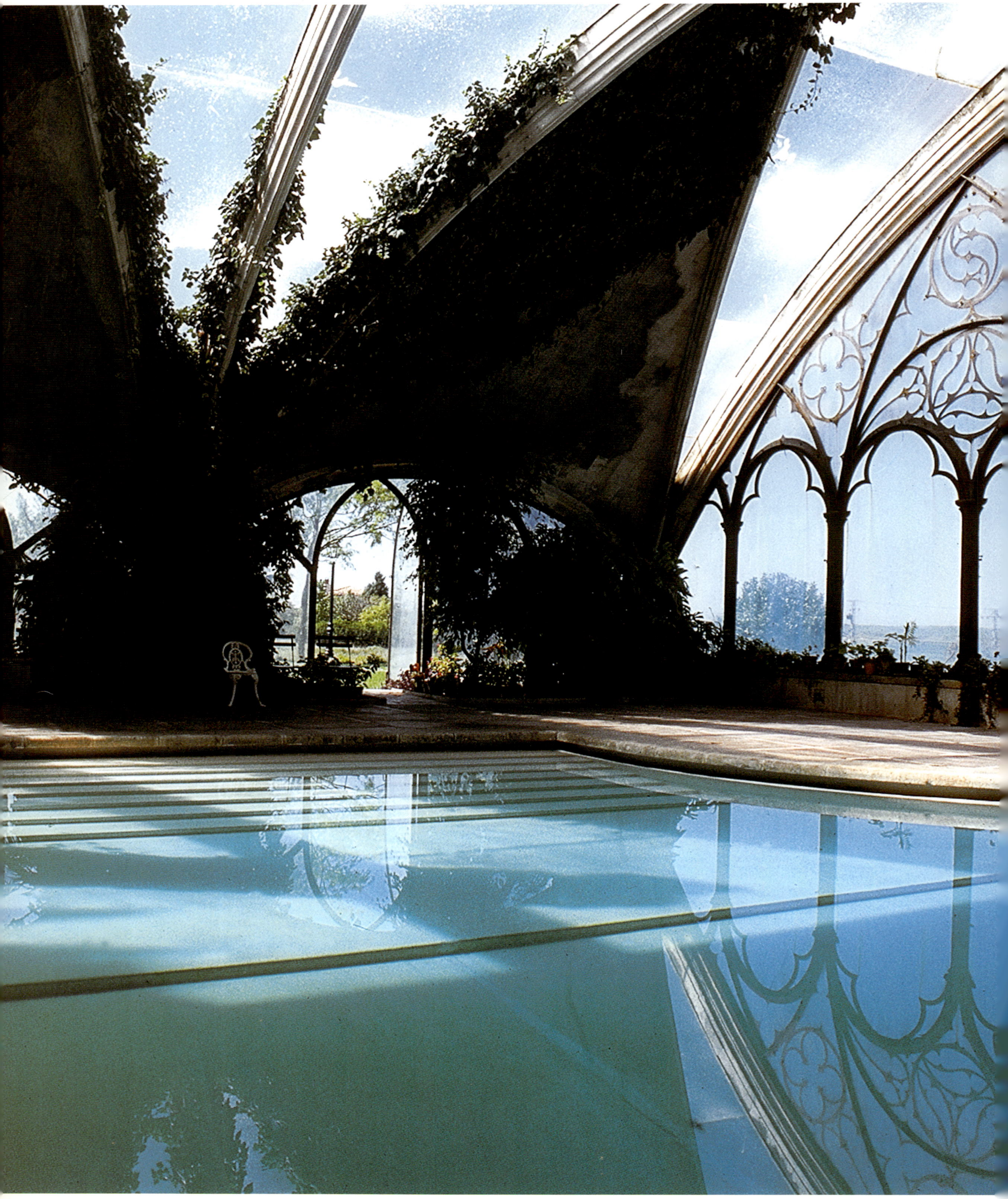

Landa Palace

Whether you drive south from the ferry port of Santander, or from Bilbao, also on Spain's northern coastline, the two roads will meet in the ancient town of Burgos, an ideal place to break your journey south towards Madrid, take a breather, and relax for a day or two before continuing onwards.

There is plenty to see in Burgos itself, but just a mile outside a special hotel awaits the traveller who appreciates the better things in life. In the village of Albillos, on the edge of Burgos and on the banks of the Rio Gabia, you'll find what you're looking for: the five star Landa Palace Hotel, a refreshing oasis of rural peace and sophisticated comfort.

You really don't have to book their 'Royal Suite' to feel suitably welcomed and pampered... every suite and every room is special; modern, certainly, but with a timeless feel that always seems to go with good design, craftsmanship and quality furnishings.

I've always said that it's worth, sometimes, forsaking the apparent convenience of air travel to experience something that more than makes up for losing a little time. This hotel is a perfect reason why a journey by road is justified.

The province of Burgos has some gorgeous beech forests in the Sierra de la Demanda, expansive areas of pines in Yecla and the Canyon del Rio Lobos boasts, as the name suggests, a deep and steep-sided caynon spread with wild flowers, the habitat of soaring eagles and other birds of prey, of deer, wild boar, and the elusive otter.

Once in Burgos itself, look out for the lovely and ancient cathedral of Santa Maria and the 14th century Gothic church of San Esteban. The Burgos Museum is housed in a pair of small but enchanting Renaissance palaces, the Casa del Inigo Angulo and the Casa de Miranda.

After installing yourself in your room at the Landa - admiring on your way the wide and opulent marble staircase that leads to the upper floors - head for the inviting indoor pool. Over your head as you cool off in the shimmering water is an amazing vaulted ceiling and, around you, arched windows giving you huge views out into the surrounding countryside.

The key to a memorable hotel, though; is the food... and the Landa is a gastronomic delight. I tried their excellent garlic soup and followed it with a delicate roast lamb served with the freshest of local vegetables, completing a very disctinctive and beautifully served meal with local cheese served with honey and nuts and a delicious pot of coffee. By the time I left the table, night had fallen and I took a little walk out onto the wide terrace in front of the Landa, with its little wrought-iron bandstand. I gazed out into the purpling distance, feeling a satisfying sleepiness overcome me, together with anticipation of the day that lay ahead, a continuing voyage of discovery into the romantic Iberian peninsula.

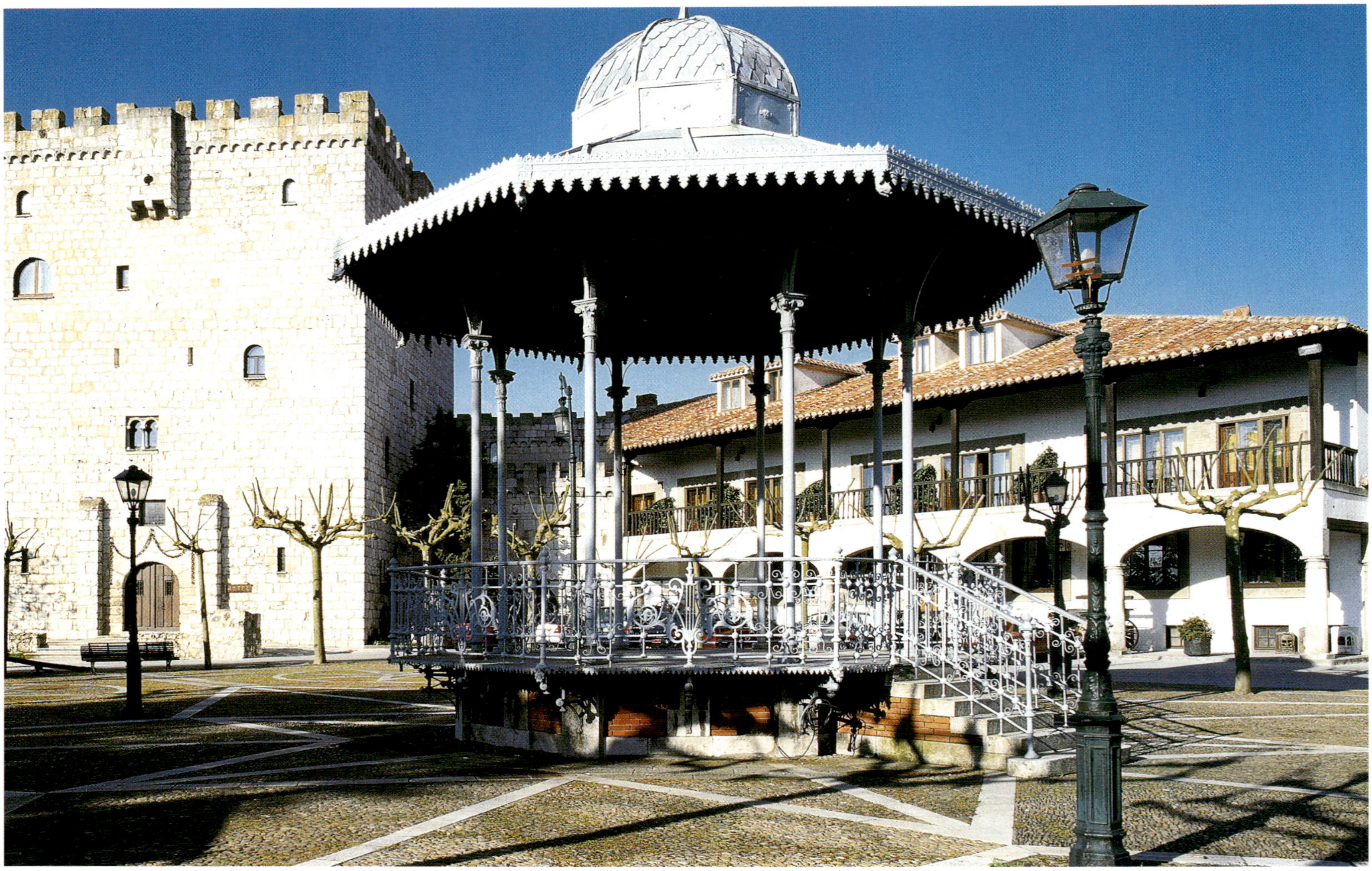

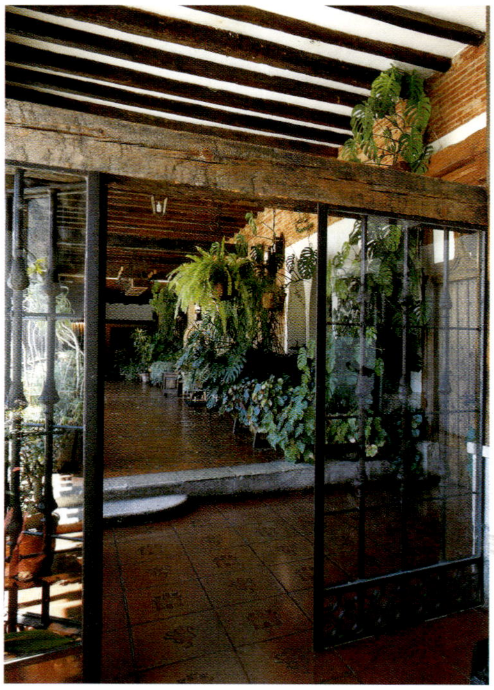

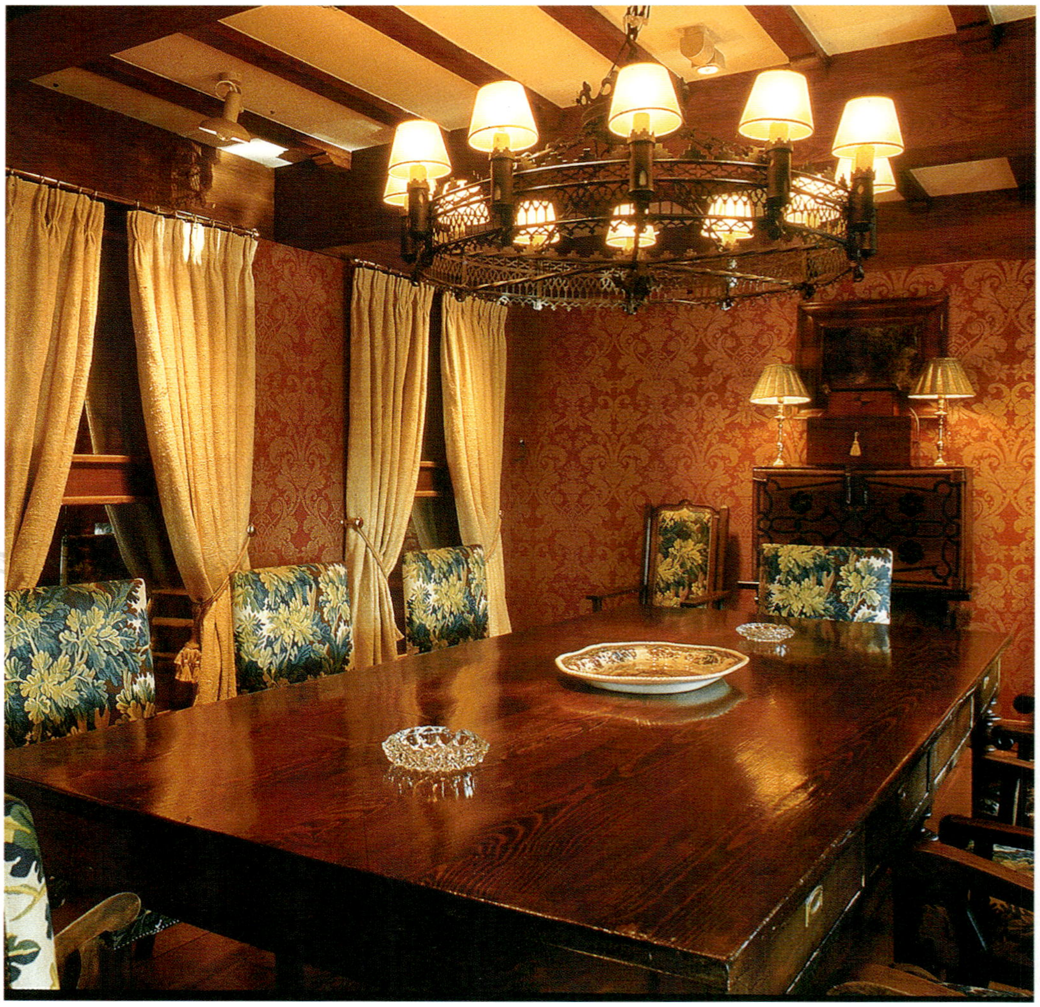

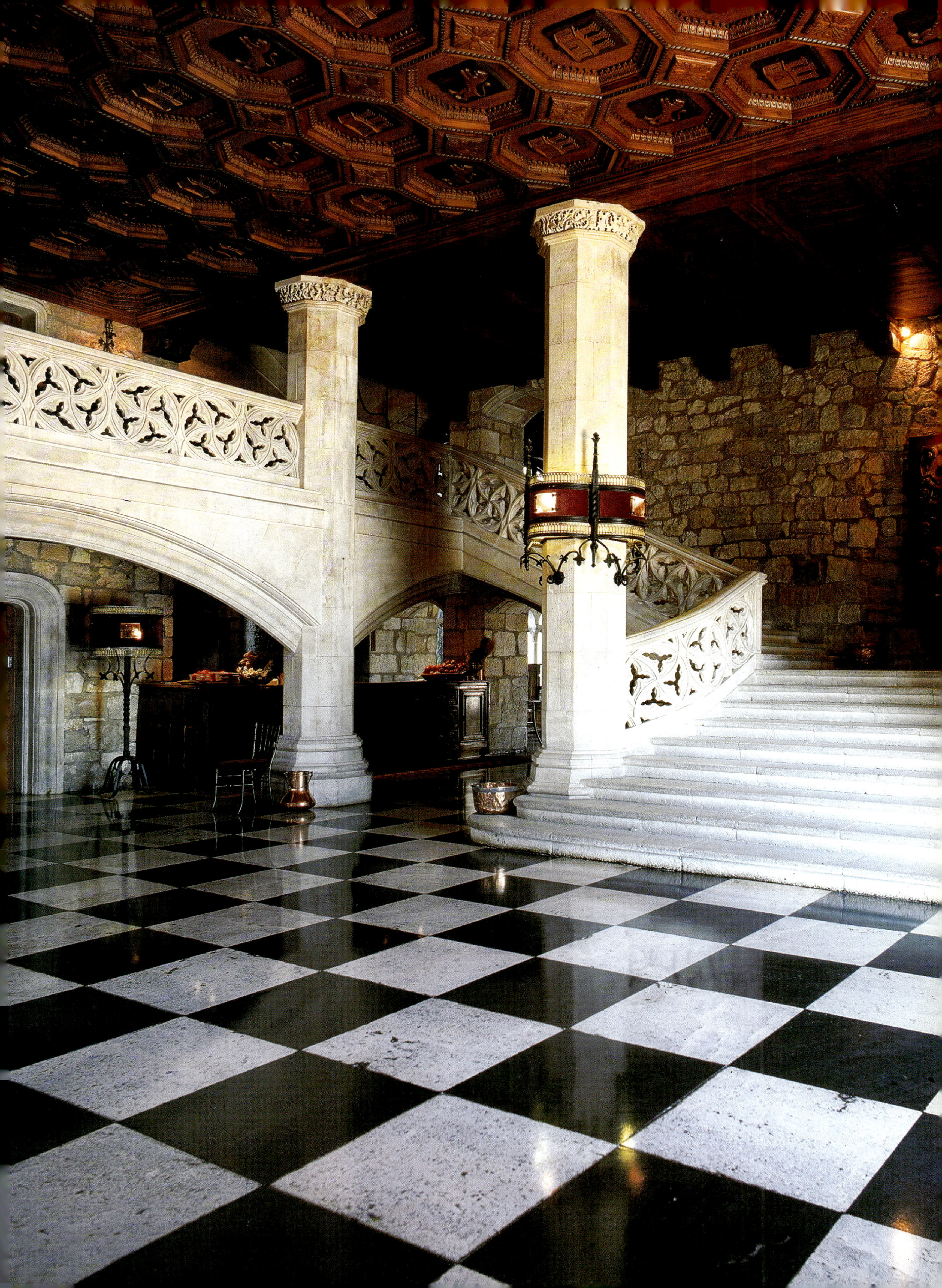

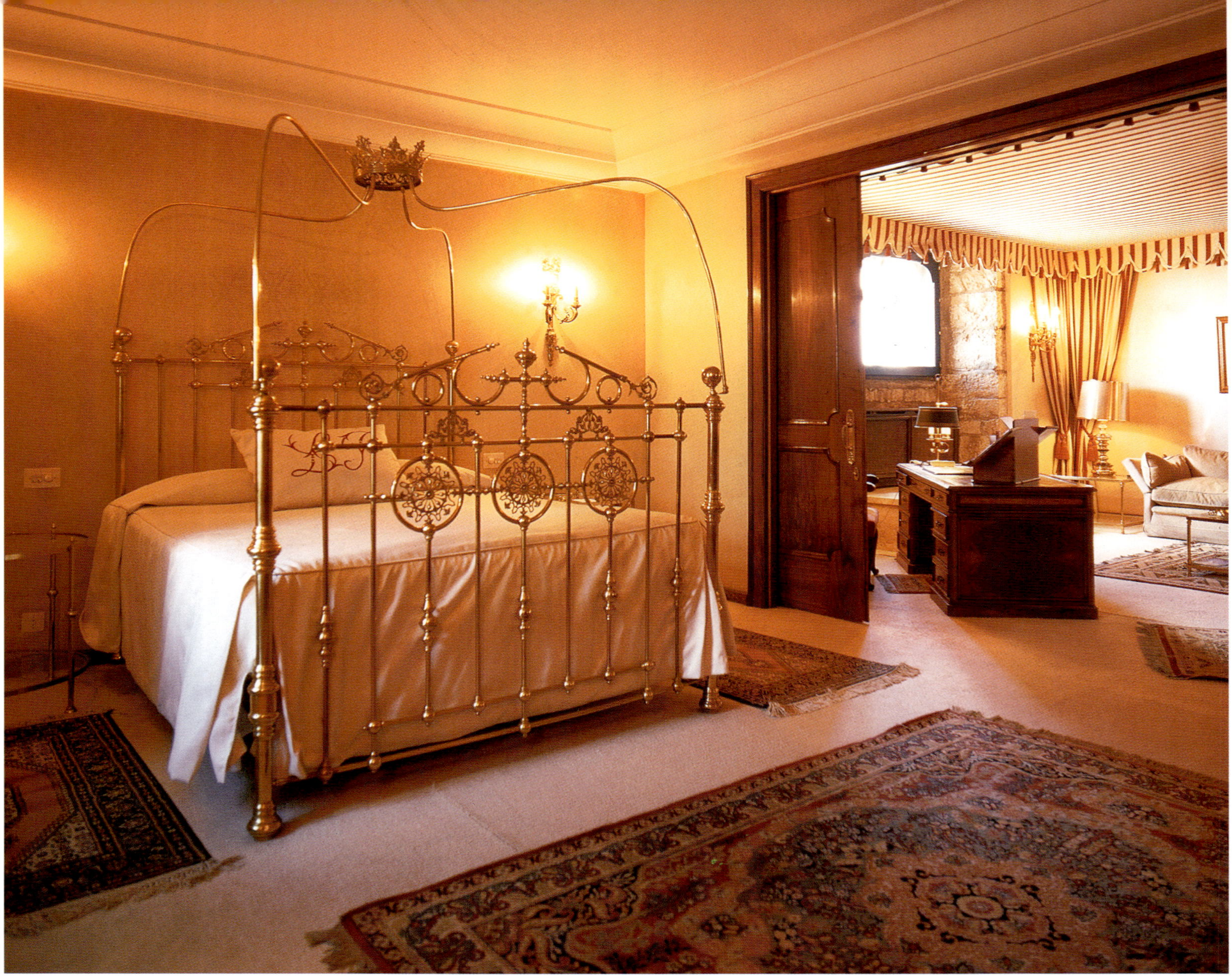

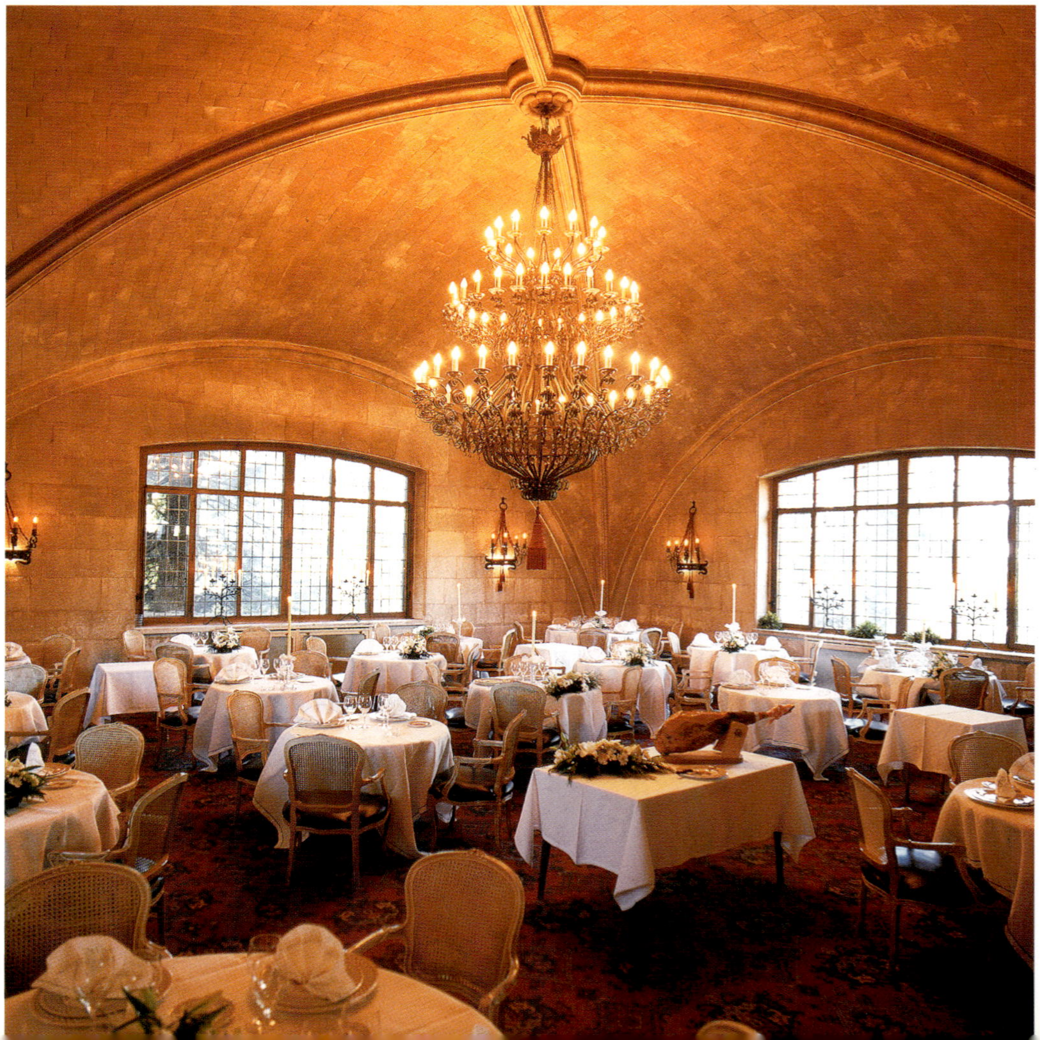

Landa Palace is an exceptional luxury hotel in Burgos.

Parador de Zamora

In the historic centre of Zamora stands a 15th century palace, now a luxurious Parador. It was built on the ruins of a Roman castle. After the Castilian wars, an inner courtyard in Renaissance style and an impressive stairway were added. The palace eventually became a children's home. In 1968 it was extensively restored and became the wonderfully-appointed hotel it is today. The medieval atmosphere of the interior, with its suits of armour, ancient wall hangings and beautiful four-poster beds is in beautiful harmony with the Renaissance style of the patio, the glassed-in wooden gallery and the many coats of arms along the walls. In the lovely courtyard garden there is an inviting swimming pool. The restaurant offers a wide array of local specialities, such as cod, trout, luscious squid, pork, a special consommé and, for dessert, wonderful Zamoran specialities or a piece of almond flan. Zamora is in Castile, not far from the border of Portugal. Here you feel you are in the real Spain. Not to be missed is the Visigoth church of San Pedro de la Nave, which dates from the end of the 7th century, and of course the lively university town of Salamanca, with its typical narrow streets and numerous monuments, with squares such as the Plaza Mayor and the cosy Patio de las Escualas, with the old 12th -century Cathedral and the 'new' 16th –century Cathedral. Other interesting features are the many convents and old university colleges.

PARADOR DE TURISMO
CONDES DE ALBA
DE ALISTE

128

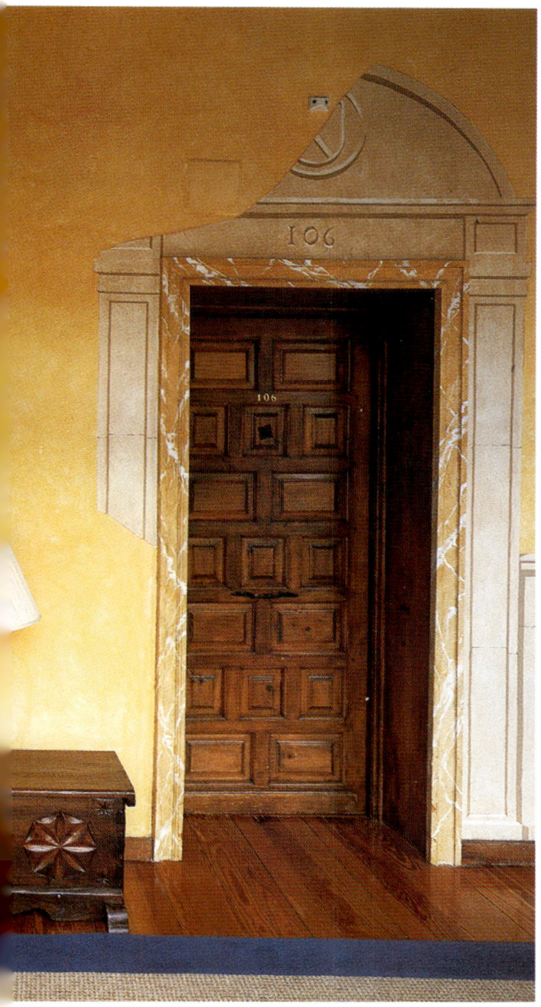
106

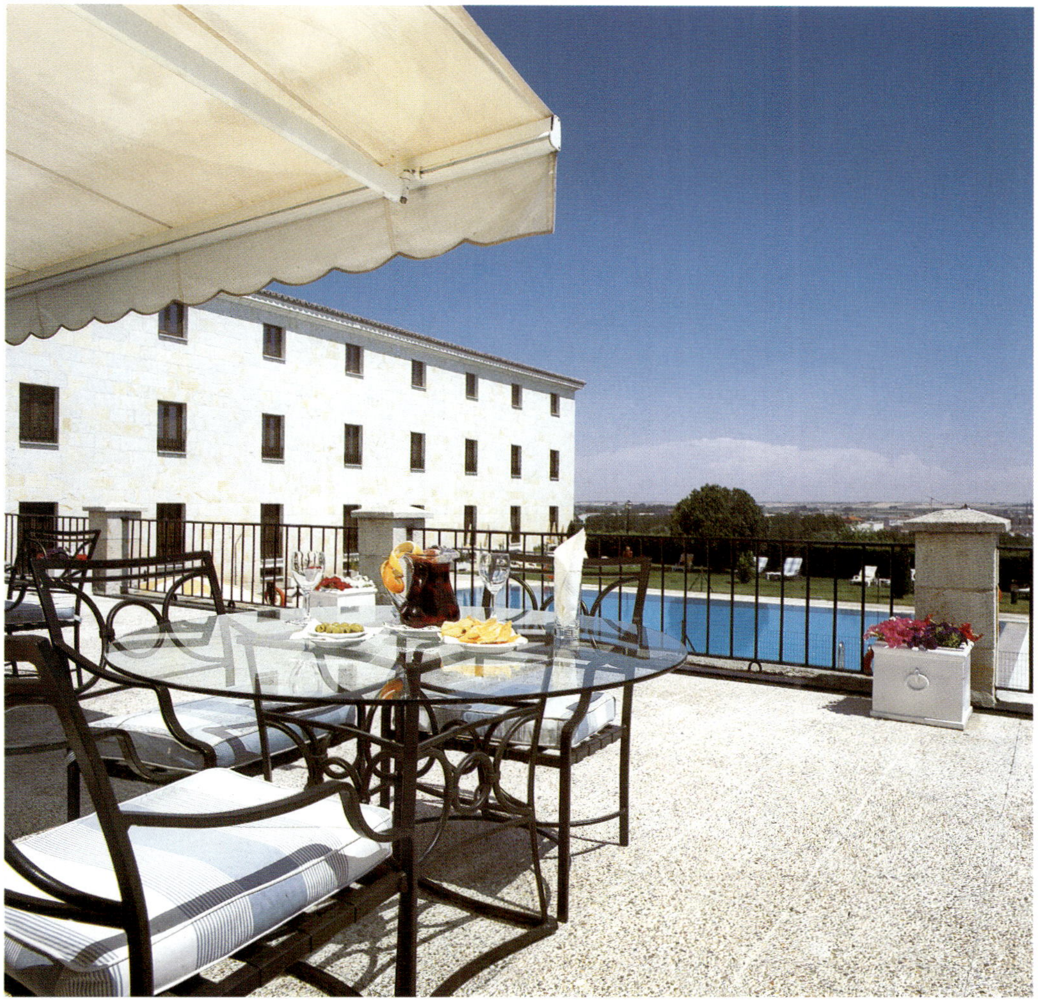

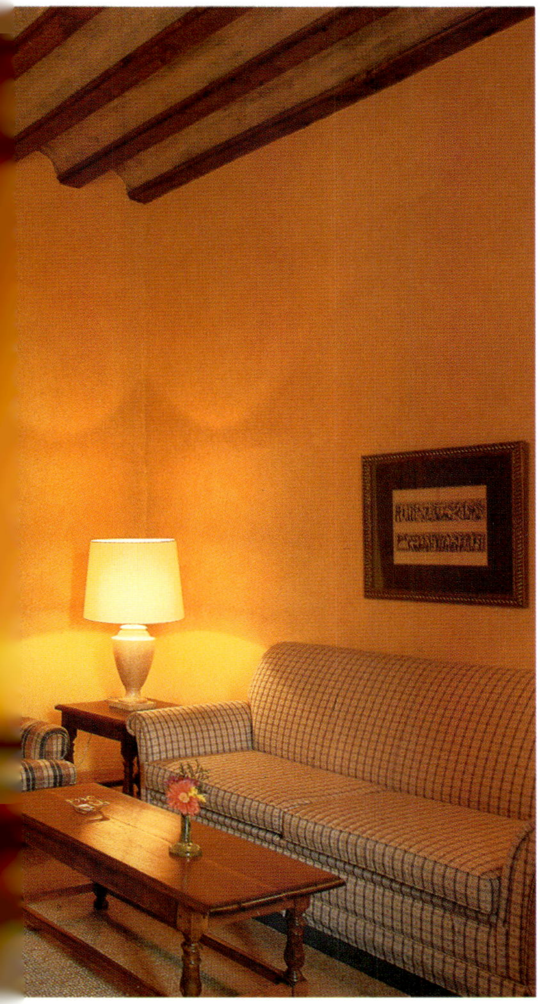

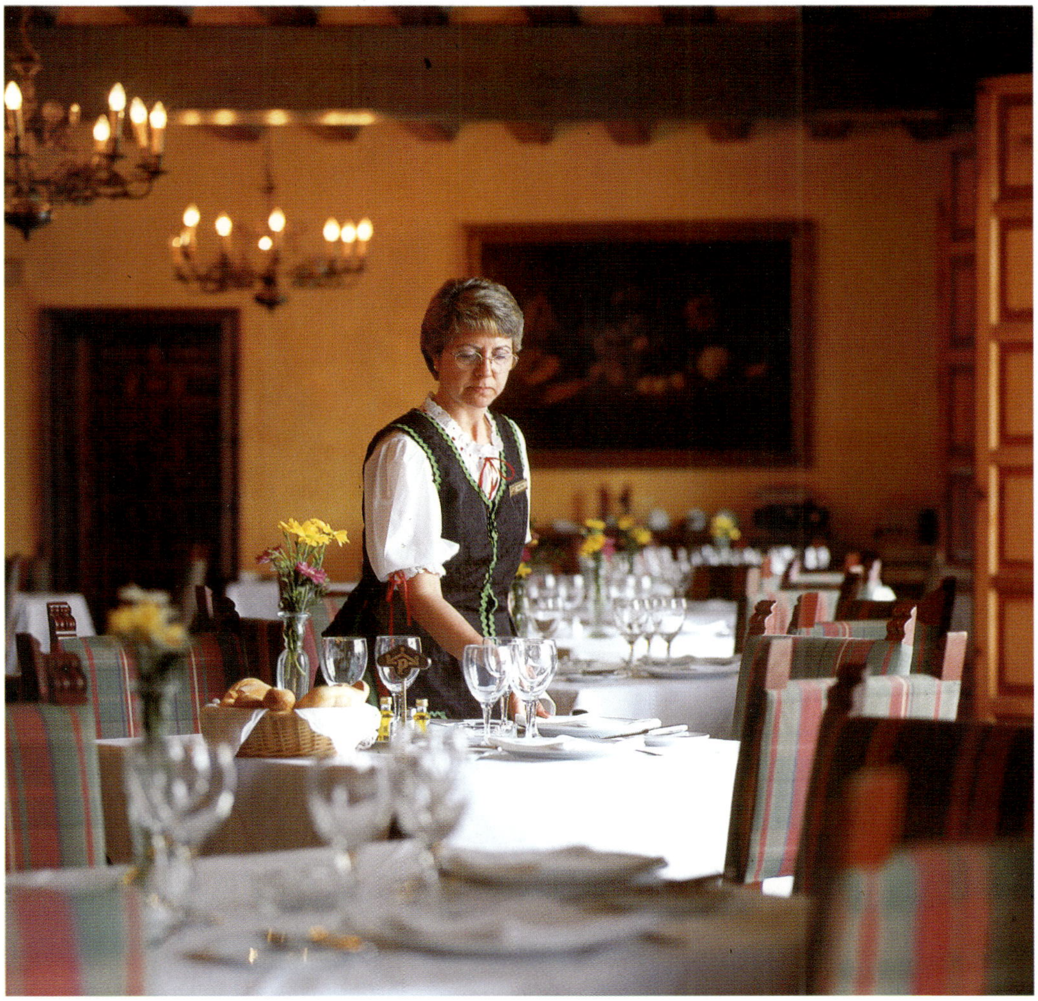

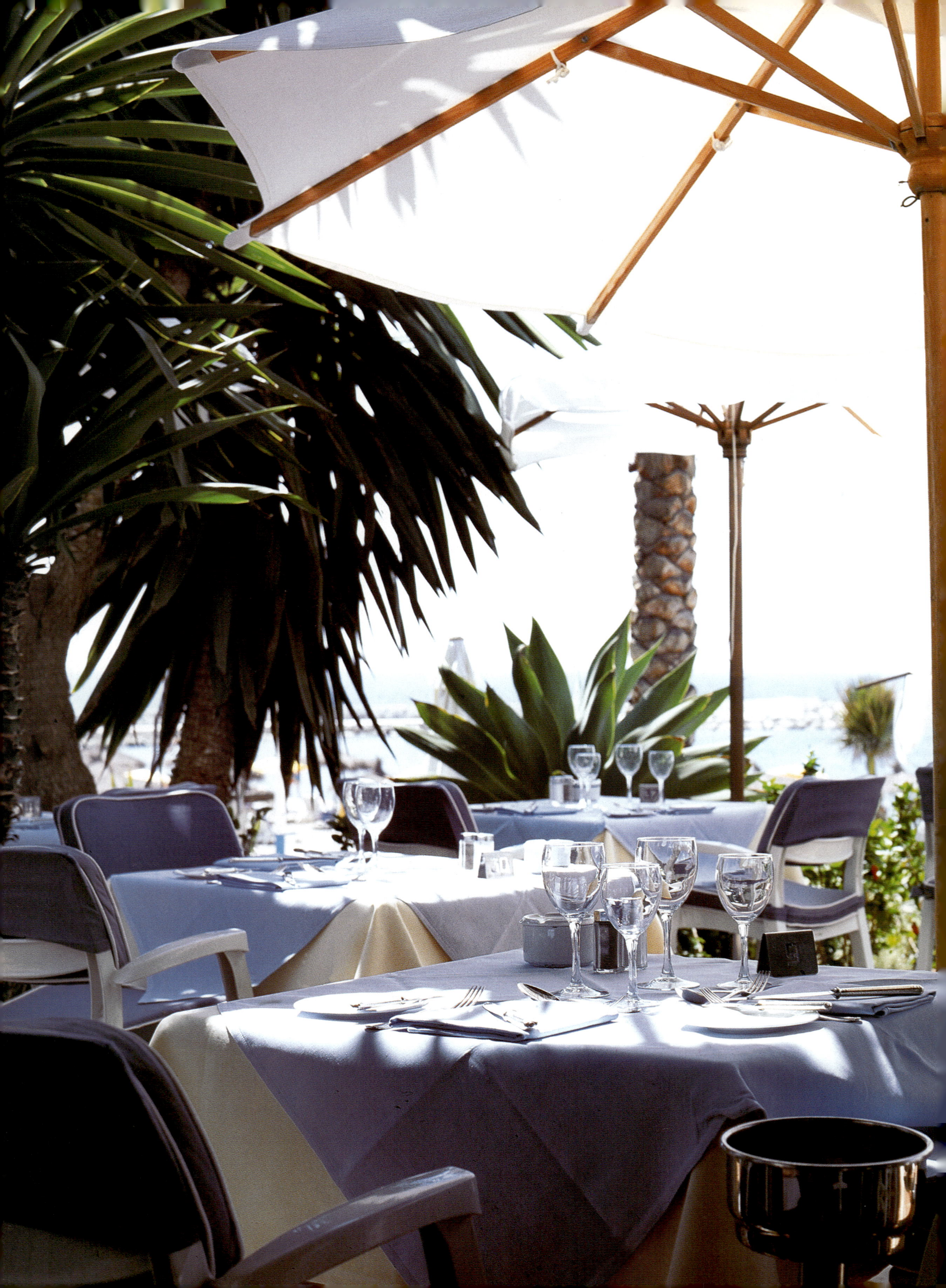

Puente Romano

There will always be something a little bit special about any hotel built beside the sea, particularly so if the warm gently-lapping waters of the Mediterranean can be seen - and heard - from your open windows. The five-star Puente Romano begins with that great advantage… and then transports the visitor far beyond such simple delight.

Marbella, once, believe it or not, a sleepy little fishing port, has been for years now a celebrated and popular destination for the rich and famous. Its crowded marina is a wonderful playground for the cosmopolitan sporting fraternity. Within easy reach of the town there are more than 30 golf courses, testifying to another of the jet-set's occupations. Encircled by the protective Sierra Blanca mountains, the town enjoys an especially cossetting micro-climate, even by the benign standards of the Mediterranean. Every square, street and alleyway is a garden of exotic and tumbling blooms; it is easy to feel blessed and rather special as a visitor in this favoured place.

Puente Romano is like an Andalusian village; a Moorish influence in both its architecture and furnishings is everywhere. There are 149 rooms and 77 suites, but they are set out in 26 separate villas, so there is no feeling at all of crowding.

Leafy vegetations allow each guest surprising privacy, enhanced even more by the private secluded terraces. Bamboo seating, marble floors and local fabrics running from cool ivory to hot yellows and reds adorn the rooms which, need it be said, contain every modern luxury.

There's no need to be a golfer, a mariner, a fitness fanatic or tennis player - though there is ample opportunity to indulge in the active life. The tennis courts, for example, are of professional standard, and Davis Cup matches are played here. A walk to the beach may be all you fancy doing, lunch at the Beach Club, a little shopping in the hotel's boutique gallery, a massage perhaps, a siesta, a cocktail in the Cascada Bar at dusk before a long and leisurely gourmet meal in the Restaurant El Puente or the outdoor La Plaza restaurant. The caring and attentive hotel staff at Puente Romano are there to ensure you have every opportunity to relax completely.

If you can drag yourself away, the hotel will be happy to suggest, and help organise, day trips for you. Tax-free Gibraltar is only an hour away, the wine vaults of Jerez a little further. Ronda and Mijas, hidden up in the mountains to the north, are charming old towns you shouldn't miss, full of romantic little streets and curious shops. And at the end of the day, the quiet pleasures of Puente Romano will be awaiting your return.

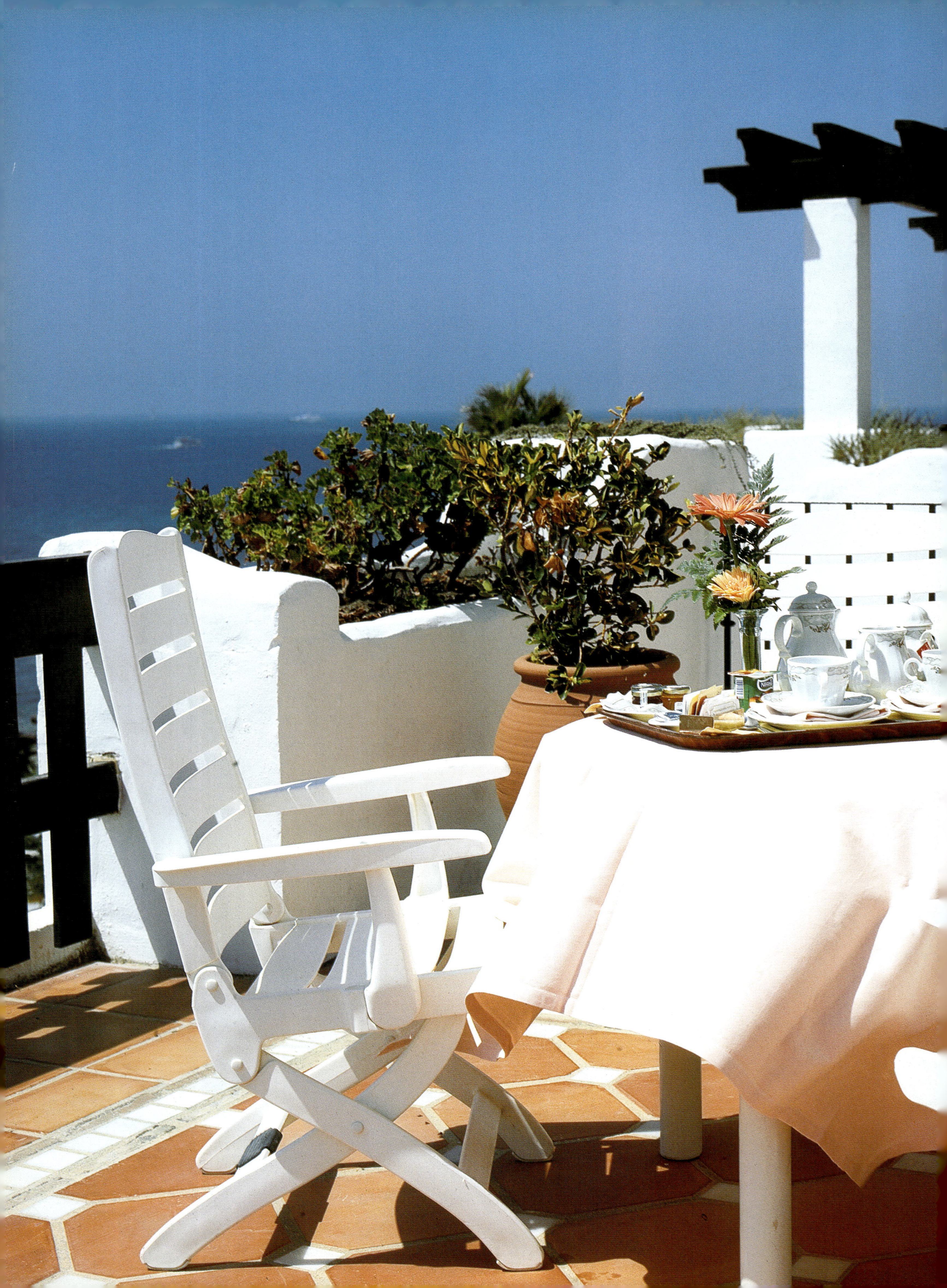

133

Puente Romano was built like an Andalusian village in sub-tropical gardens.

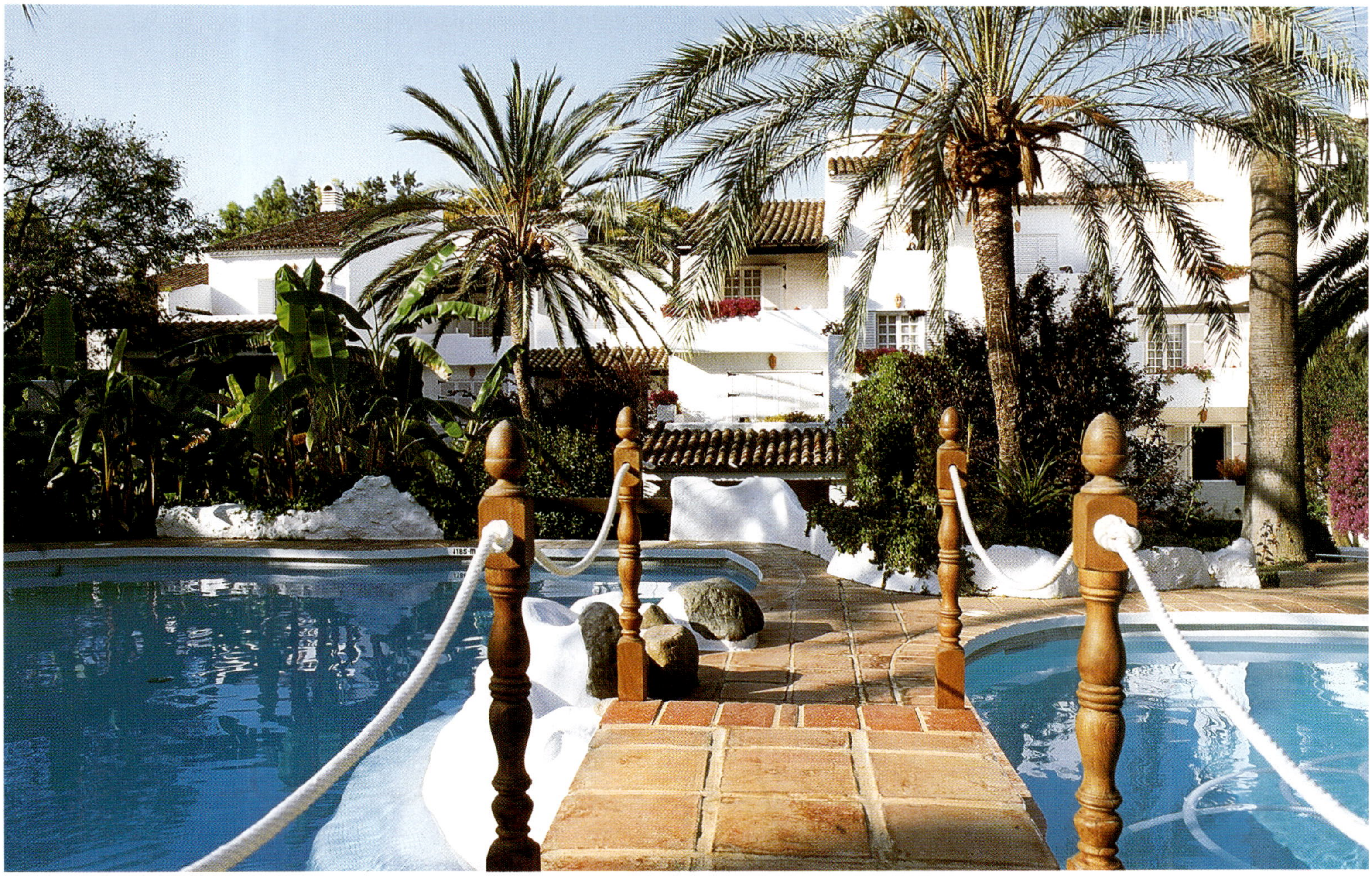

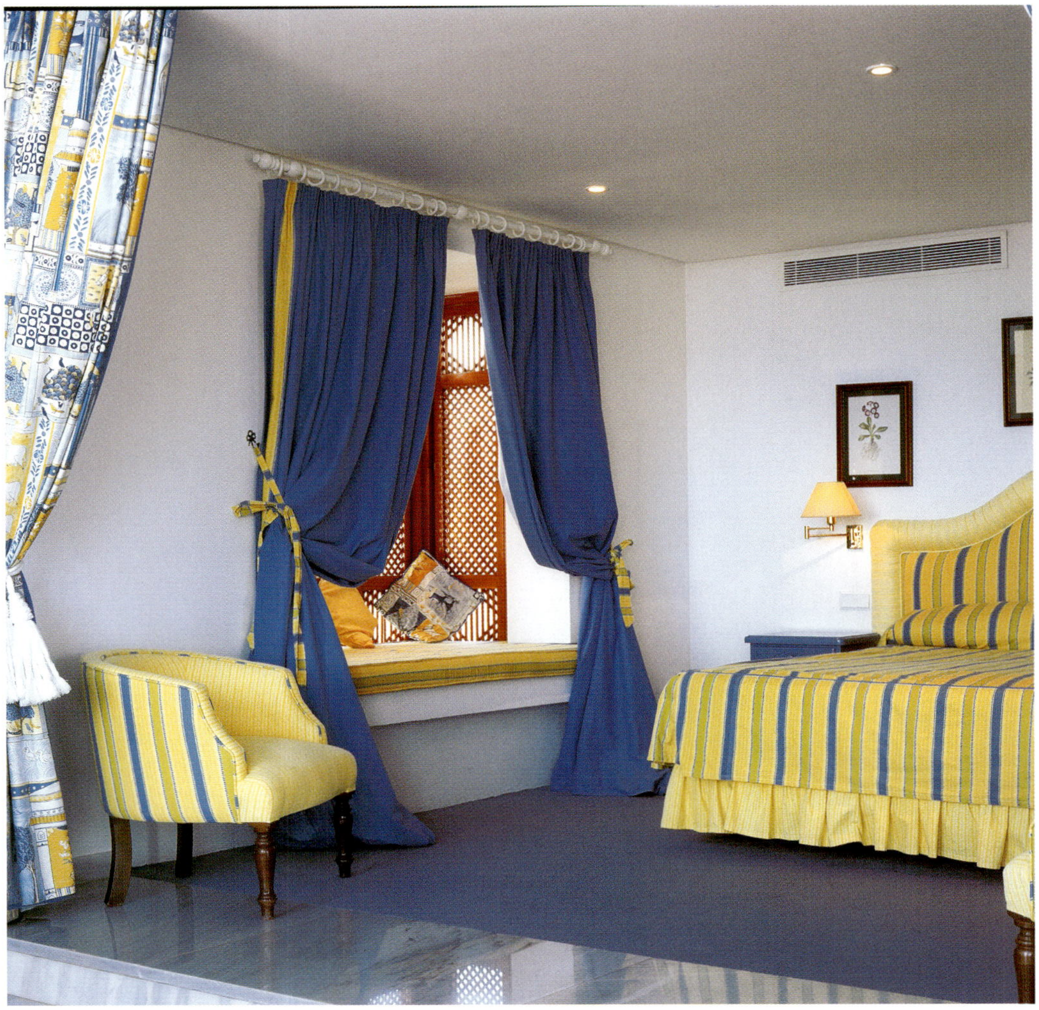

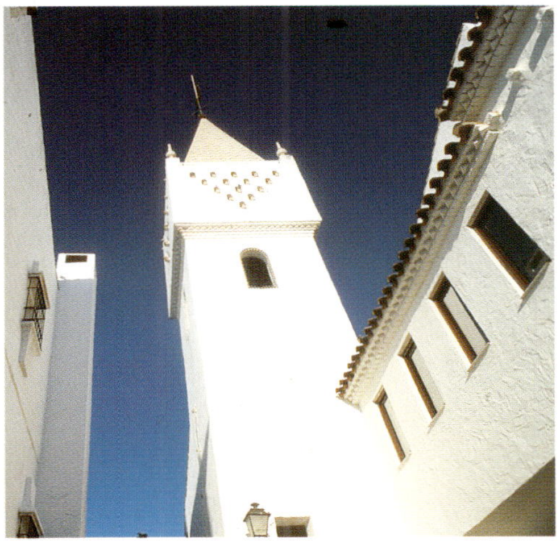

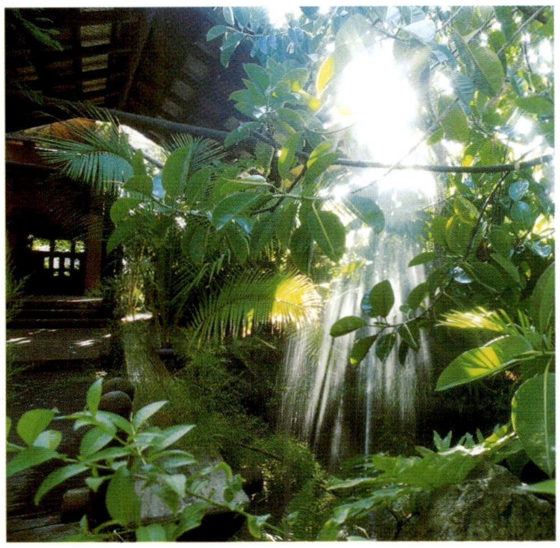

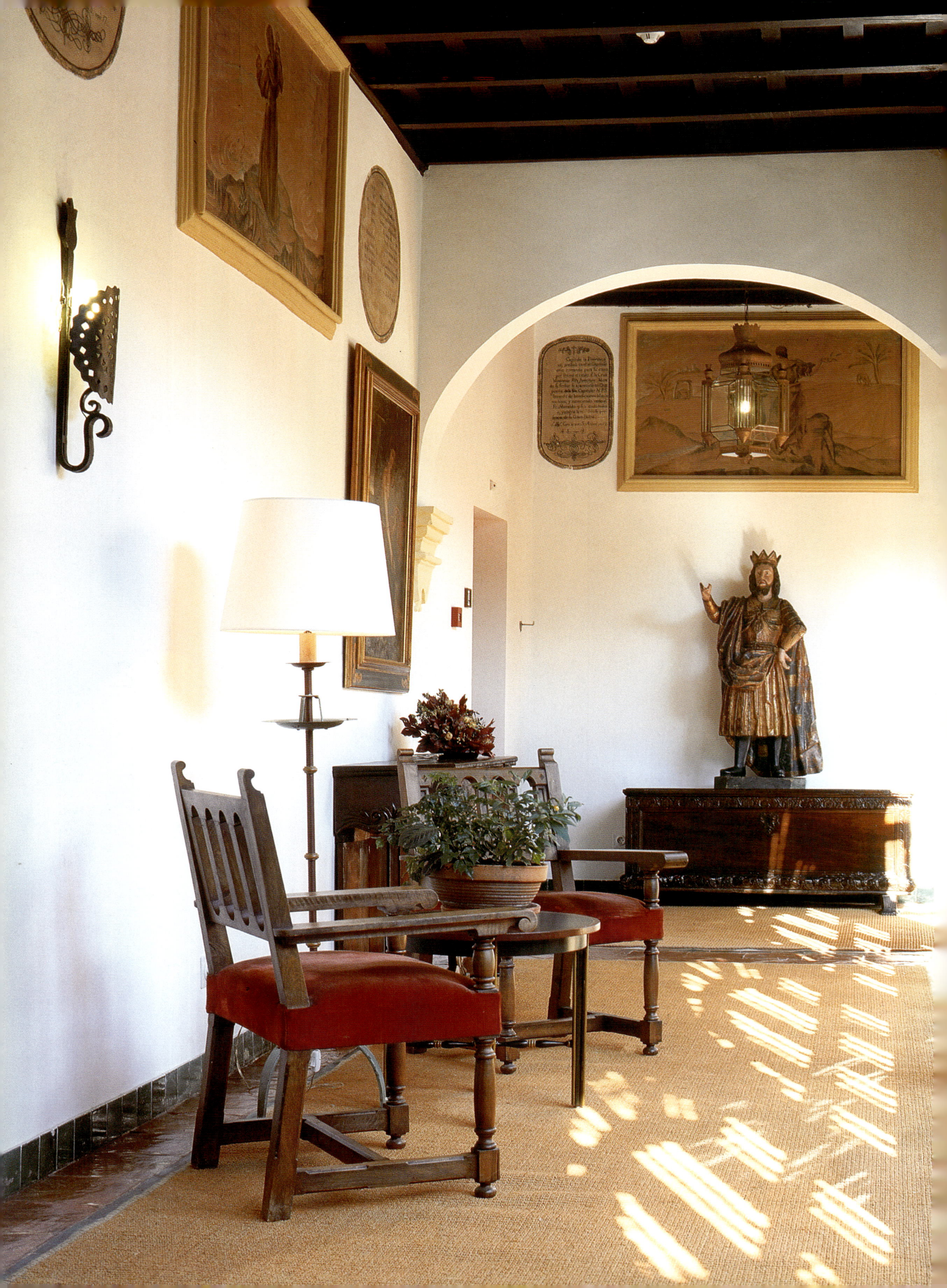

Parador de Granada

The wonderful Granada Parador was once, centuries ago, a Franciscan convent, built by order of the Reyes Católicos when they came to Granada in 1492, on a mission to drive out the Saracens. There had been a mosque and a palace, built by the Islamic king Yusuf I in the 14th century. The hotel is a fascinating blend of cultures. Nowadays, the landscaped gardens and beautiful vistas offer a splendid view of the Alhambra, the wonderful fountains of the Generalife and the red walls of the Albaicín. And the distant panorama of the white peaks of the Sierra Nevada, rising high into the sky, is simply breath-taking. The Parador was officially opened at the end of the war, back in 1945. Every room is different; all of them are stylish but simple, like a former convent should be. The whole building exudes a peace and serenity that influences the mood of the hotel guests: this is a place to find rest and relaxation. All the tastefully-furnished rooms offer a view of the Generalife, the Albaicín, the Sacromonte or the wonderful gardens of Secano.

For your meals, you can choose between the dining room with its high, imposing ceiling- a wonderful example of craftsmanship - and the shady summer terrace, where you can enjoy Andalusian gazpacho, tortilla Sacromonte or Santa Fe pionos. Find out for yourself what wonderful dishes they are! The Arabs left behind them a large array of herbs, which, all these centuries later, the chef makes ample use of to give the wonderful regional produce that extra flair. The many kinds of fresh local vegetables, the wonderful fish, the famous Granada meats and the Trevélze ham… no wonder the cuisine at the Parador de Granada is renowned far and wide!

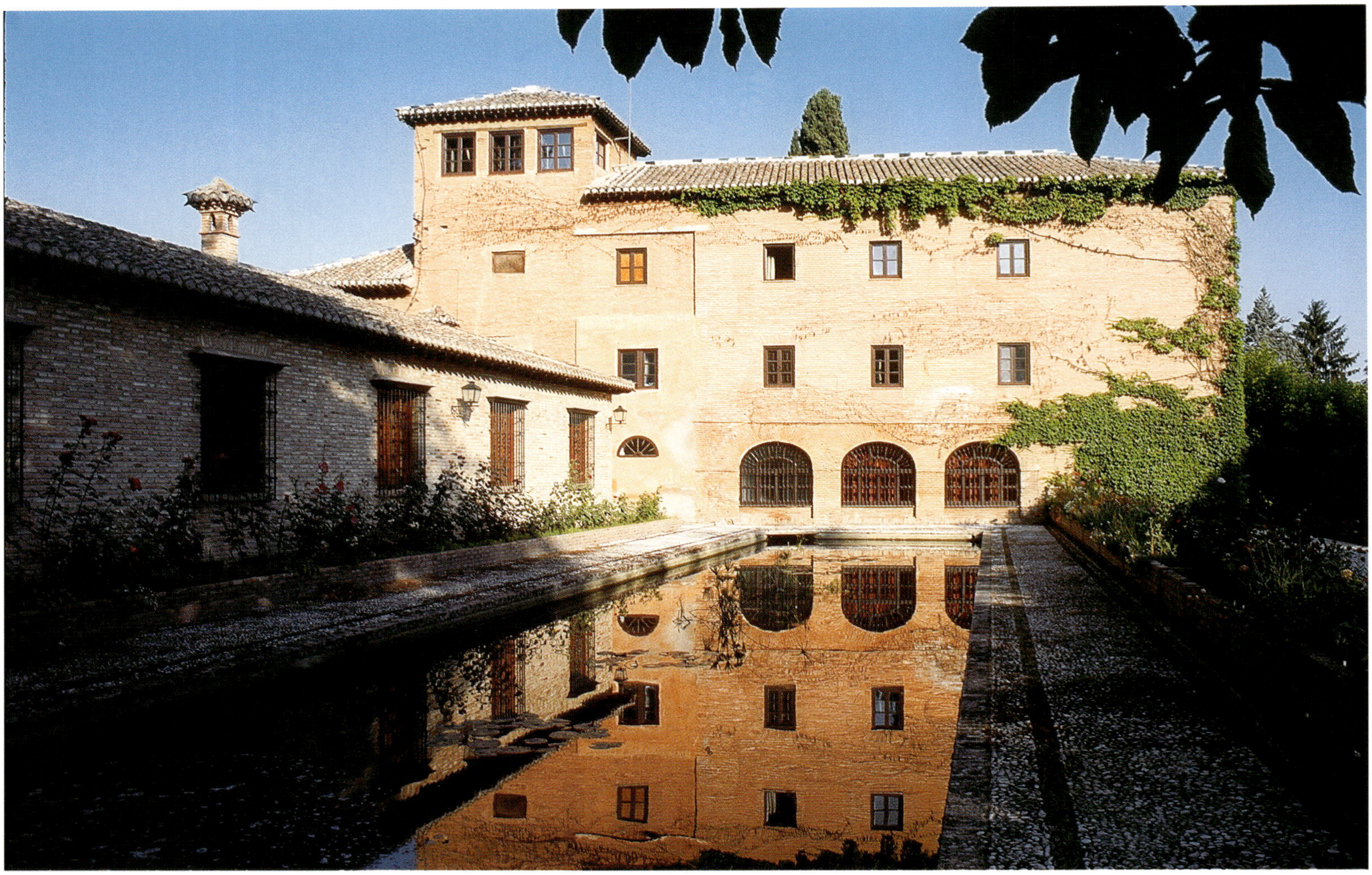

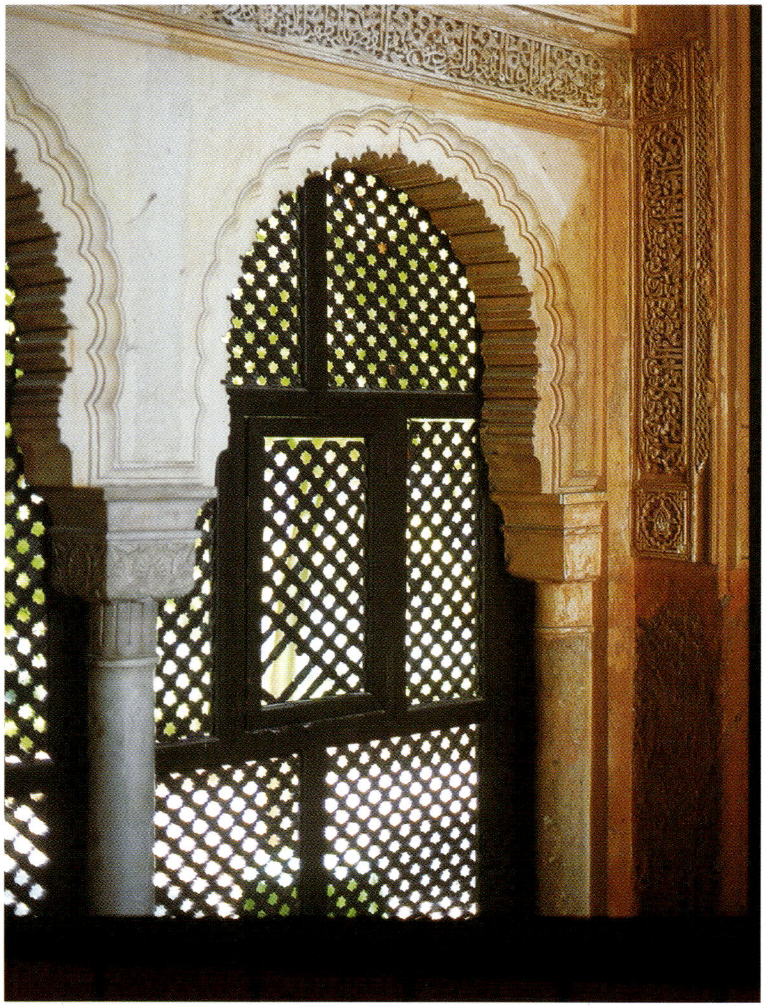

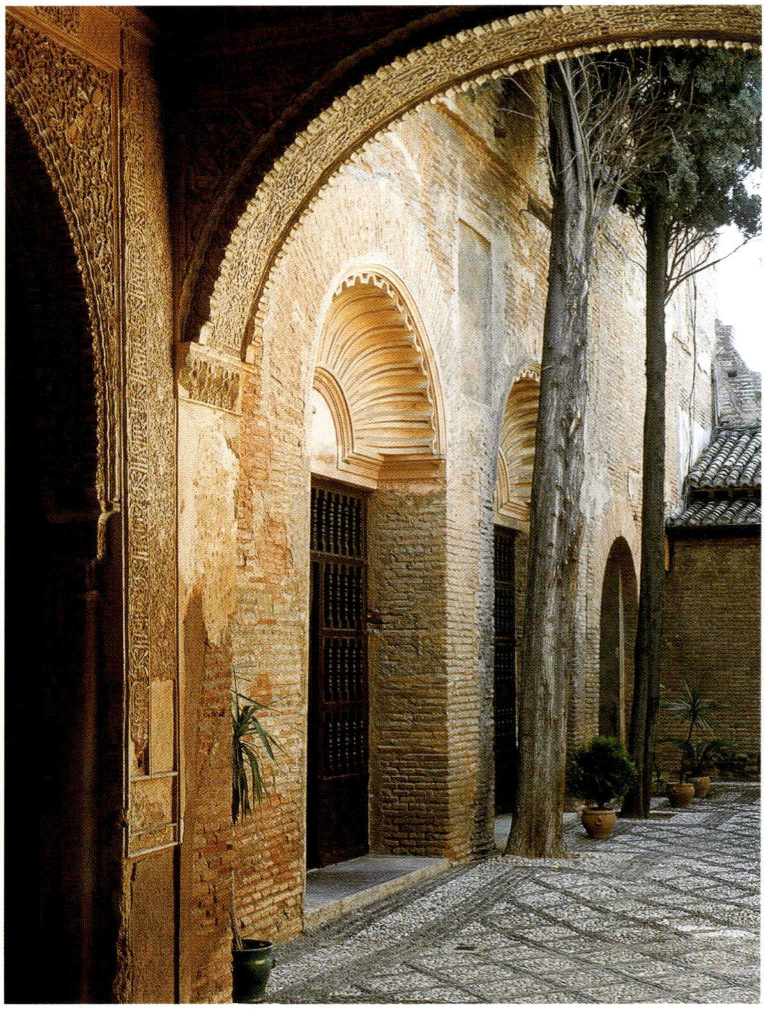

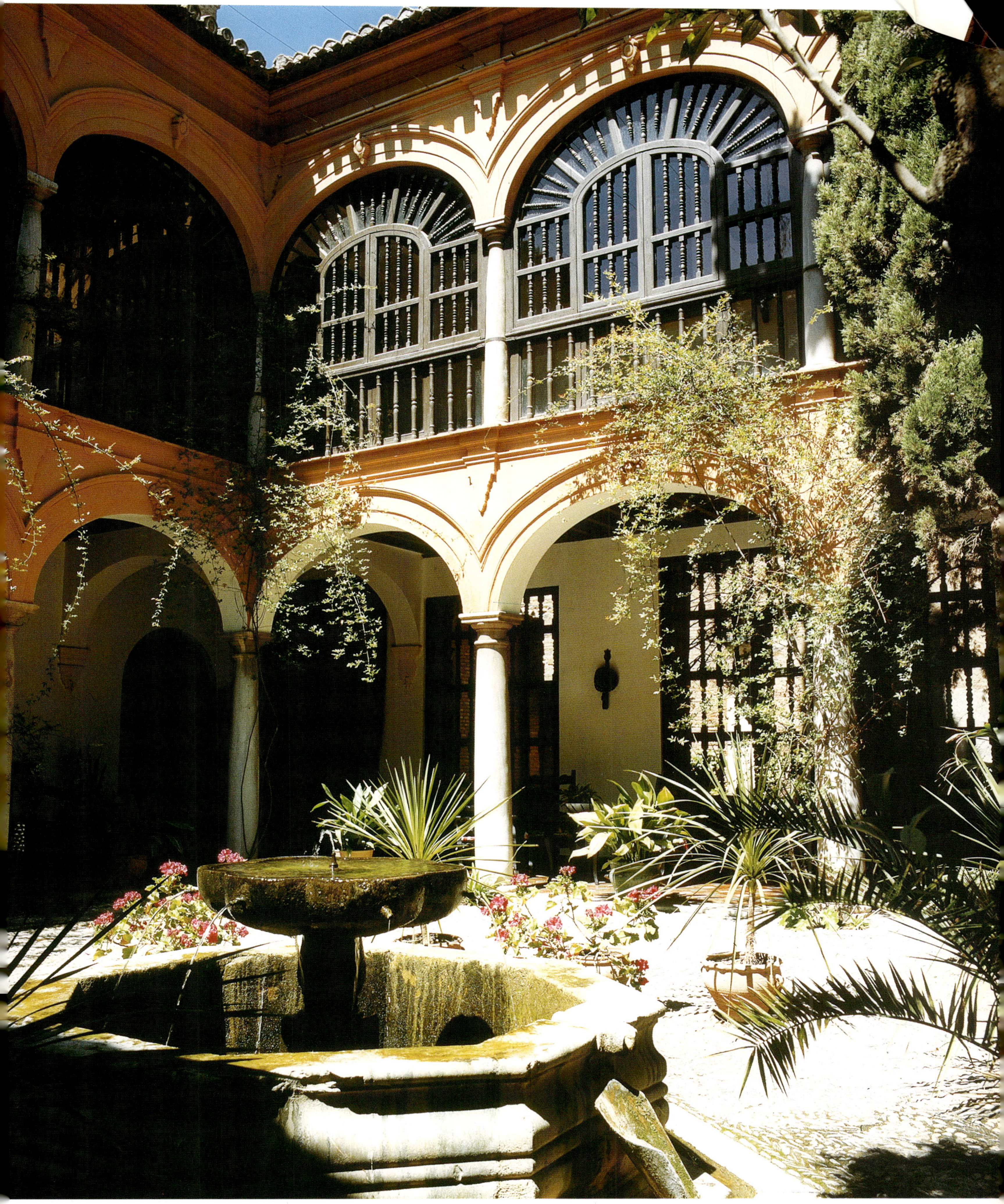

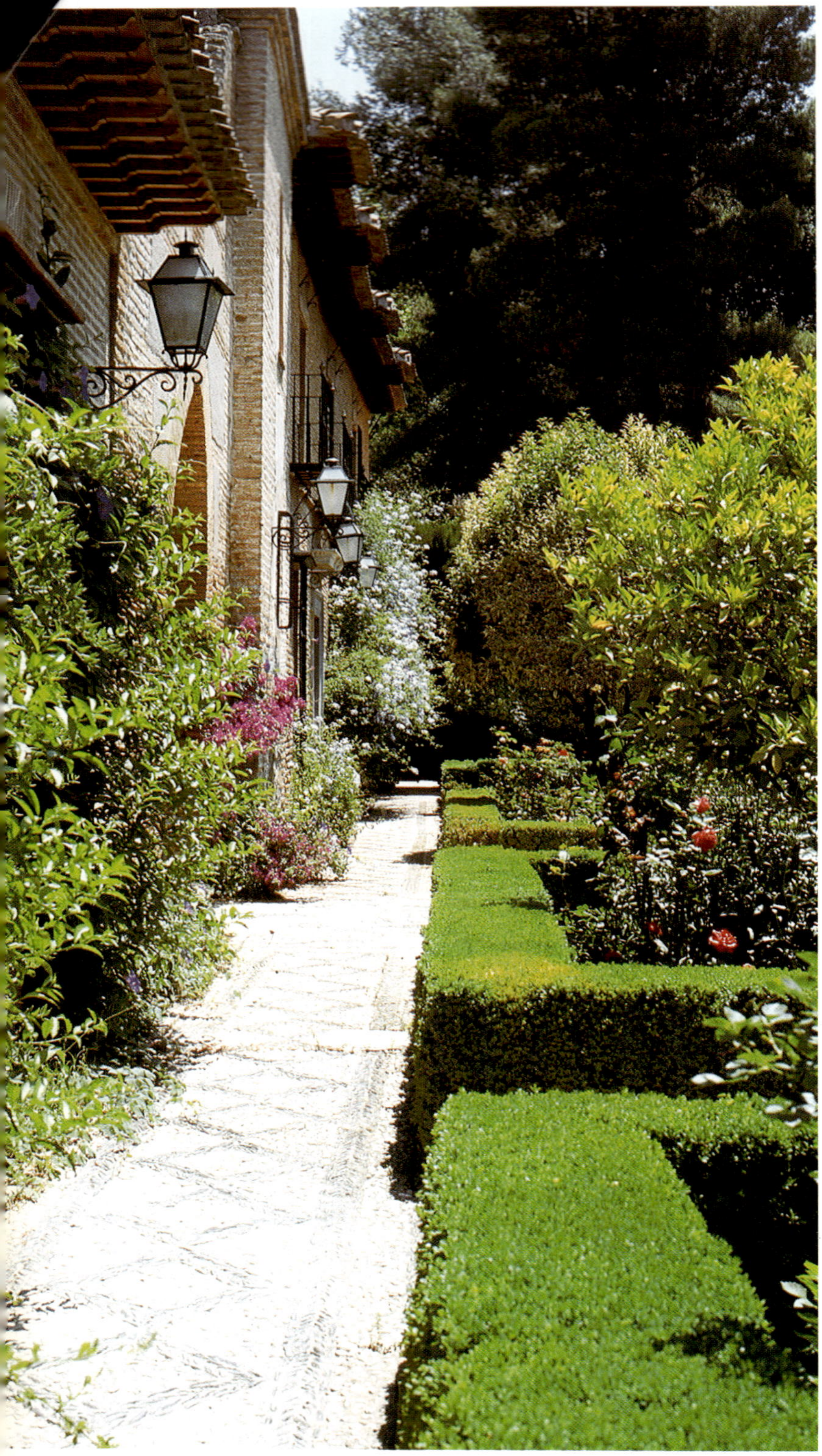
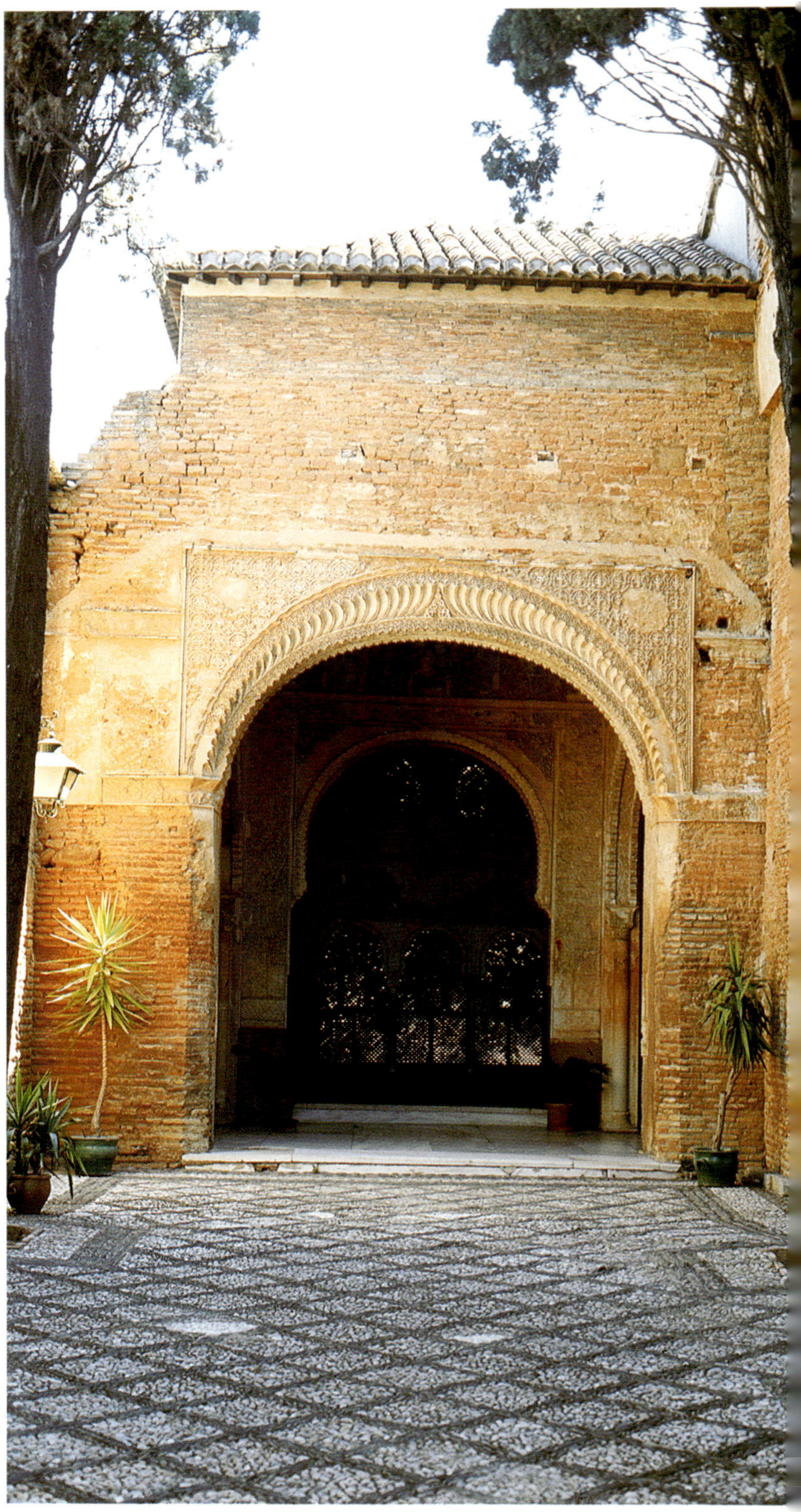
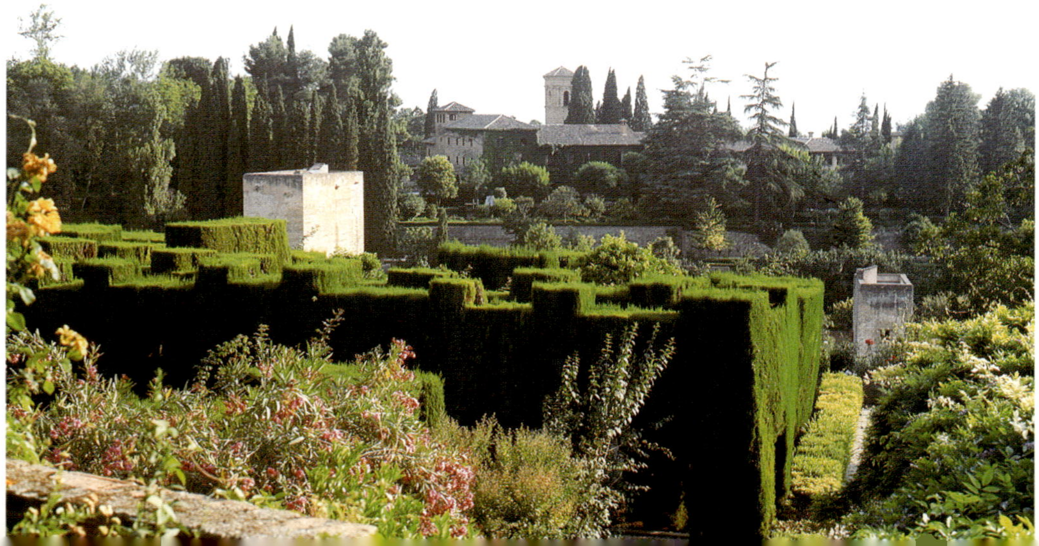
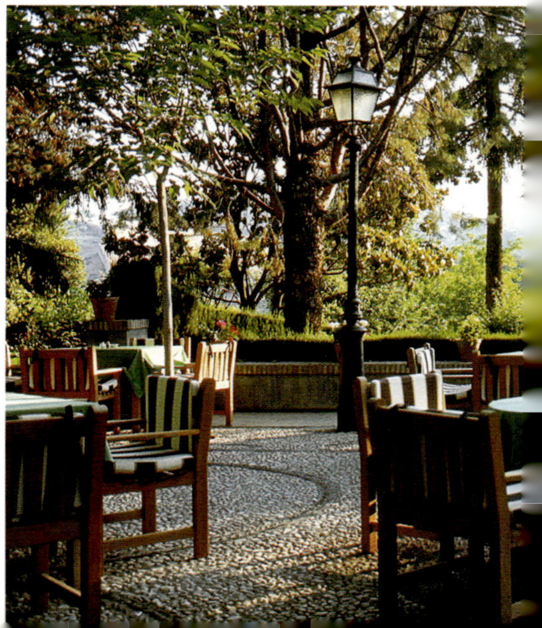

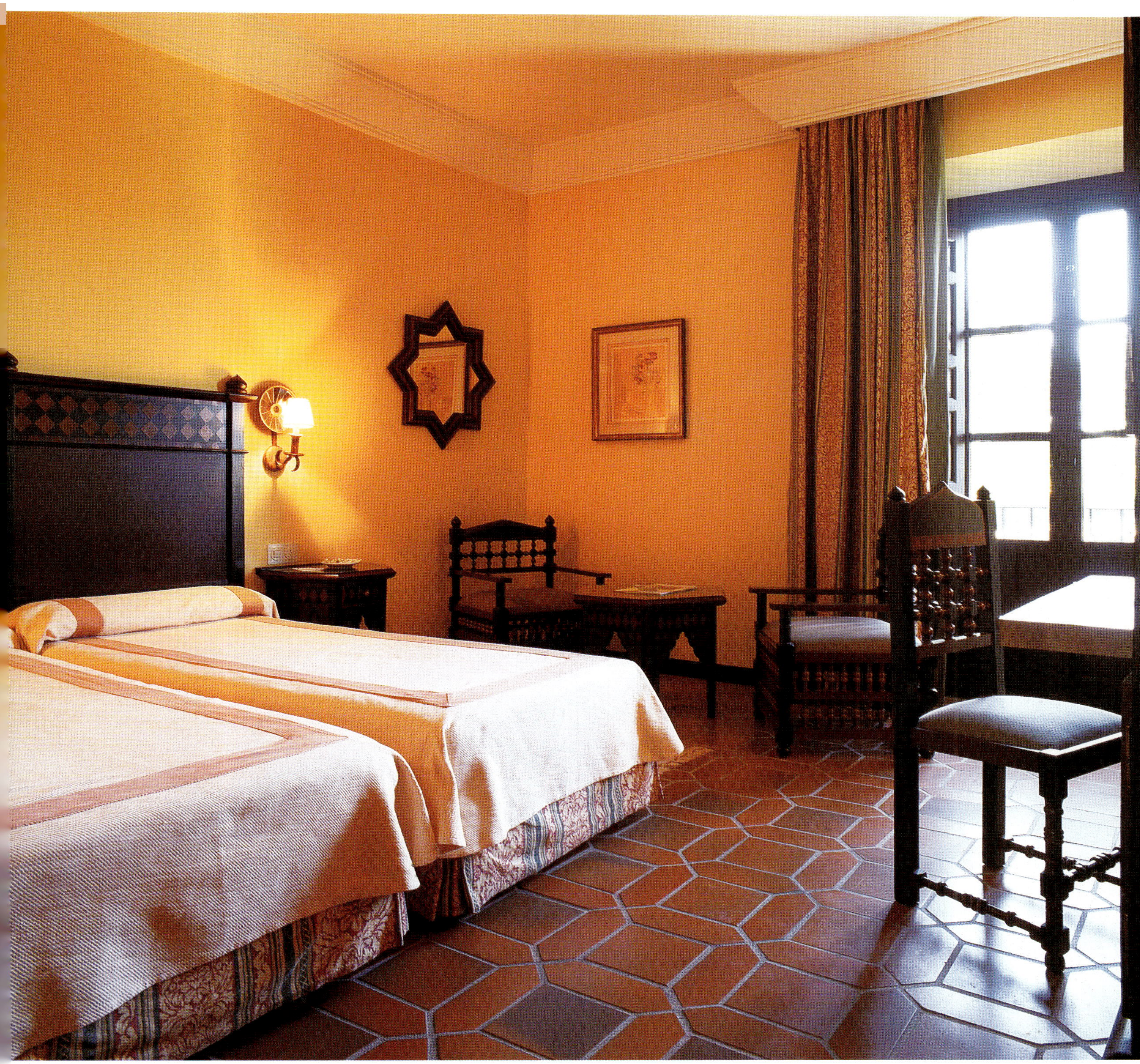

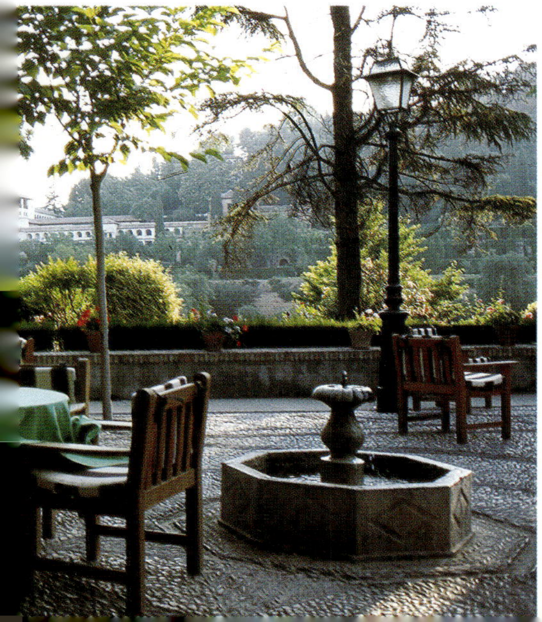

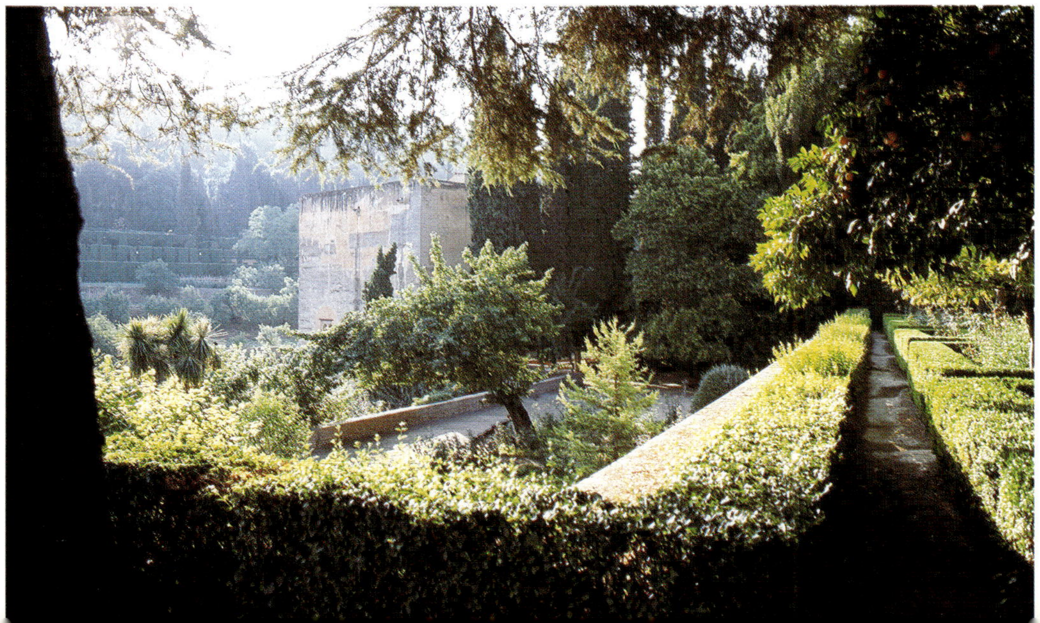

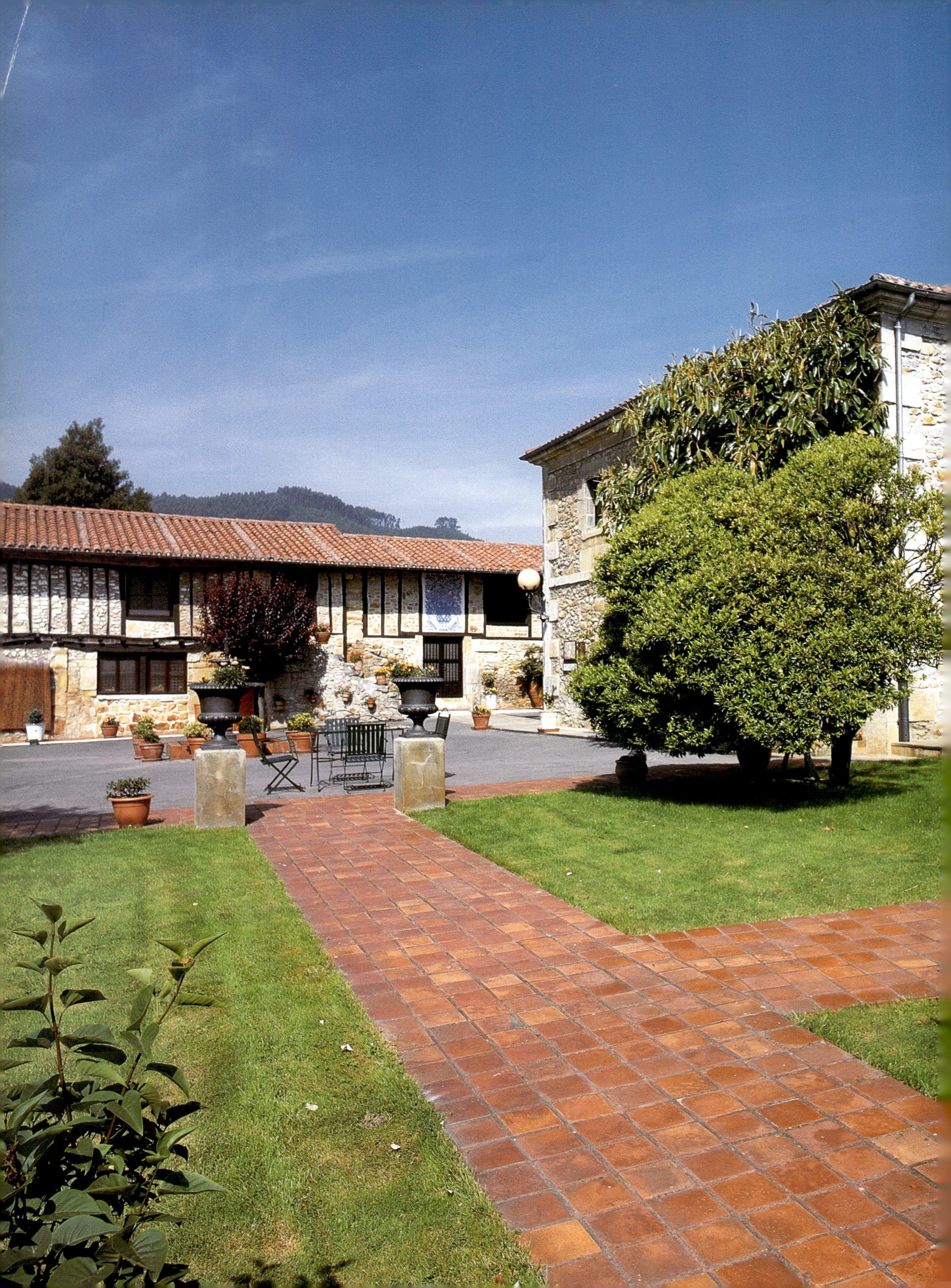

San Román de Escalante

You'll find this lovely hotel up in the north-west corner of Spain, 40 miles from Bilbao, which lies a stone's throw from the French border and only 22 miles from Santander. Hotel San Roman de Escalante would make an ideal stopover for your first night in the country of El Greco, Pablo Picasso and Pablo Casals. The trouble may be that you will surely want to extend your visit and enjoy a little longer everything this place has to offer.

It is a top-class hotel, first and foremost - but it is also a museum and a rather splendid botanical gardens and arboretum. The hotel is fortunately set in an area that enjoys an especially favourable micro-climate, with warm western winds flowing in off the Atlantic ocean.

The proprietors are three life-long friends, who have a great love of antiquities and horticulture, and the San Roman de Escalante affords them the opportunity to exercise their imaginative flair and wide knowledge in these fields. Everywhere you find yourself, you will come across gorgeous antiques, treasured examples of old furniture, and furnishings that complement the design of each very individual room.

Cantabria is a small but attractive coastal province and it is well worth pausing here before launching yourself southwards. If you have arrived by car ferry, make your way around the great inlet on which Santander lies, to Solares, and then take the highway towards Bilbao. It's a fun road, with great views and many twists and turns, but at Gama you turn seaward and are soon at the gates of San Romano.

On the grounds is an exceptional 12th century chapel, once a simple hermitage, whose name has been adopted by the hotel, which was previously an artists' hideaway. There is still work on the walls by influential Spanish painters, and sculptures, too, abound, both indoors and out. Should you by chance have space in the boot of your car, you can actually purchase what you like best and take it away with you.

A restaurant was constructed from the old stables, which quickly acquired a Michelin star and then the hotel, too, grew apace, until now it offers 20 spacious and comfortable rooms, some with lovely oak balconies, all with cosy and luxurious bathrooms, antique furniture and eye-catching paintings on the walls.

Once you've settled in, it's time to make another voyage of discovery, from the intimate bar to the peaceful library and finally out into the gardens where pillared walkways, hung with climbing roses, and monastic-like shaded cloisters frame lush lawns and trees of many unusual varieties. The evening meal that awaits is the responsibility of a young and gifted chef who presents traditional Spanish dishes with a special personal flair all his own.

Beyond the ancient walls of San Romano, there's watersports and fishing, rocky tidal pools to peer into, soft drifts of sand, and an interesting expanse of salt marshes. Golfers should slip off to Pedreña, where the professional at the 18-hole course is no less than Ballesteros, a name known even to myself, who never lifted a club in my life.

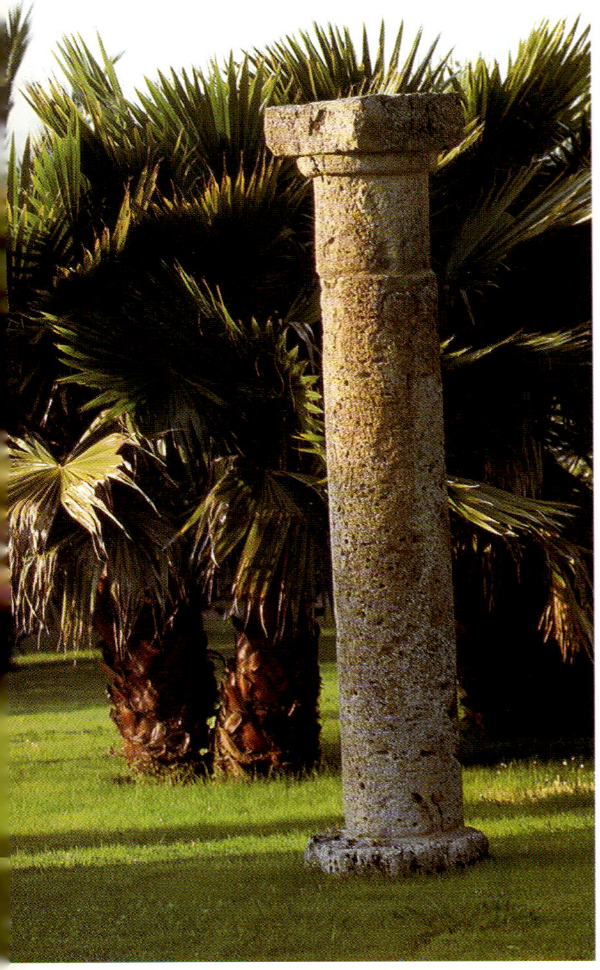
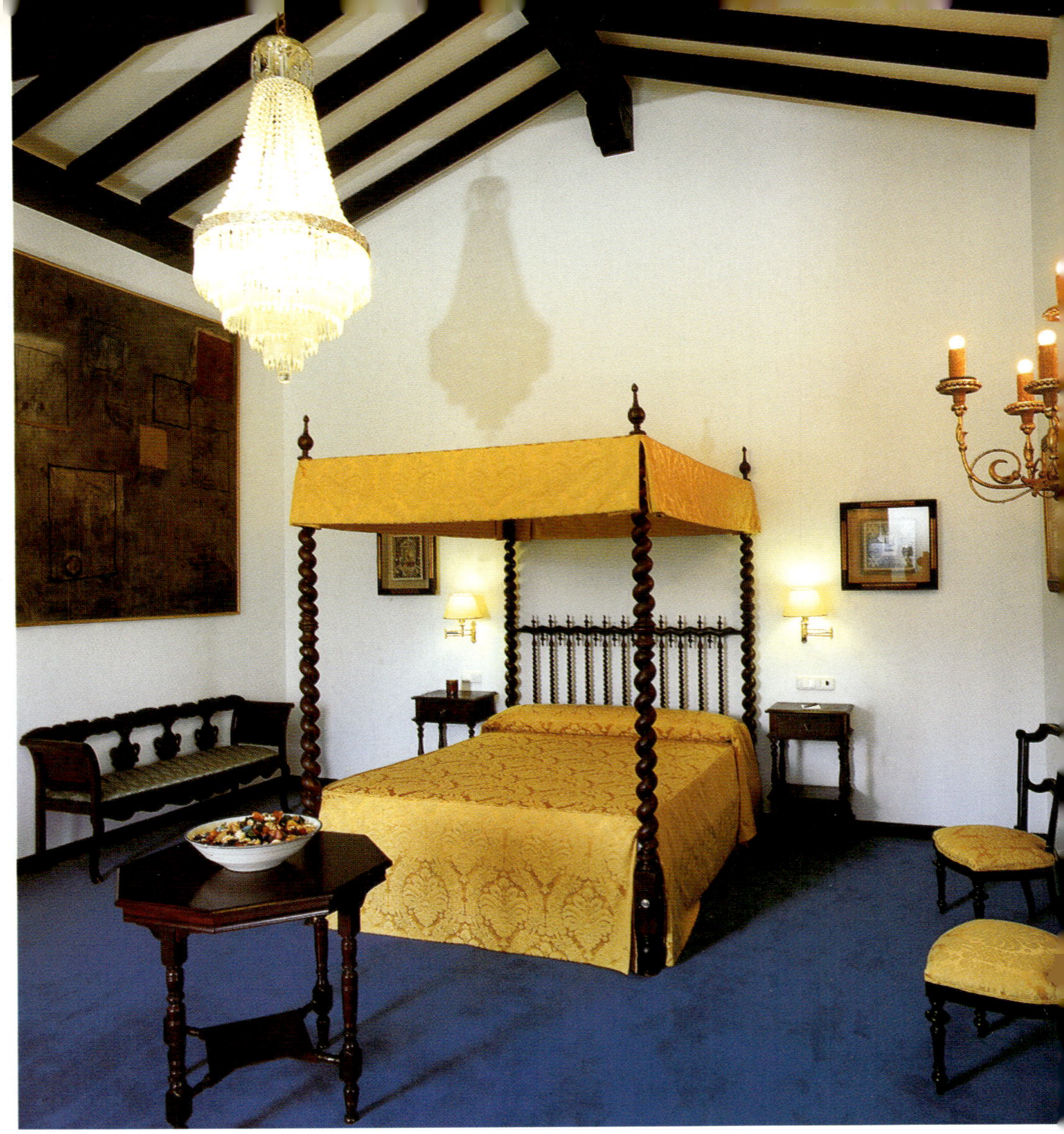
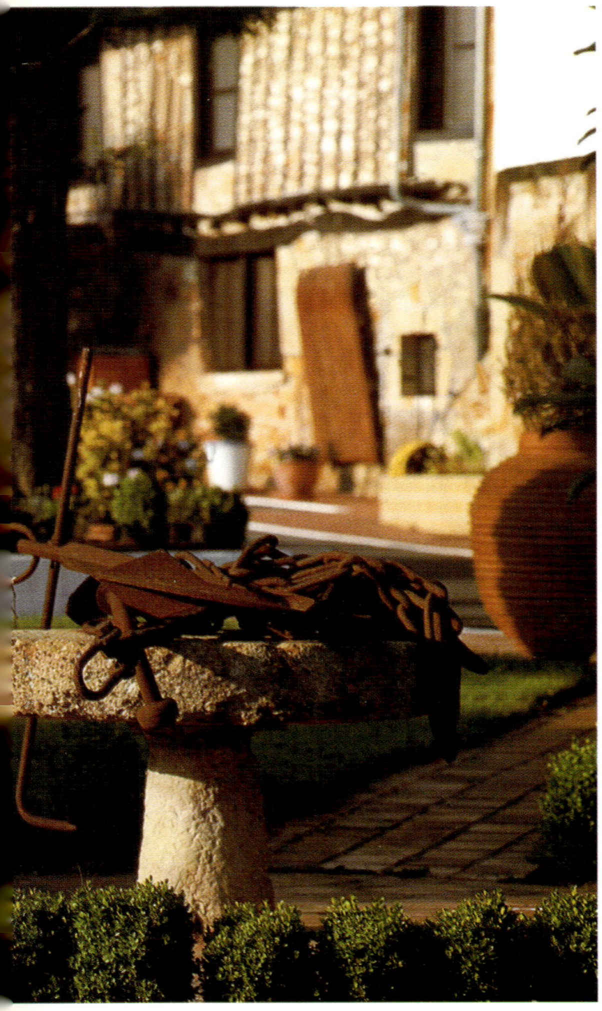
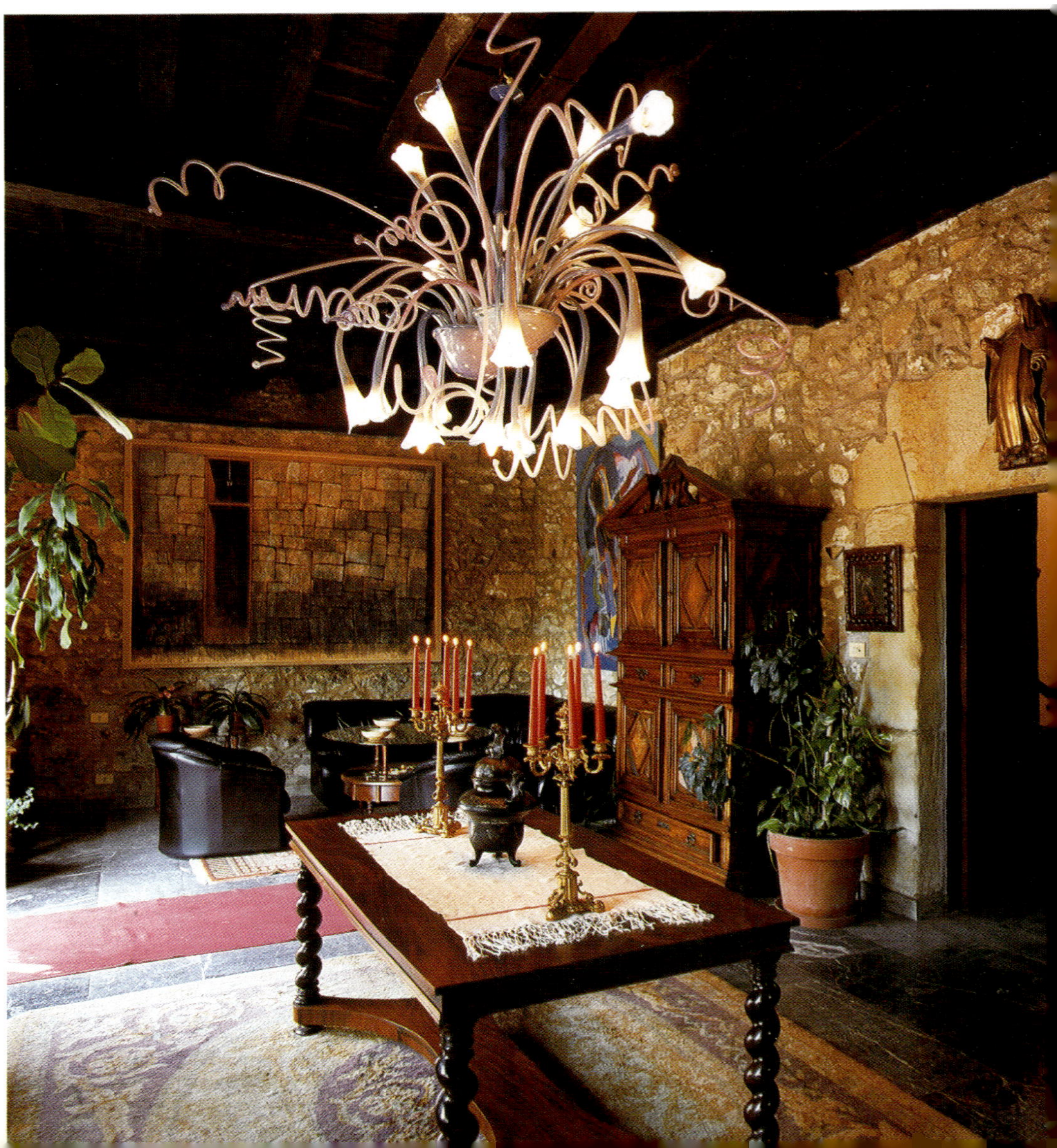

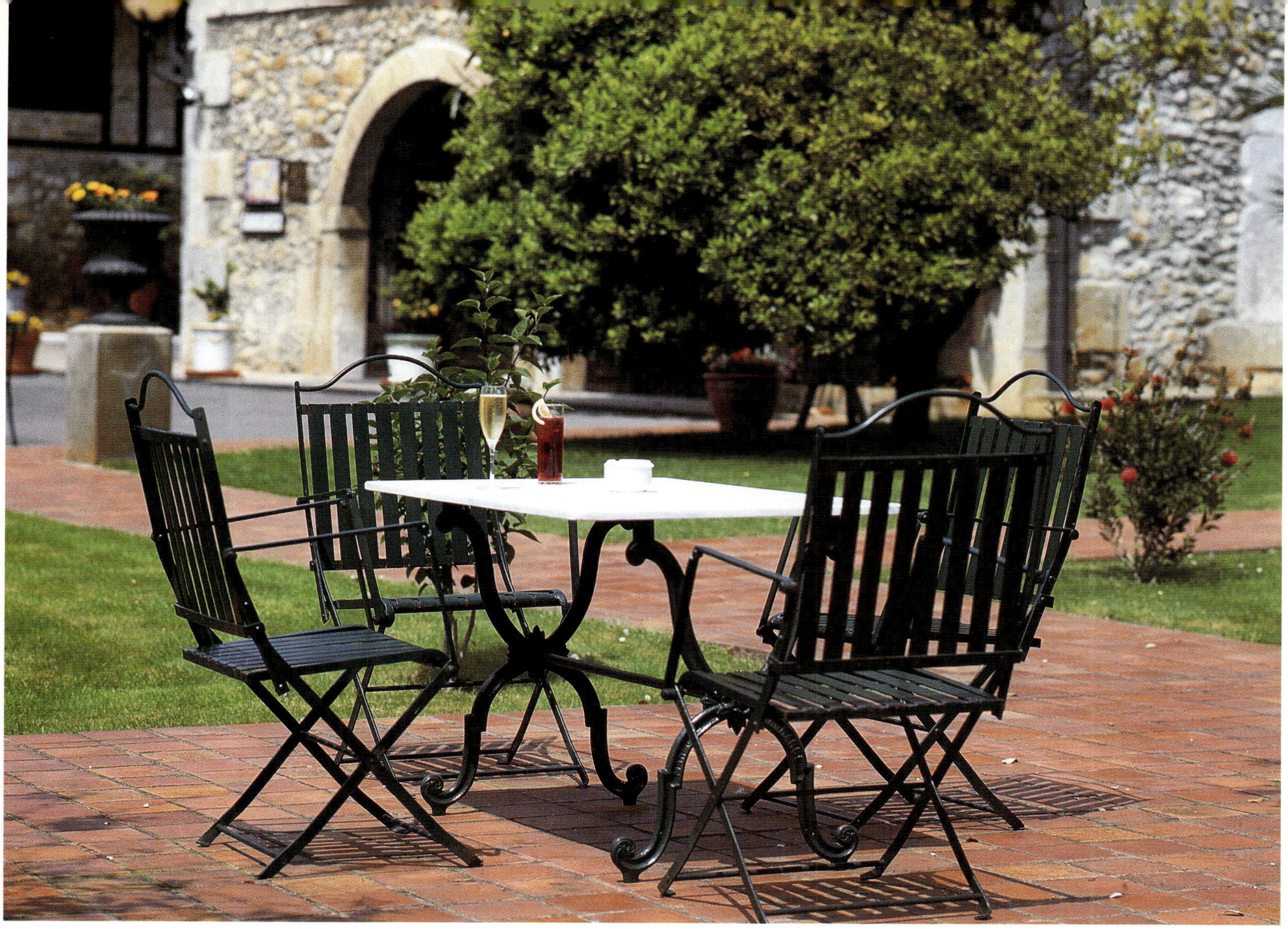

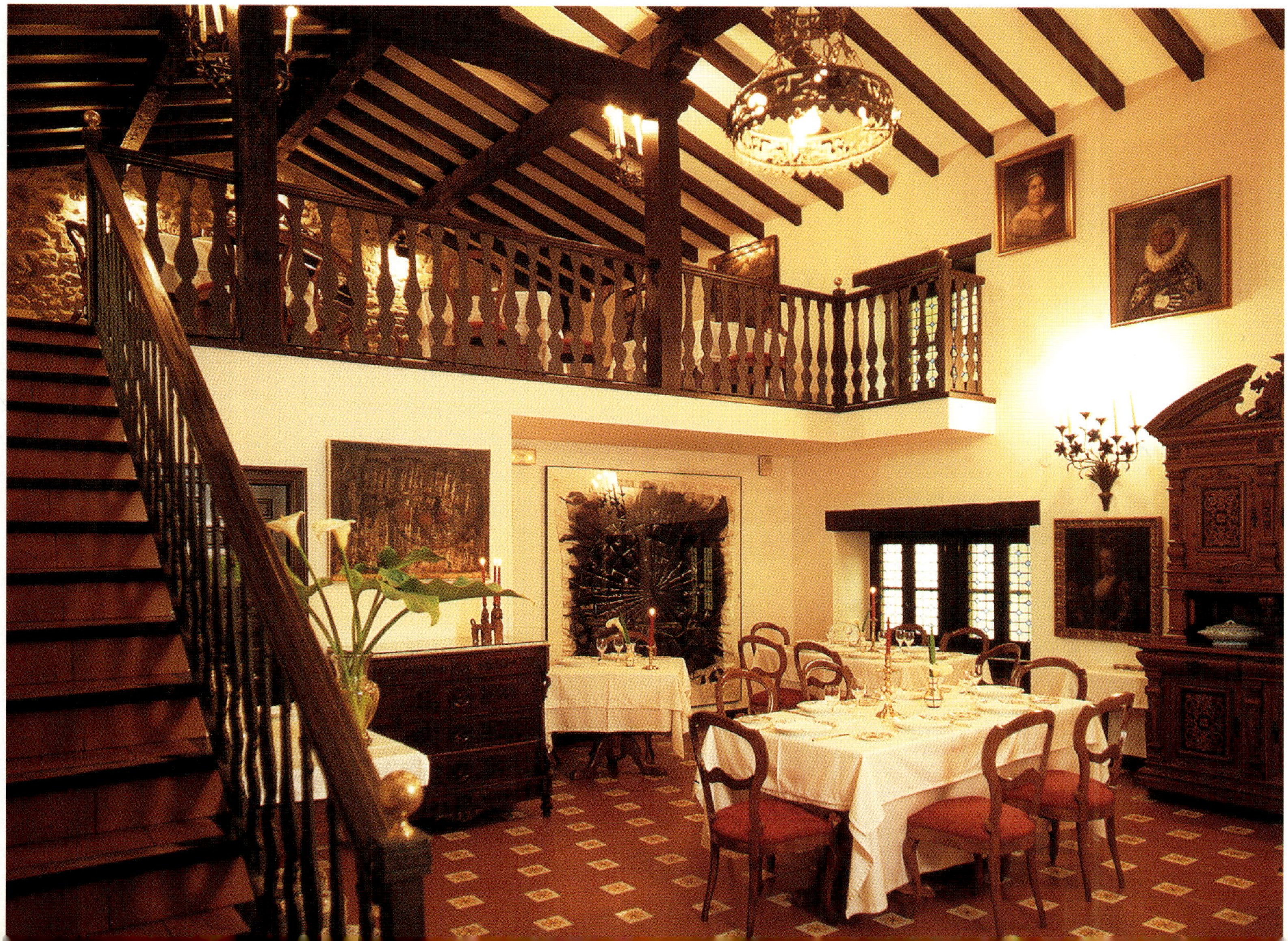

Parador de Santiago

The magnificent Parador of Santiago de Compostela with the wonderful name 'Hostal Reyes Católicos' was once a royal hospital and refuge for pilgrims.

The impressive building is a fine mixture of history, art and tradition, the dream of all pilgrims and the very symbol of Santiago. It stands on the Plaza del Obradoiro, and first opened its doors as a hospital in 1499. It was meant to provide shelter, too, for the numerous pilgrims who came on pilgrimage to Santiago. In 1954 it became a Parador, one of the oldest in the world and perhaps the most luxurious and most beautiful of all. Your stay here will be an unforgettable one.

Fernando de Aragón and Isabel de Castilla ordered the construction of the original building, putting it in the hands of Enrique Egas and Diego de Muros. The façade is the work of French masters Martin Blas and Guillén Colás. In 1678 it was renovated under the leadership of Brother Thomas Alonso. He was convinced the façade would not be complete without a gallery, and he constructed one of great beauty, running either side of the impressive main entrance. The vast, simple façade is in stark contrast to the sculptured entrance. Flanked by the coats of arms of the founders, it consists of several rows of carved figures: Adam and Eve, Santa Catalina, Santa Lucía, the twelve apostles, and many more.

The interior of the hotel is wonderfully rich, with beautiful ceilings, courtyards, fountains, large windows, remarkable wood carvings, beautiful wall hangings and four-poster beds in the guest rooms... all astounding feats of craftsmanship. The ancient chapel in the centre of the building is surrounded by galleries.

In the luxurious Libredón restaurant, you can choose from a variety of Galician fish and meat dishes, prepared from age-old recipes: pies with root vegetables and pork, fish with Iberian bacon, a stew with spaghetti and lobster, scallops with sea-urchin and seaweed in puff pastry, all served with the popular local Santiago bread. And for dessert, there is the famous Santiago cake to savour. No pilgrim of old ever had it better.

HOTEL
HOSTAL
DE LOS
REYES CATOLICOS
HOSTAL
DOS
REIS CATOLICOS

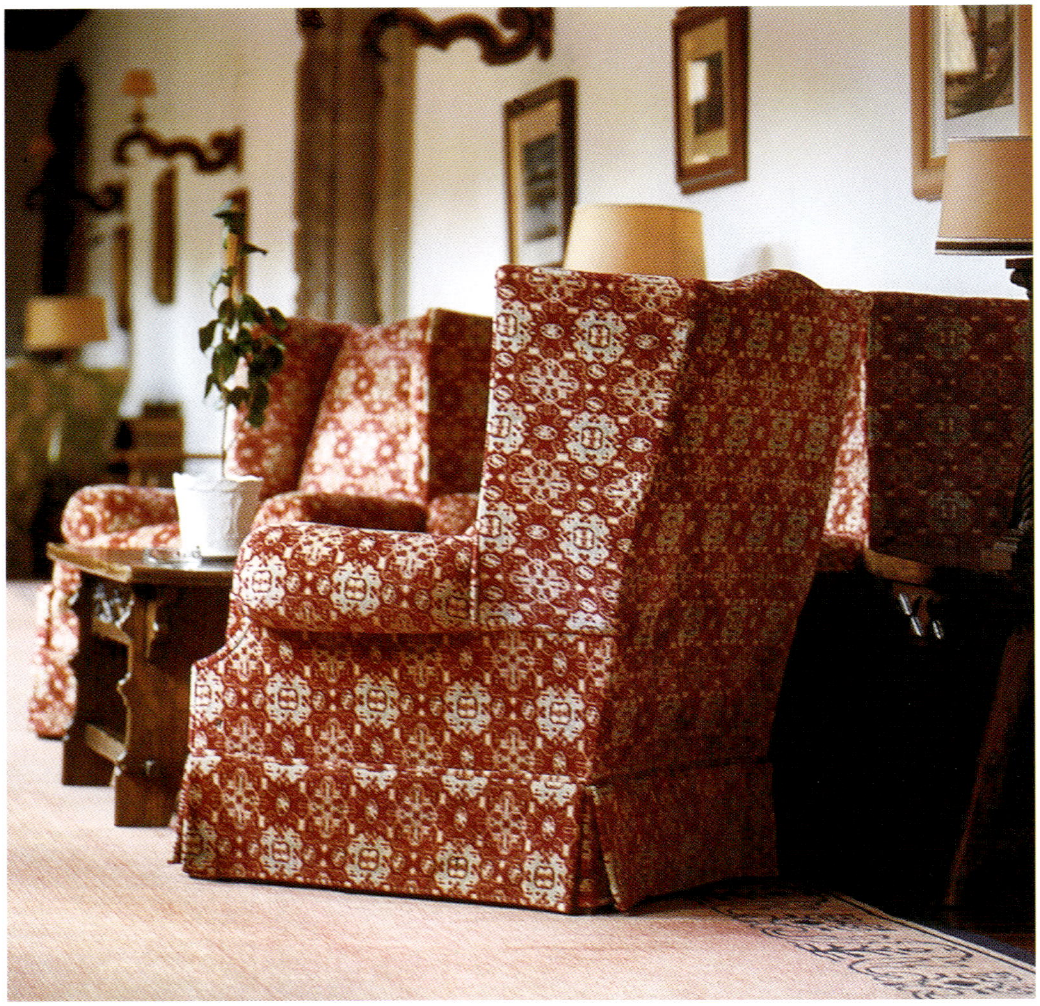
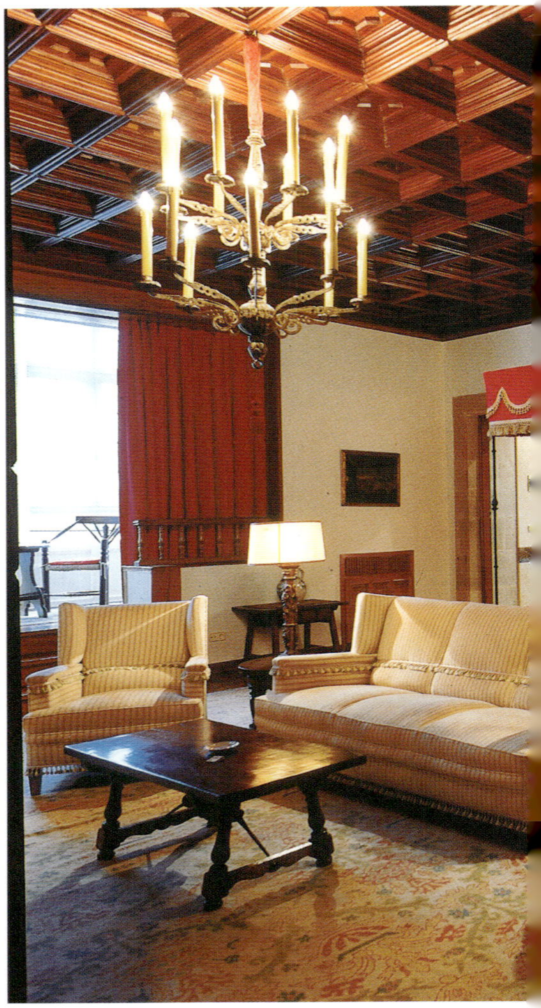
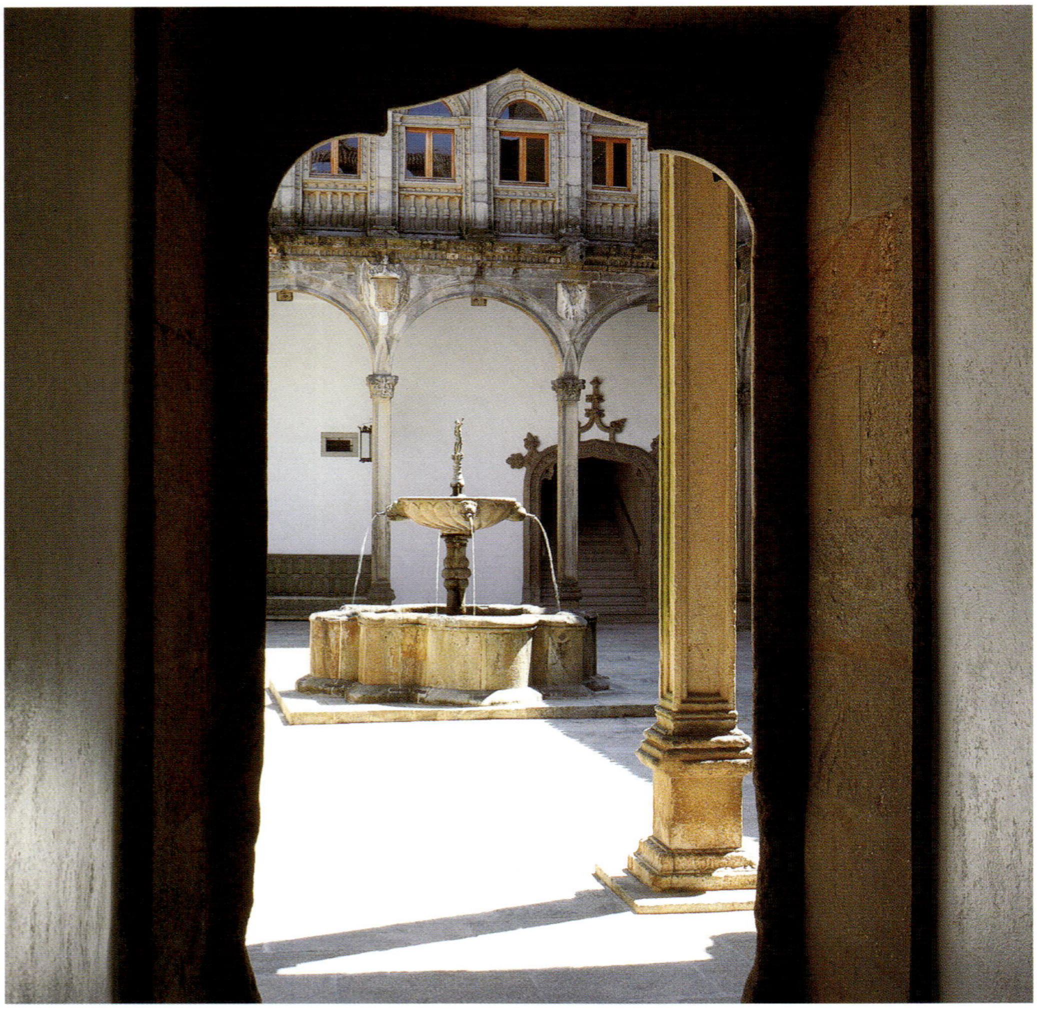
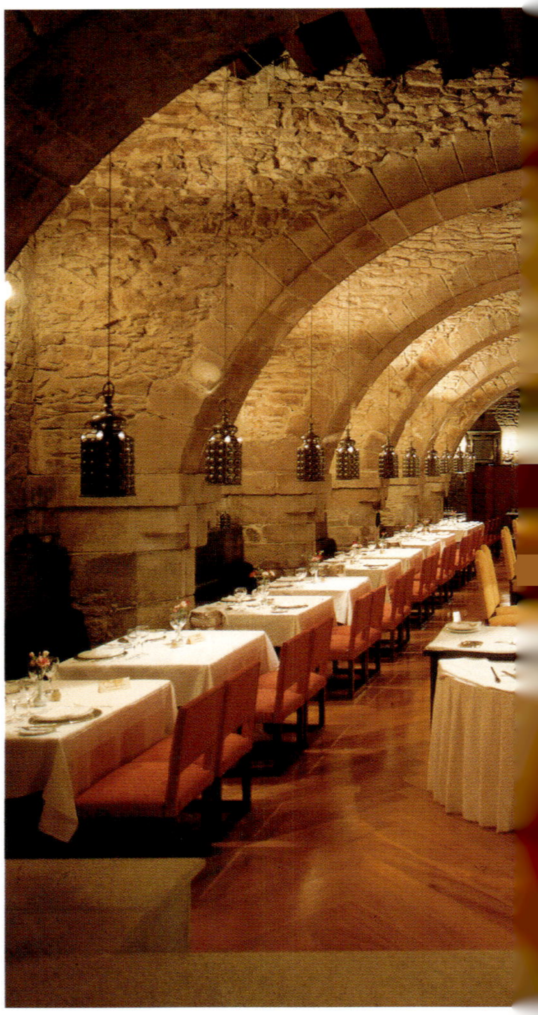

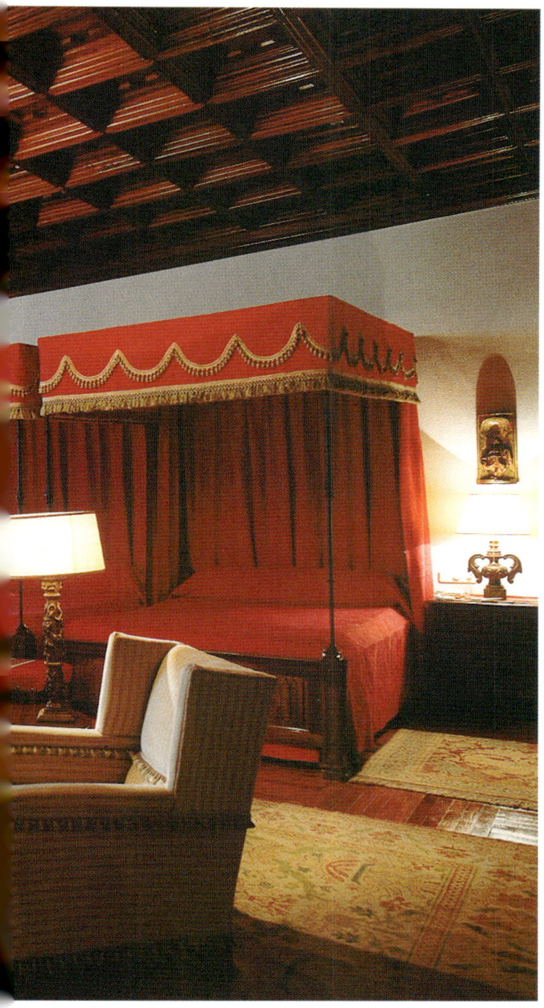

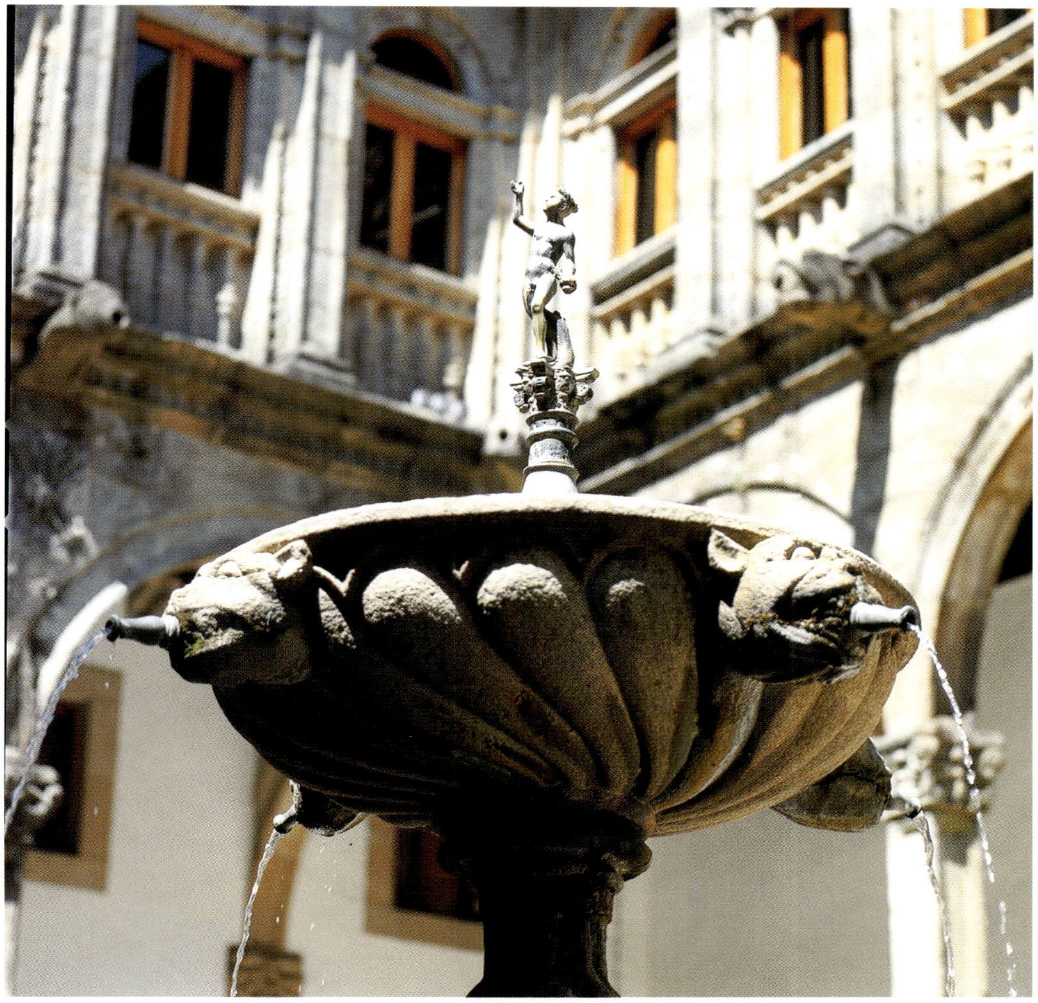

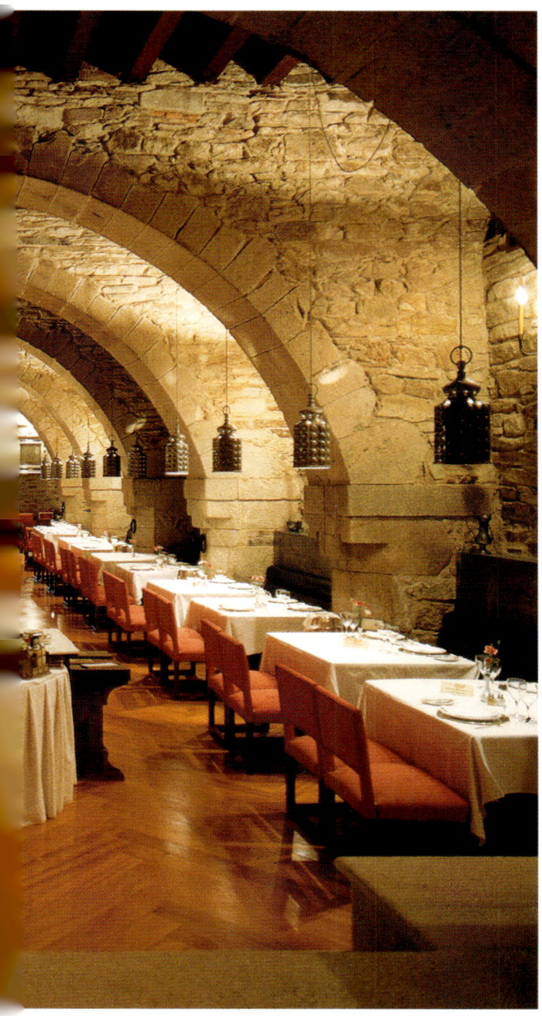

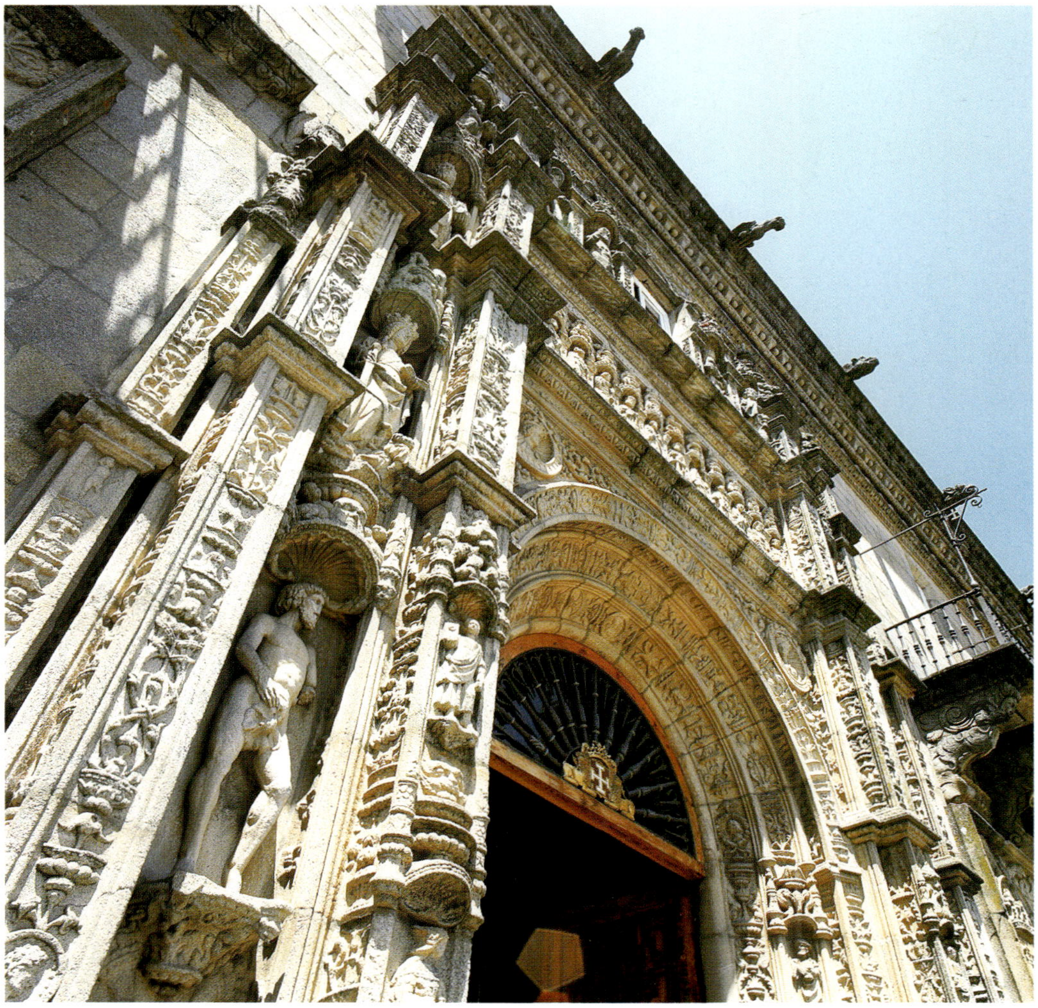

Marbella Club

Marbella is a name synonymous with luxury and success, blue seas and white yachts, long sunny days and vibrant champagne nights. This public image is very close to the truth and situated right on the coast, in the middle of what's become known as 'the golden mile', you'll find the Marbella Club Hotel, a favoured and classic resort with a distinguished pedigree.

Just after the war, the celebrated and fabulously wealthy Hohenlohe family acquired Finca Santa Margarita, an extensive estate of olive trees and vineyards. There was an estate residence of some grandeur, but yet it was not really big enough for prince Alfonso von Hohenlohe, his large family, retinue and numerous friends, so the house was enlarged, and then extended further.

Alfonso was a dedicated gardener and accomplished landscape architect, and it was he who planned and executed the lovely sub-tropical gardens that today surround the hotel and run down to the beach itself. His ideas for the estate developed eventually into creating an exclusive 'club' of some 16 rooms. Now the whole luxurious complex comprises far more than even the prince envisaged.

There are 130 guest rooms altogether, comprising executive and garden suites, junior suites and nine detached villas –some with private swimming pools- and bungalows, with two or three bedrooms each, as well as 84 superior and very comfortable rooms.

The hotel, as it developed, was always conceived in the traditional Andalusian style that best suits this part of Spain. It has been marvellously and meticulously designed to offer the very best to a knowledgeable international clientele, its success reflected in its inclusion among the Leading Hotels in the World and its list of prestigious awards over the past decade. The fine gourmet restaurant and the exquisite gardens, as well as the hotel itself, have each been recipients, and worthy ones most certainly.

The Marbella area has plenty to offer for those who love golf. There are no less than 30 excellent professional courses to be found, but the Marbella Club Hotel has added one more of its own, designed by one-time Ryder Cup player Dave Thomas, who has stopped at nothing to provide one of the very best and most challenging courses on the Spanish coast.

Tennis, too, is well catered for and in winter skiing parties into the Sierra Nevada are organised. Swimmers can enjoy the two hotel pools or step into the cool and welcoming surf of the Mediterranean itself.

In the year 2000 the Marbella Club Spa was opened, with a pool, sauna, steam room, jacuzzi and 10 beauty treatment rooms including massages, scrubs etc.

Most luxury hotels know how to mix business and pleasure, and the Marbella Club does this with considerable panache. There are several well-appointed meeting rooms, for conferences and lectures. Every imaginable aid is available. Ask, and it shall be given to you; the Marbella Club is a hotel that esteems service. And that, I think, is the key: to success, to white yachts, to the mystique that creates a Marbella and a beach hotel fit for princes.

151

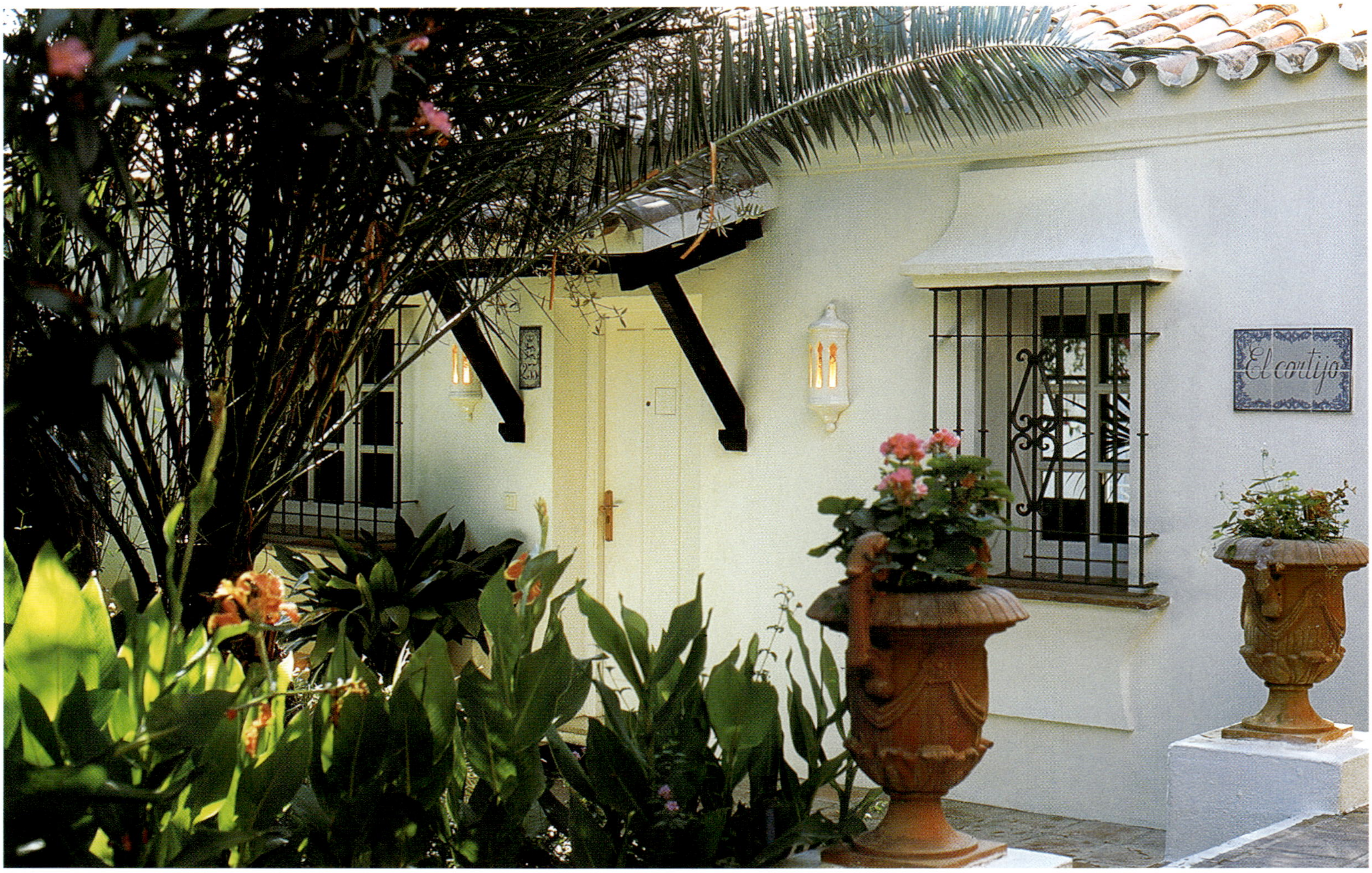
El cortijo

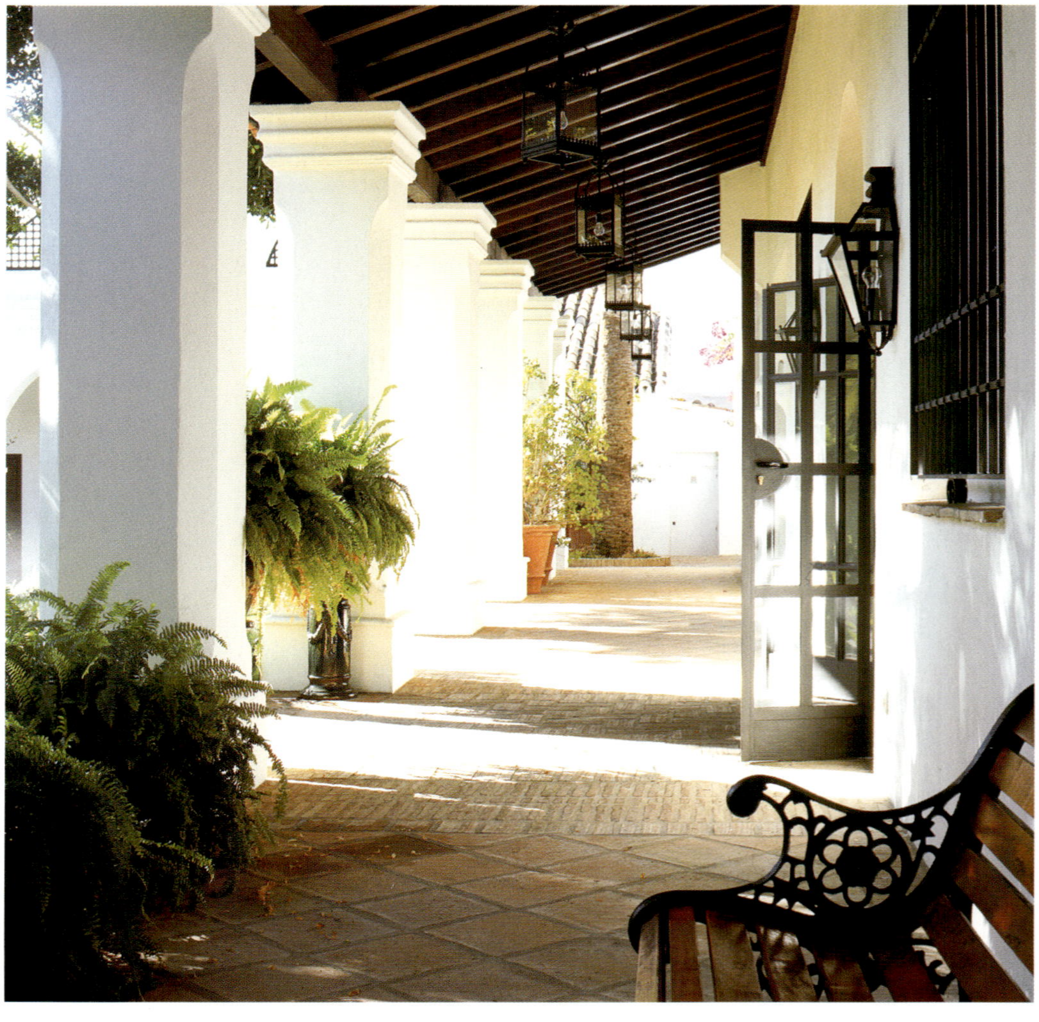

Marbella Club: an Andalusian estate on the Mediterranean beach.

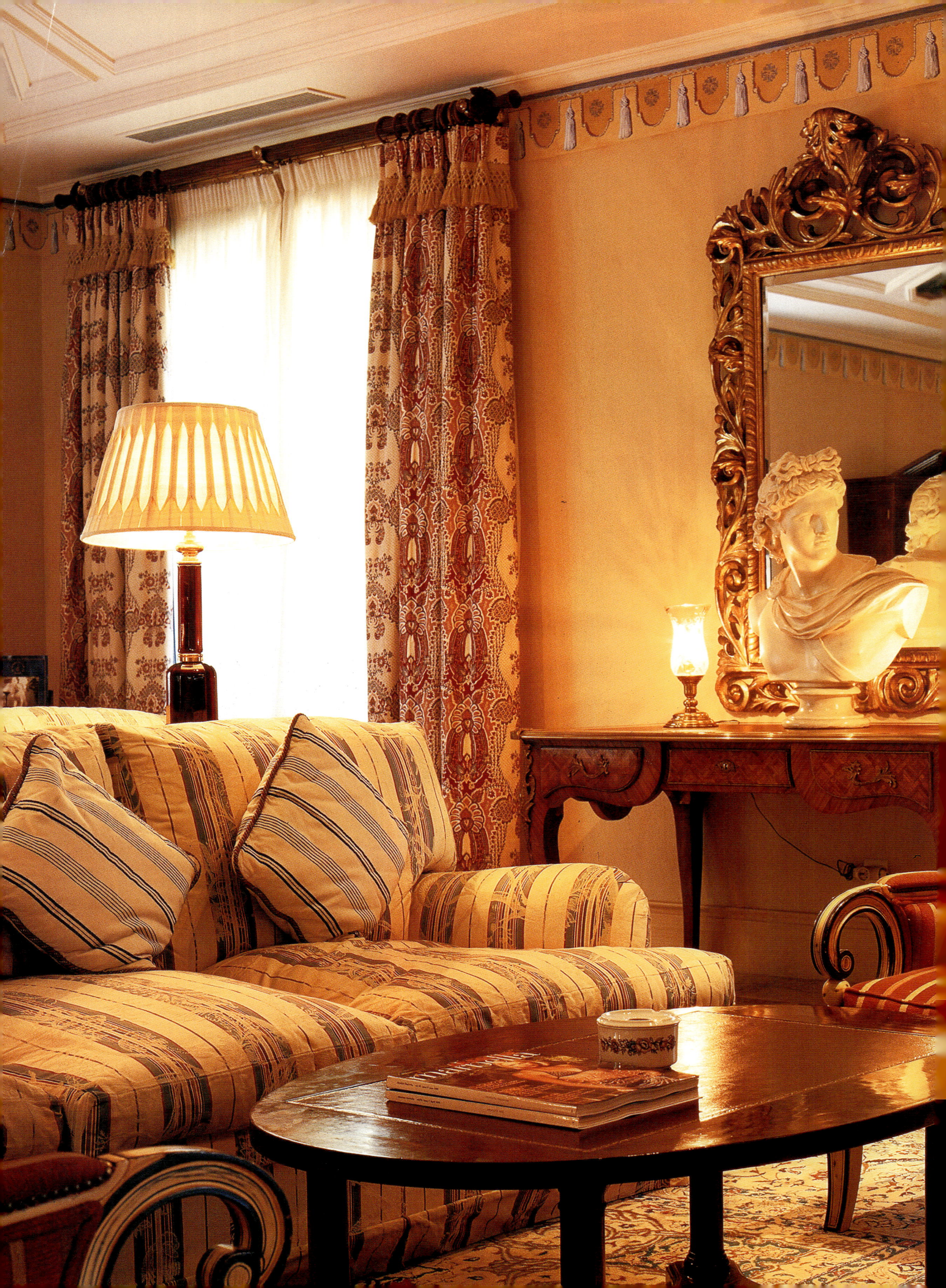

155

Villa Real

Madrid, like a heart, is set deep in the body of Spain and when I got there, after a long drive, I felt hot and tired, but also elated - an adventurer arrived at his oasis. The Villa Real, my destination, is indeed just that, an oasis of quietude, on the grand scale - cool Carrara marble underfoot, with Persian rugs laid down upon it, tapestries on the walls and, here and there, antique stone figures striking beautiful poses.

The Villa Real, unusually for a five-star hotel in Spain, is almost brand-new, only a decade old, though standing before it, you'd not think so. It fits seamlessly into its historical surroundings. Whilst never actually a palace, it is palatial, with a distinguished pedigree, since 1996 one of the select Derby group of hotels - a certificate, in itself, of absolute luxury, elegance and fine service. It stands conveniently central both for the tourist and the businessman, on the Plaza de las Cortes, opposite the Parliament building.

A statue in the square caught my eye, a man in costume giving pretty ladies and plump gentlemen an equally quizzical look. Next morning, early, I took a turn around the plaza end inspected the statue more closely. Miguel de Cervantes! Author of one of my favourite books. How often I've felt I was also tilting at windmills.

After a wonderful breakfast, I stepped out a second time and walked to the Prado Museum. It took just five minutes.

I use galleries to dream in, to linger in, imagining the past, in its pain and beauty. I let three hours go by, and saw so little and so much.

Back in my room at the Villa Real, I sat on my balcony, gazing out over the rooftops of one of Europe's most beautiful cities, sipping a very cold white wine, and imagined Don Quixote and his sidekick completing their exploits, as it was, in a metallic green Seat saloon.

This building would have amazed our protagonist. He would have loved it. The 96 double rooms all have split-level sitting areas and balconies like mine. The 19 'grand-luxe' suites have hot bubbling jacuzzis as well.

There are several small but elegant dining-rooms for every kind of private or business occasion and an excellent restaurant, serving a varied and accomplished international cuisine, and some excellent wines.

Business is a world the Villa Real understands, and serves well. For a start, it is located at the financial heart of the capital, has a tailor-made selection of meeting rooms of different sizes, as well as a lively coffee shop on the ground floor that serves as an ideal *ad hoc* informal meeting place.

Next day, I didn't really want to leave, there was still so much in Madrid to enjoy, but I had another appointment far to the south... but not too far, you can be sure, from the comic and melancholy shade of the great Don Quixote.

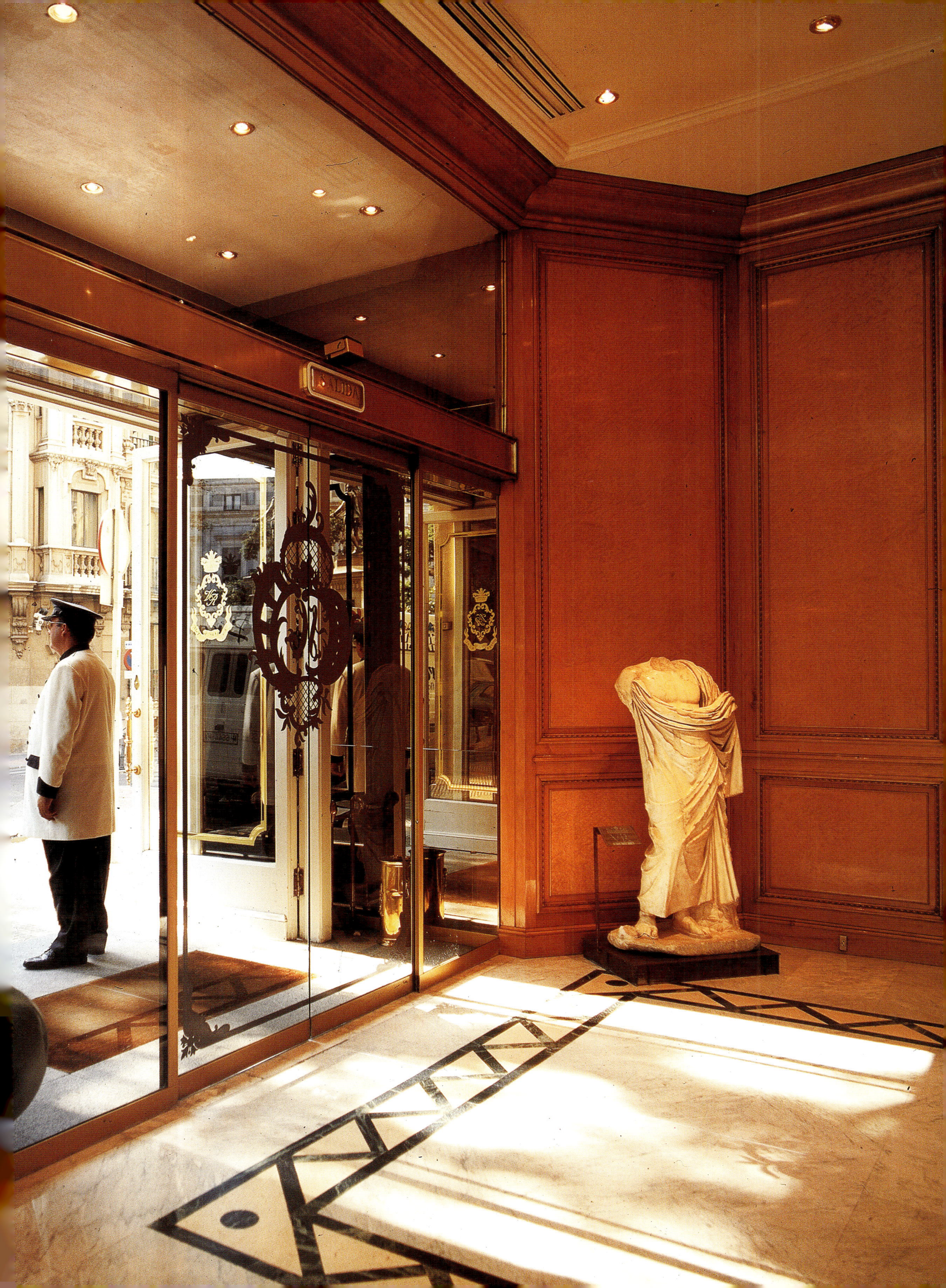
SALIDA

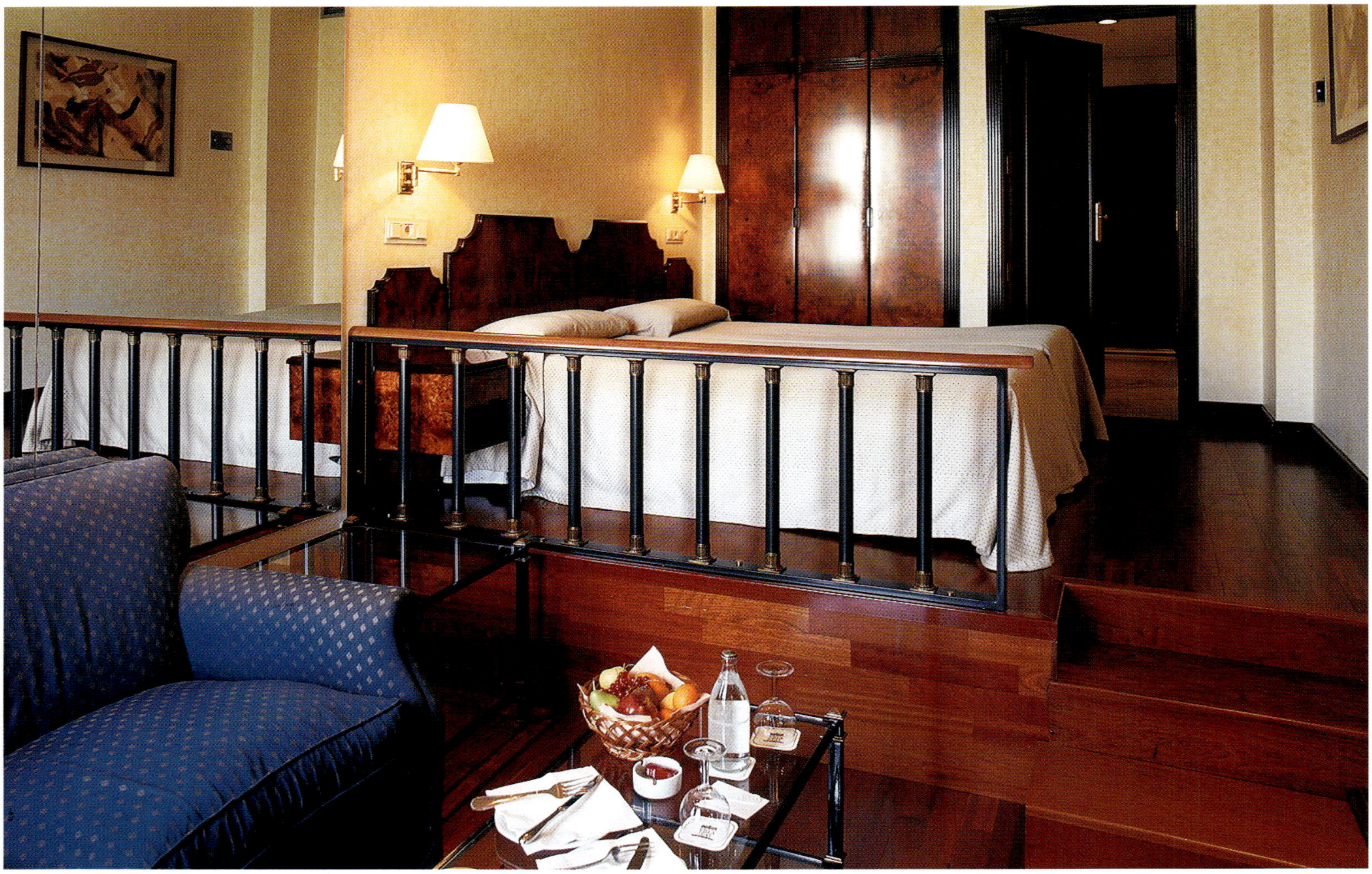

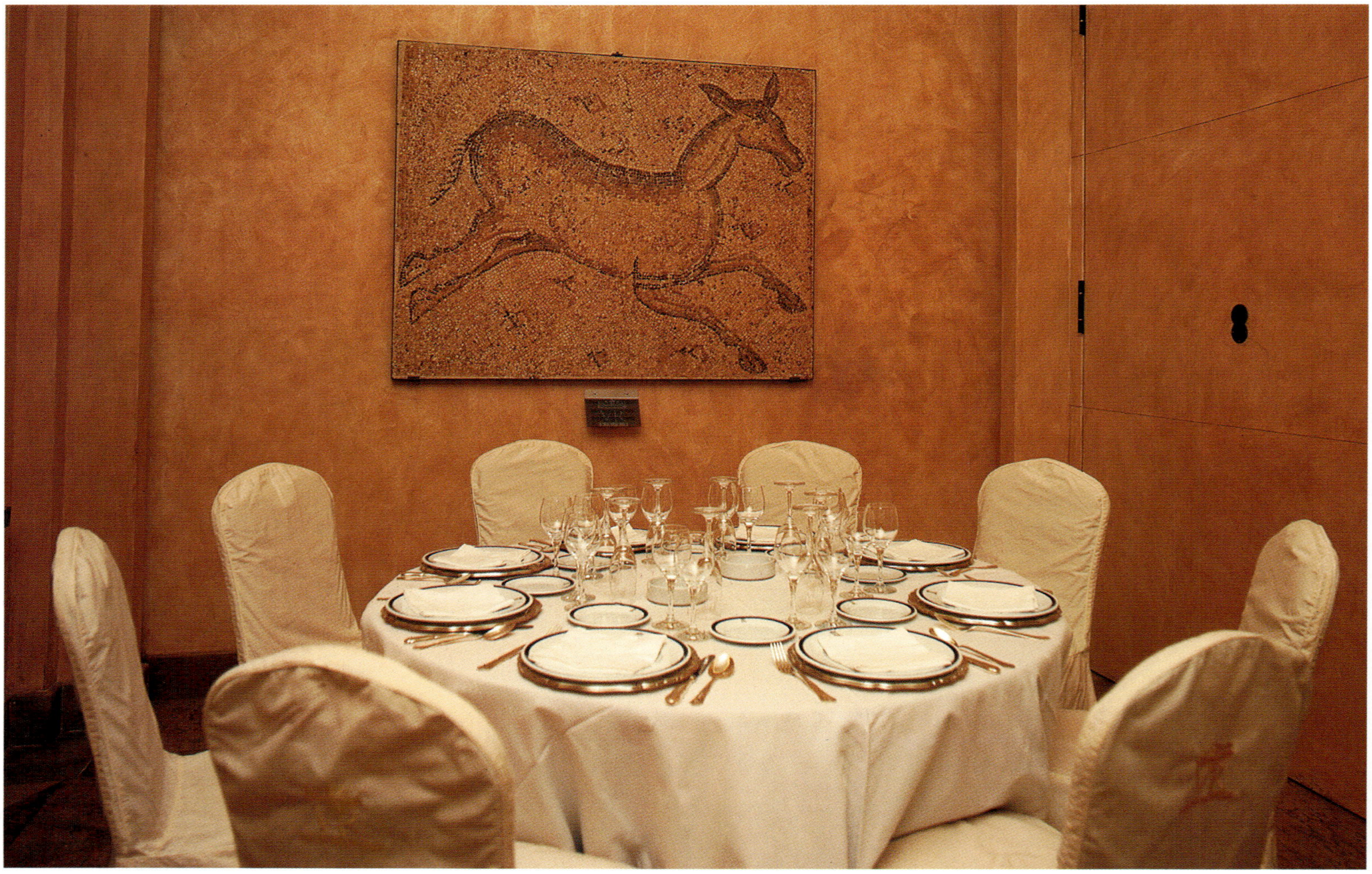

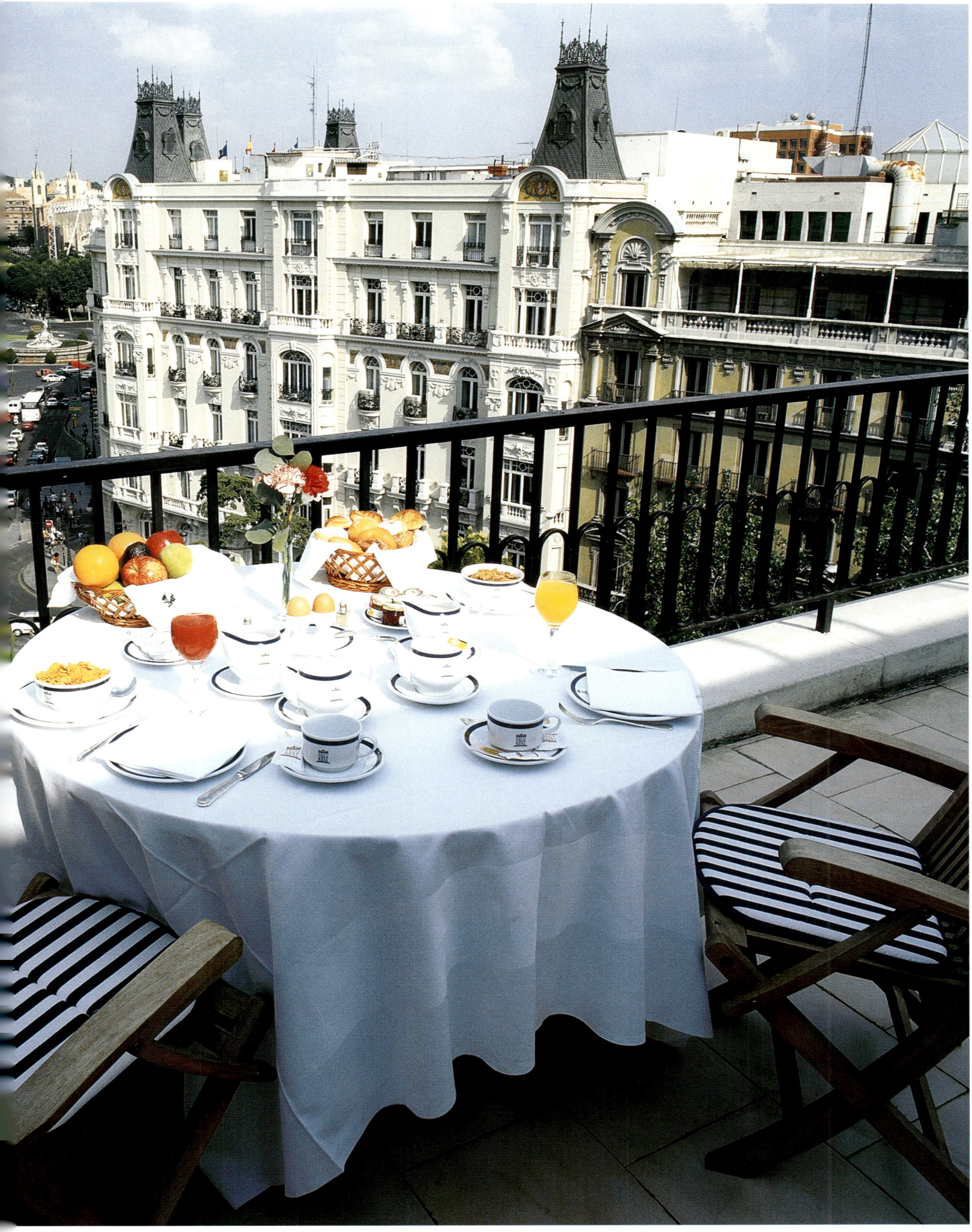

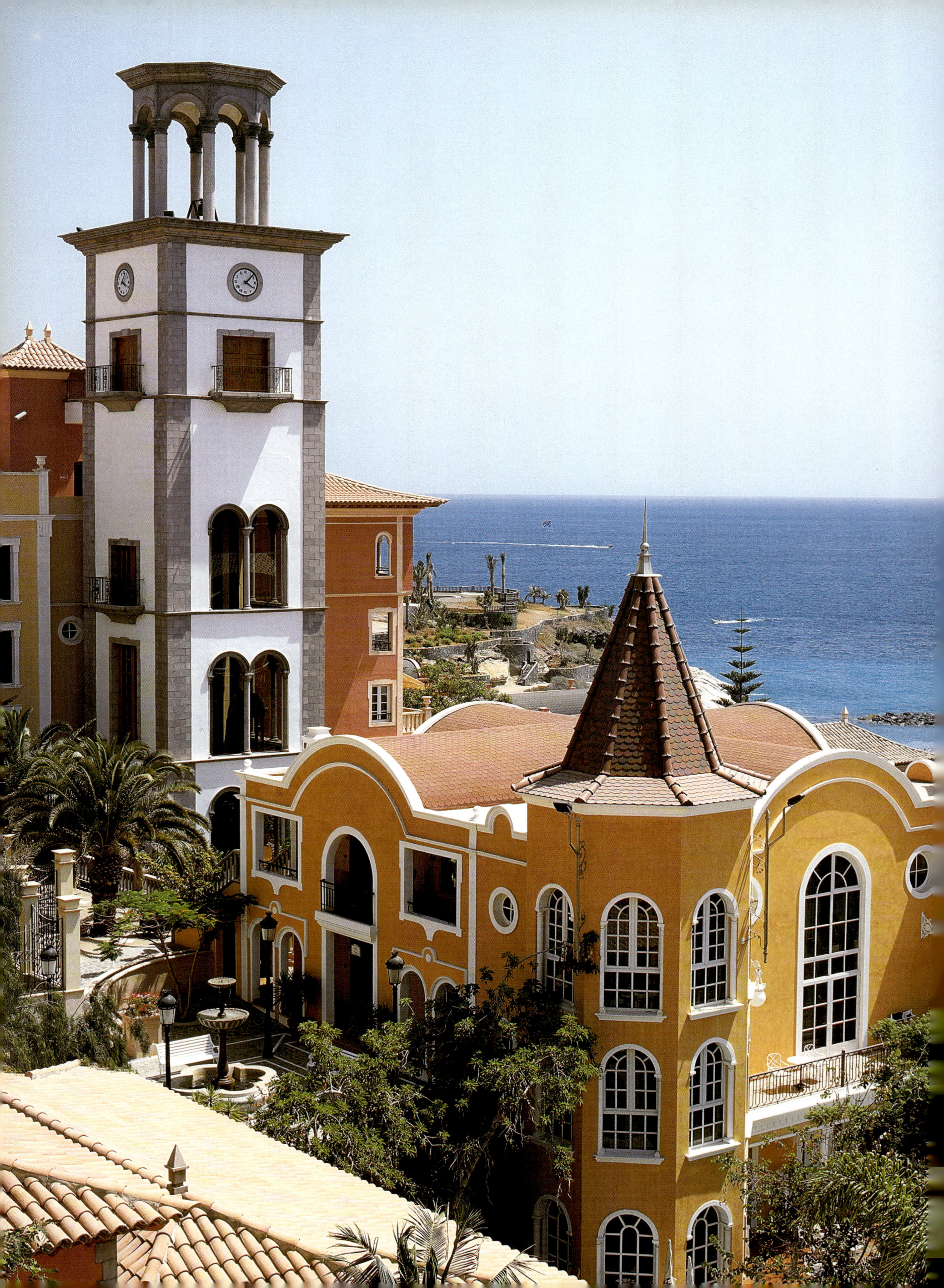

Gran Hotel Bahia del Duque

The five-star Gran Hotel Bahia del Duque, in Costa Adeje, on the southernmost tip of Tenerife, is a beachside village, an estate, a semi-tropical botanical garden, an oasis, a breathtakingly grand and vivid concept carried through to completion with verve and great style.

The many buildings that comprise Gran Hotel Bahia del Duque are an historical essay in the varied influences - a happy blend of Venetian and Victorian - that constituted the architecture of the Canary Islands some hundred years ago. There are echoes, everywhere, of Tenerife's capital town, Santa Cruz.

To begin with, you will certainly need a map to help you get your bearings. There are no less than 324 rooms and 38 luxurious suites, spread through 19 guest buildings. Four of them are called 'Las Casas Ducales' (The Manor Houses), which offer amenities including butler service, a separate reception desk and breakfast room, amongst others. The hotel also provides 19 conference rooms, to accommodate every size of business meeting, eight restaurants, each offering a different cuisine, five swimming-pools, eight bars, an Internet C@fé, where guests can surf the net, all kinds of outdoor leisure activities, both on land and on the water… and an observatory, with a telescope, stronger and more penetrative than most laymen will ever have met with before. The skies above the Canary Islands are renowned for their purity and astronomers the world over come here to study the stars at a series of state-of-the-art observatories across the islands.

The 'club house' is the nerve centre of the hotel, located at the front approach to Gran Hotel Bahia del Duque. Here, helpful staff will welcome you, take you to your room and guide you through the myriad choices of entertainment, sports, relaxation and culinary delights on offer, by day and by night, both on the hotel campus and beyond.

From the club house, the buildings and exotic gardens fan out towards the waters of the sparkling blue Atlantic, fringed by a wonderfully soft sandy beach. Most rooms, and all the suites, offer a private terrace facing the sea. I can't think of a better place to take a leisurely breakfast, while you plan the day ahead.

There is really so much to divert the guest at Gran Hotel Bahia del Duque itself that the world beyond its walls can understandably be forgotten, but not far away inland is the Cañadas del Teide National Park, with its spectacular and fascinating volcanic landscapes, and the Teide crater itself: visitors to these islands shouldn't miss such an opportunity. Excursions into the wilderness area can be organised by minibus, by jeep, or even helicopter.

Try to fit in a visit to the picturesque old village of Masca, northwards up the coast road from the hotel. Los Gigantes, the aptly named cliffs you will encounter there, offer dizzyingly panoramic views.

At the conclusion of your day of adventure, you will return to Gran Hotel Bahia del Duque's welcoming estate, and prepare yourself for the evening ahead. It is only as dusk falls across this intriguing hideway of a thousand faces that its romance begins to truly reveal itself.

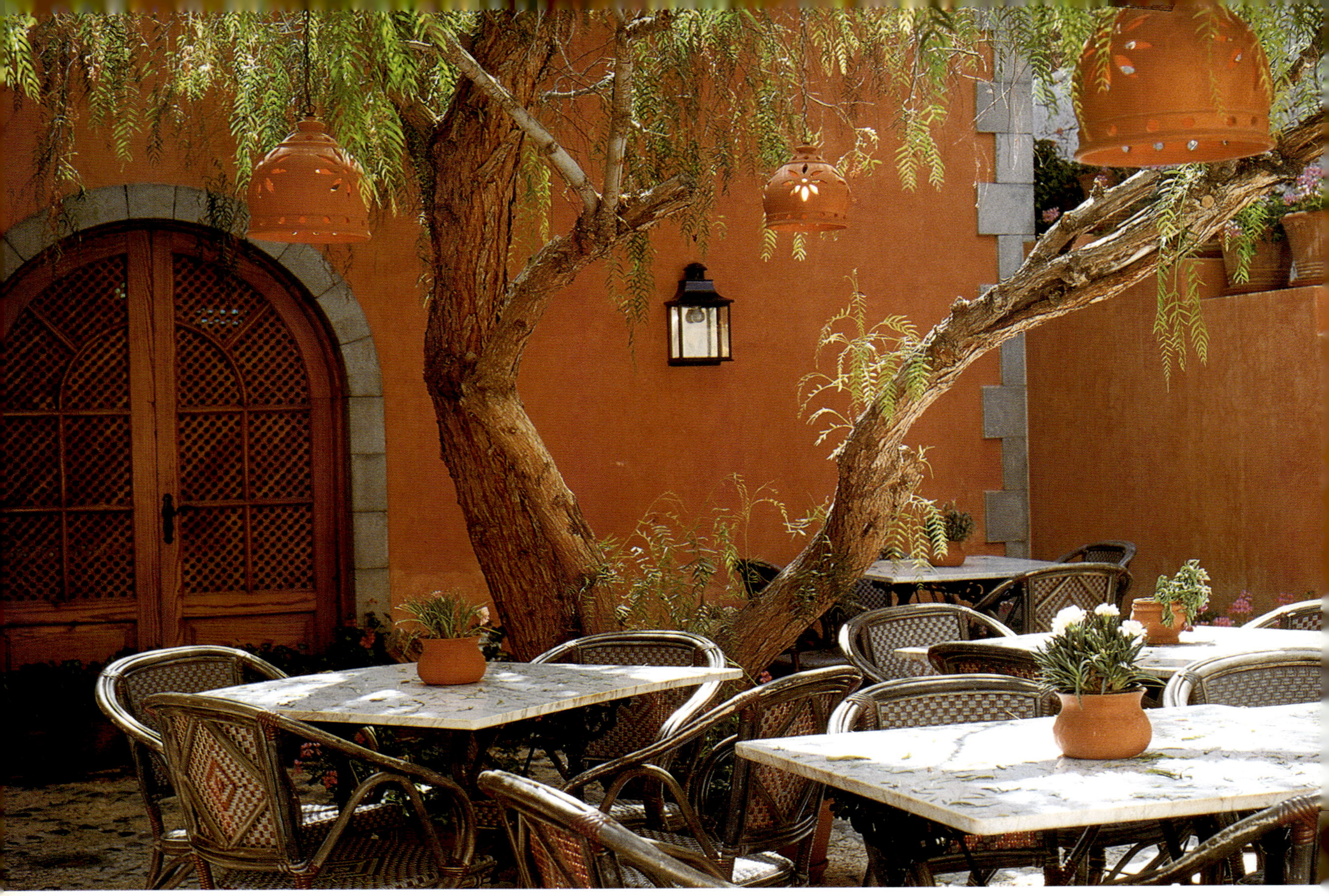

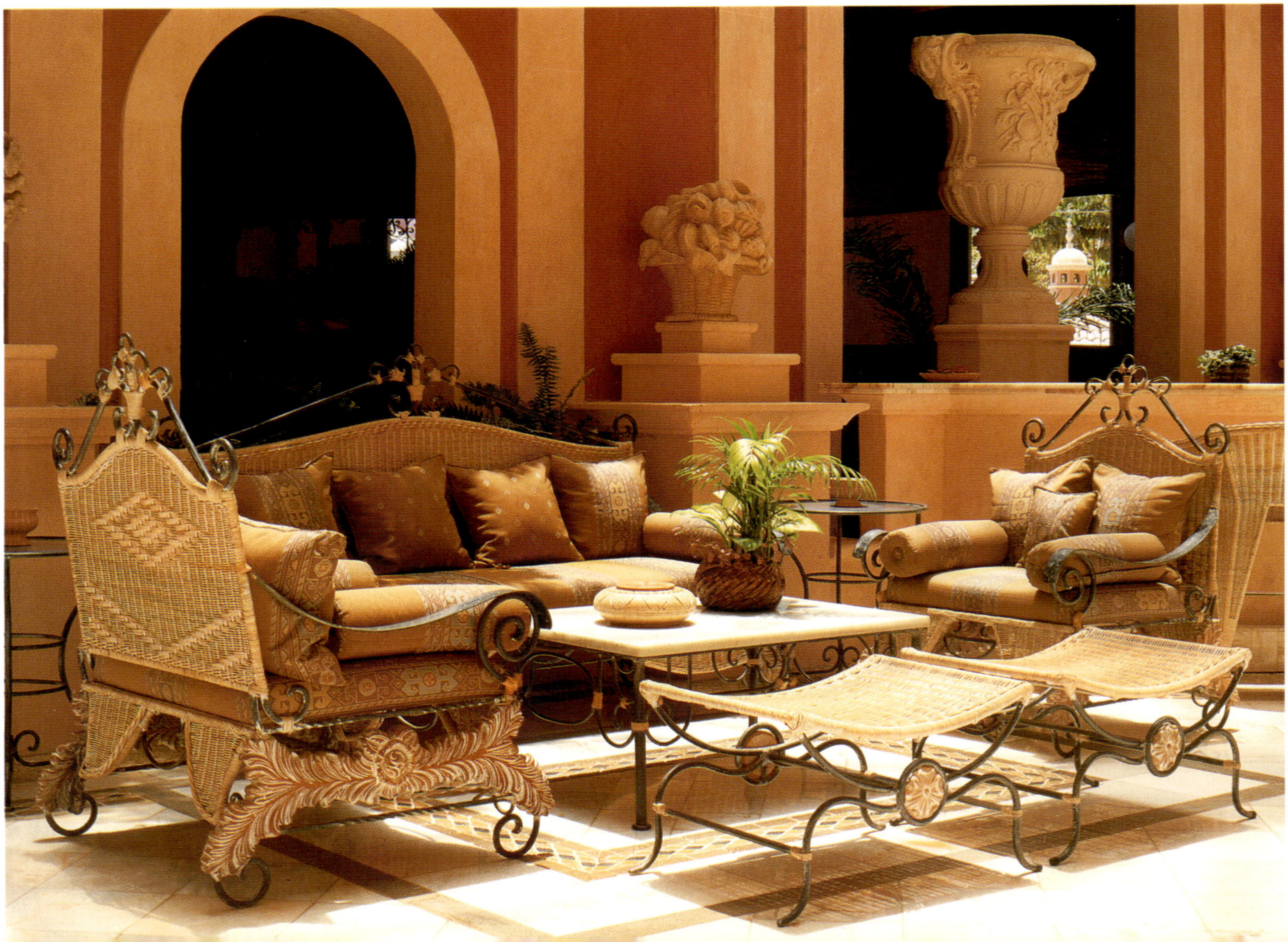

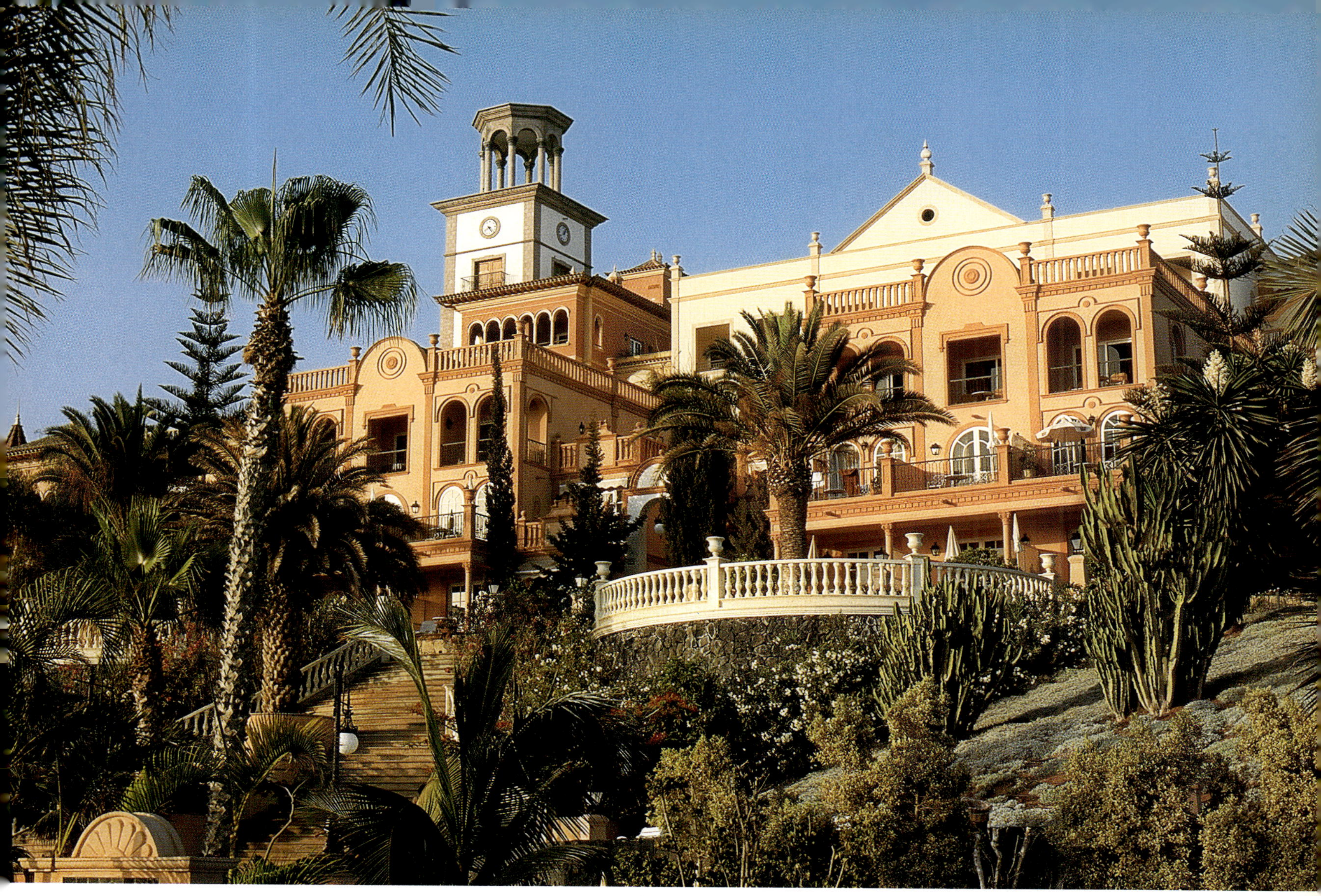

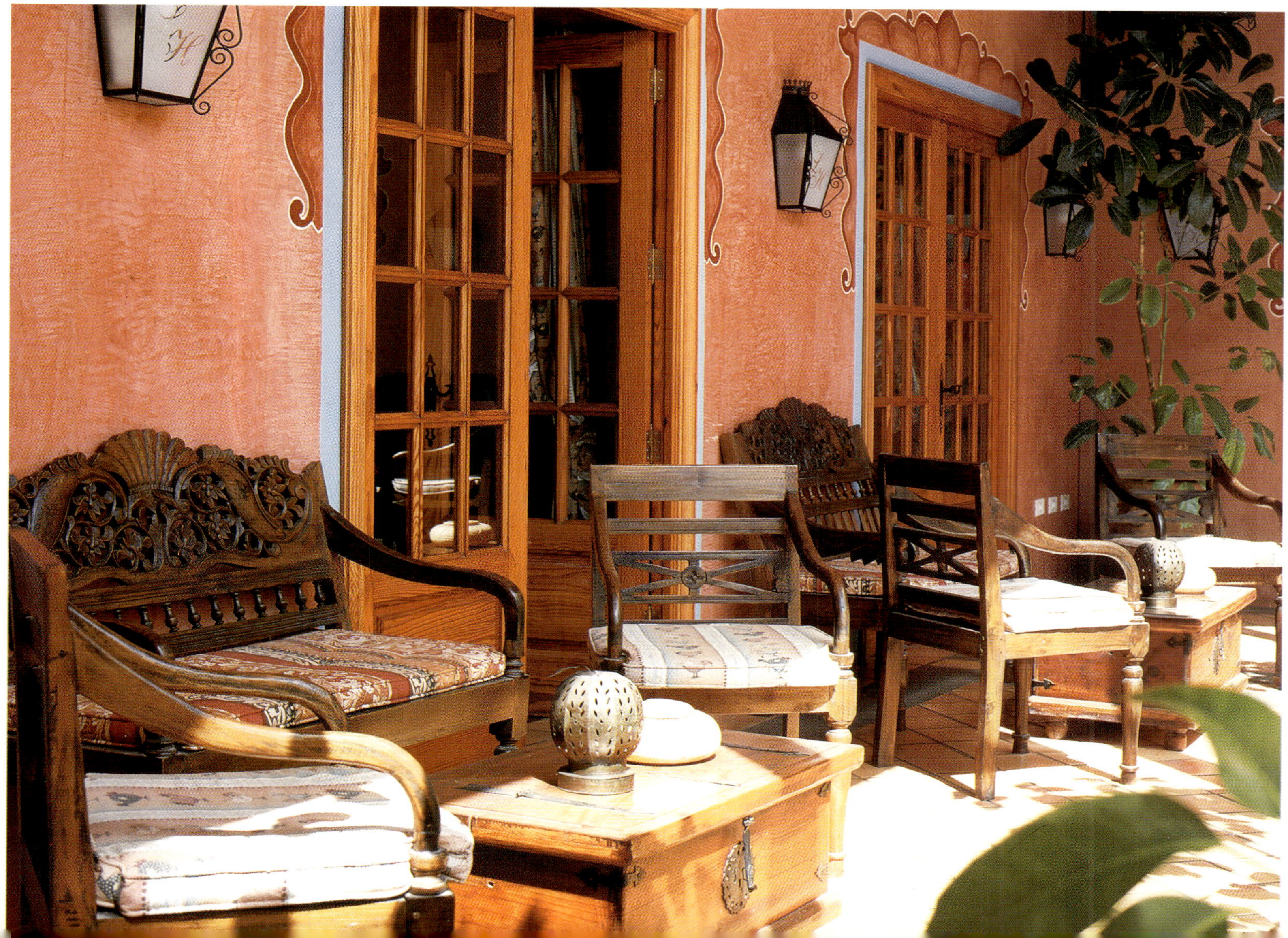

The hotel offers a summary of all the architectural influences of the Canaries.

165

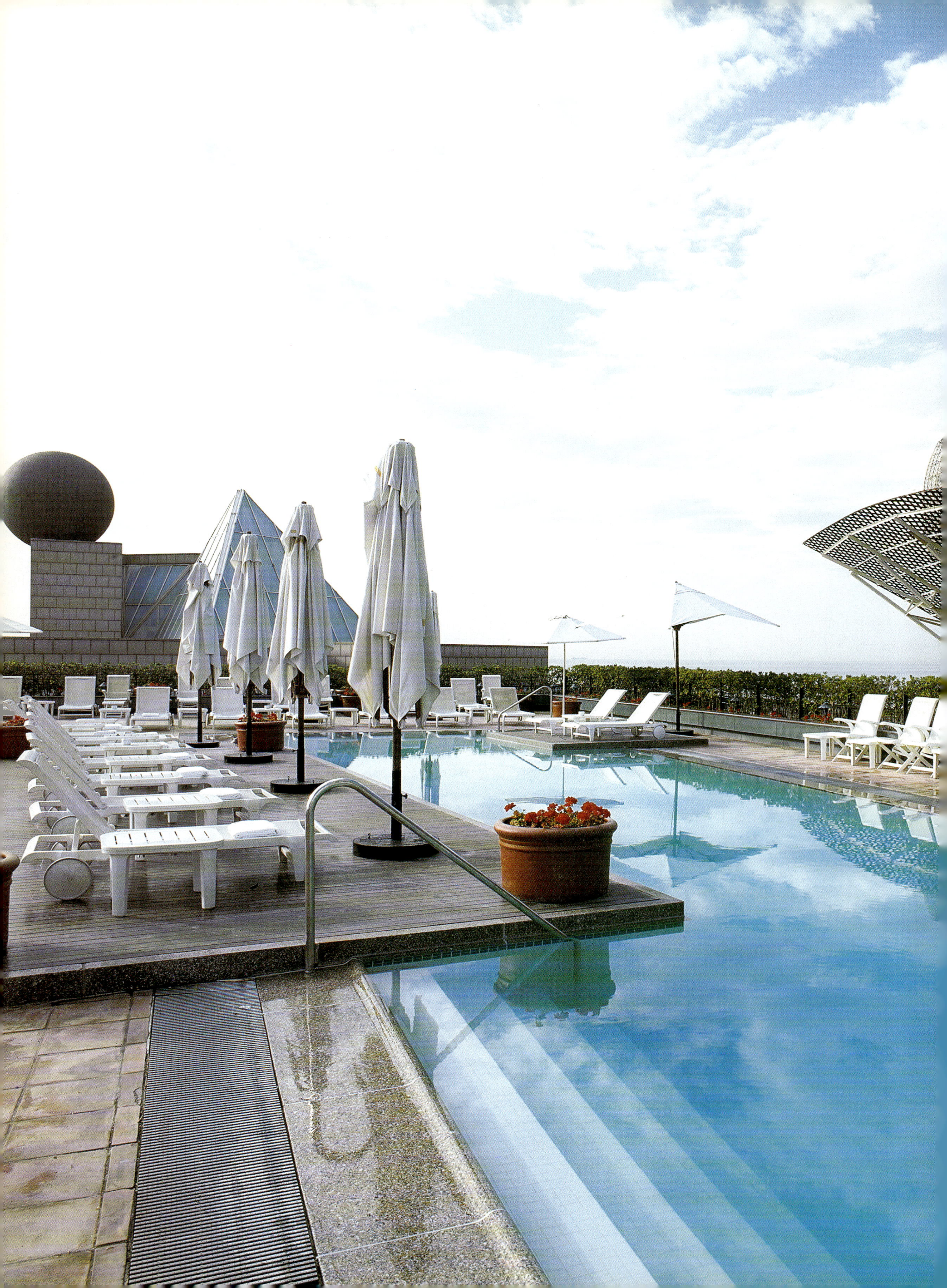

Arts

Many of the world's great hotels are created from ancient buildings, restored to combine a sense of history with modern standards of luxury and convenience that would surely astound and impress its earlier occupants. I love the timelessness of such places as much as anybody, but you can be led to assume architecture today lacks the skills of the master builders of generations gone by. I for one enjoy discovering this isn't so.

Opened as recently as 1994, the Hotel Arts in Barcelona's Olympic Village area, overlooking the azure waters of the Mediterranean, has a modern, even an avant-garde, soul and is proof that architects today possess every bit as much vision, daring, grace and skill as those in the past we honour so highly.

Stepping through its impressive portals was enough to make me feel happy to live in these times. Poetry resides not only in the shadow-filled cloisters of the past, but is equally at home in the clean, energetic lines of chrome and stainless steel that define the Hotel Arts. At home in any century are classic materials such as marble and hardwoods, and these you'll find in profusion at the Hotel Arts. The interior design matches the adventurous exterior.

Make no mistake, this is a hotel on the grand scale. It stands 44 stories high, at present the tallest building in all of Spain. There are 455 rooms altogether, 397 double rooms, 56 executive suites, a Japanese suite and a Presidential suite. That's not all: the top 10 stories, named The Club, are devoted to luxurious apartments, spacious and the very pinnacle of luxury… with the services of a personal butler. Haven't we all of us at times imagined such a pleasure? Now, it is within reach, at least for the duration of your stay at Hotel Arts.

In my own room, perched high over Barcelona, as if on a clifftop, far beyond the reach of traffic noise, I stood awhile and admired the magnificent view through my plate-glass window. The lights of the city twinkled below, the water tonight still as glass. On my coffee-table, a plumply generous bunch of clean white lilies, set beside not one but two brimming fruit bowls. From another window the gentle curve of the beach stretched away into the distance. Big modern paintings by living Spanish artists hung on my walls… and this is maybe how the hotel found its name: all through the Arts Hotel there are fine works that celebrate, like the fabric of the building itself, the spirit and vision of modern man.

There was much to see in Barcelona, but the Hotel Arts, so quiet and so privileged an environment, gave me pause… I could indulge in a little uncharacteristic *mañana*. I took a long hot bath, wrapped myself in a wonderfully fleecy robe, and rested. Then, I called a lift that took me down to the restaurant, where I enjoyed an unforgettable and delightful meal full of Catalan brio, served with every attentiveness. The modern world as defined by the Hotel Arts is an honourable and comfortable place to live in. Its extensive list of awards confirms that I'm not alone in my enthusiasm. During my stay; I told myself: 'History is bunk'.

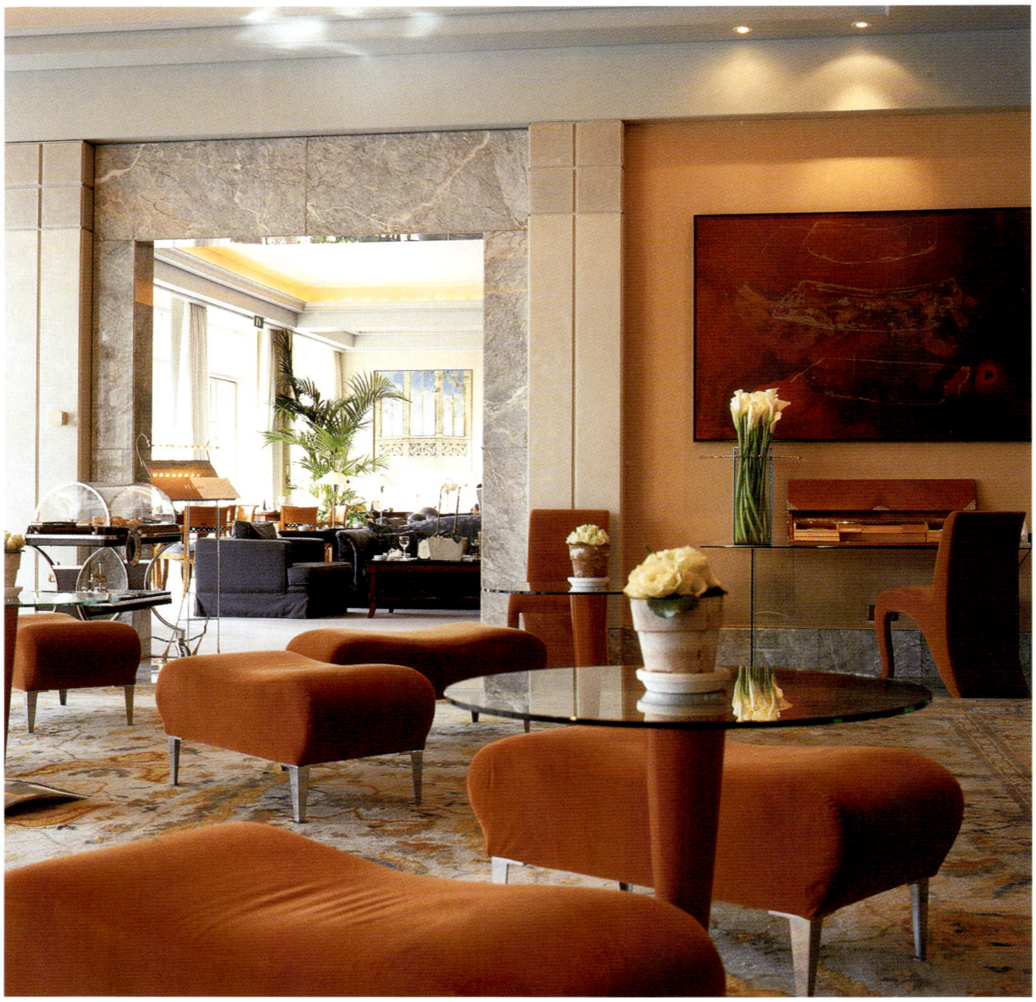

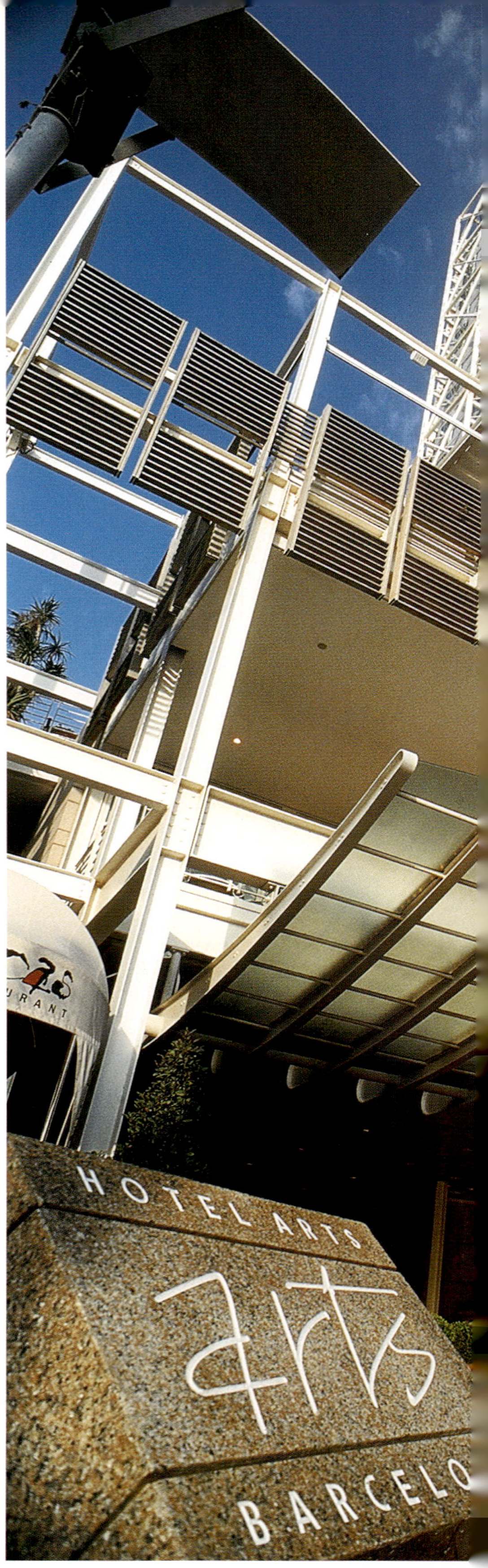
HOTEL ARTS
arts
BARCELO

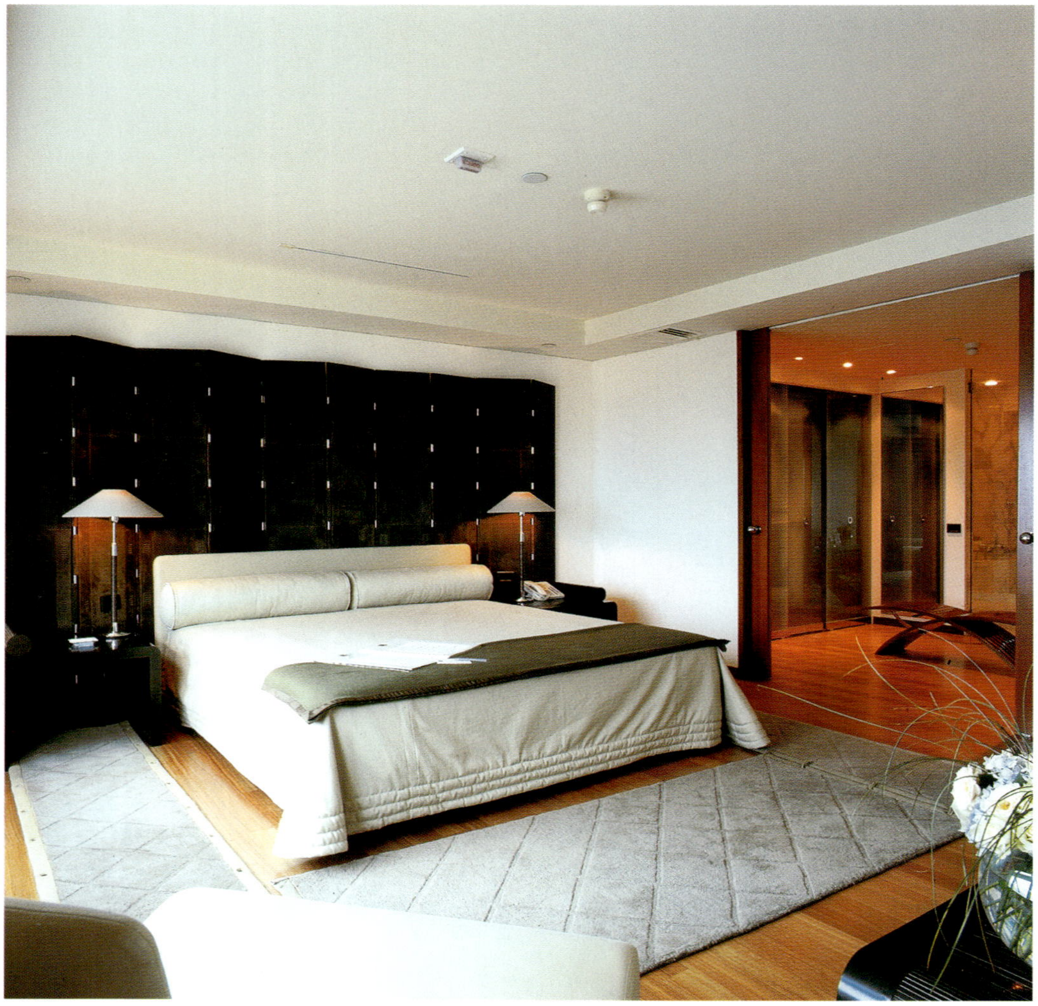

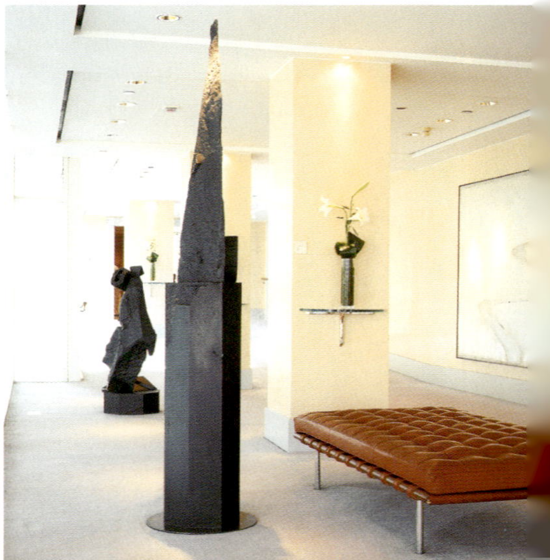

169

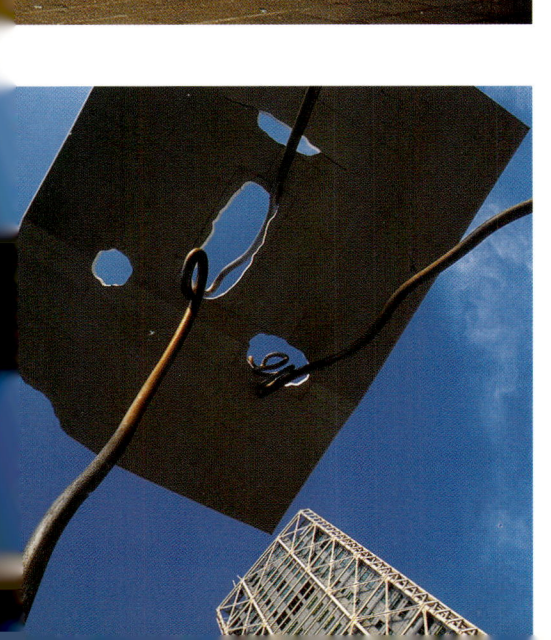

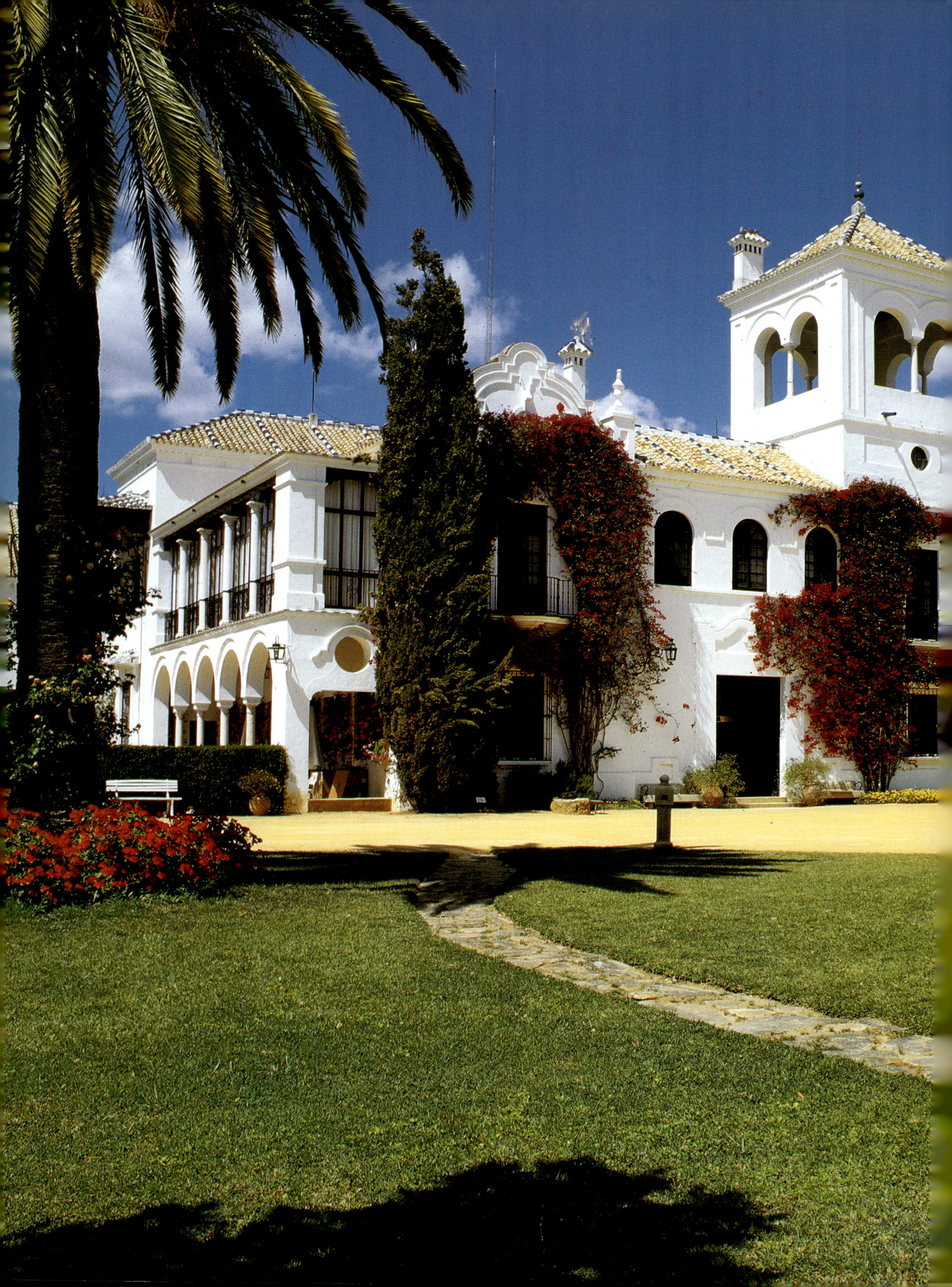

Cortijo El Esparragal

El Esparragal, near Seville, is unique amongst hotels... its boasts its own bullring. Indeed, it leads a double life - as a fascinating and quite superior holiday hideaway and a workmanlike and successful cattle-breeding station.

This is a country estate, a *hacienda*, on the grand scale, with an illustrious history that goes back to the 14th century, and before - right back to Roman times. After the Saracens were ousted, in the 15th century, the property was awarded by King Juan II to one Don Fernando Medina.

Two centuries later, his descendants sold it to the Hieronymite Order of monks, who built themselves a monastery and a chapel on the site, which are the earliest buildings still remaining today.

It was the monks who developed El Esparragal into a thriving farming community, growing cereals, keeping vineyards and planting olive groves, as well as breeding the splendid Spanish Berber horse, which, right up to the present day, has a central role in sporting, cultural and religious events right across Spain.

The haciendas in this part of the country were organised in a series of expansive patios, around which were grouped stables, barns, mills and presses for wheat, wine and olive oil, and the workers' dwellings. El Esparragal was no exception.

The system of country estates like these lived on into the 1960s, when the Spanish government finally re-organised agricultural production into larger and more economic groupings. *Haciendas* had to re-invent themselves. Some introduced new crops, others opened their doors to tourism.

El Esparragal sensibly embraced both these avenues. Today the estate are significant breeders of pedigree horses and cattle!

The hotel at El Esparragal has been made over with flair and great charm to appeal to the sensibilities of the luxury traveller.

Outside, there are wide, brilliant-green lawns, banks of thriving plants and colourful flowers. Cool fountains play under venerable trees. Within, the rooms are graced by 19th century antique furniture, the guest rooms are high, light and airy, with thick walls.

The city of Seville is within easy reach, full of fascinating museums and historic buildings and crowded with lively pavement cafés and eating-houses. What better way to relax, after a day in that bustling city, than to return home, full of new impressions, to your own country estate, sit down to a fabulous meal, and afterwards, as evening falls, stroll, enthralled, around the farm and the lovely gardens, into the acres of woodland, listening to the lowing of cattle and the soft calling of birds, and end up, perhaps, by the azure swimming pool, and sit awhile, dreaming, under the tall and imposing palm-trees.

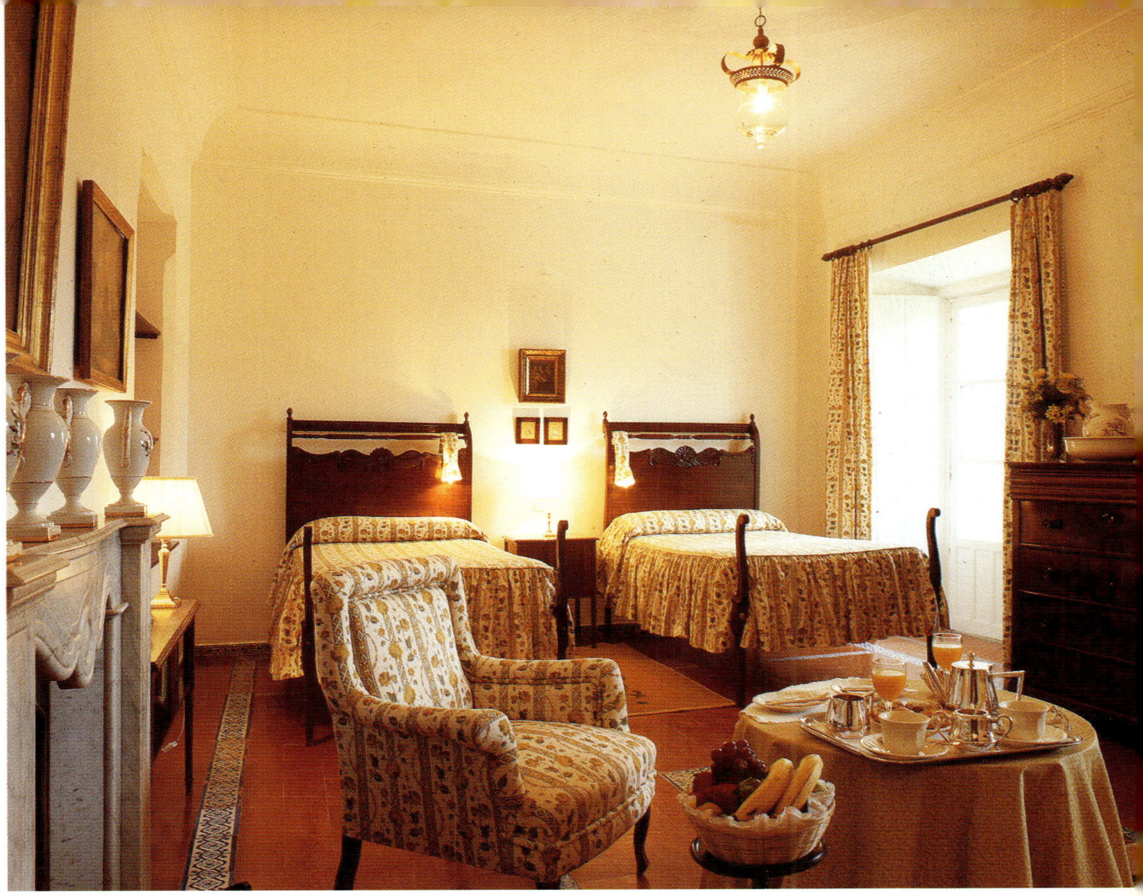
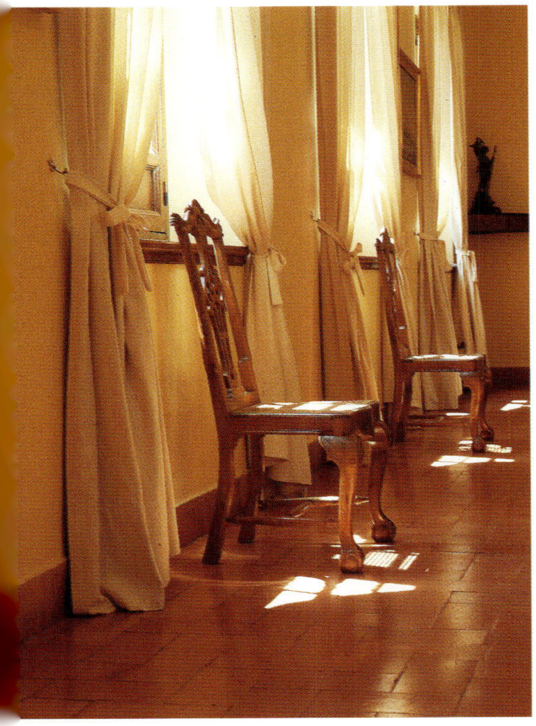
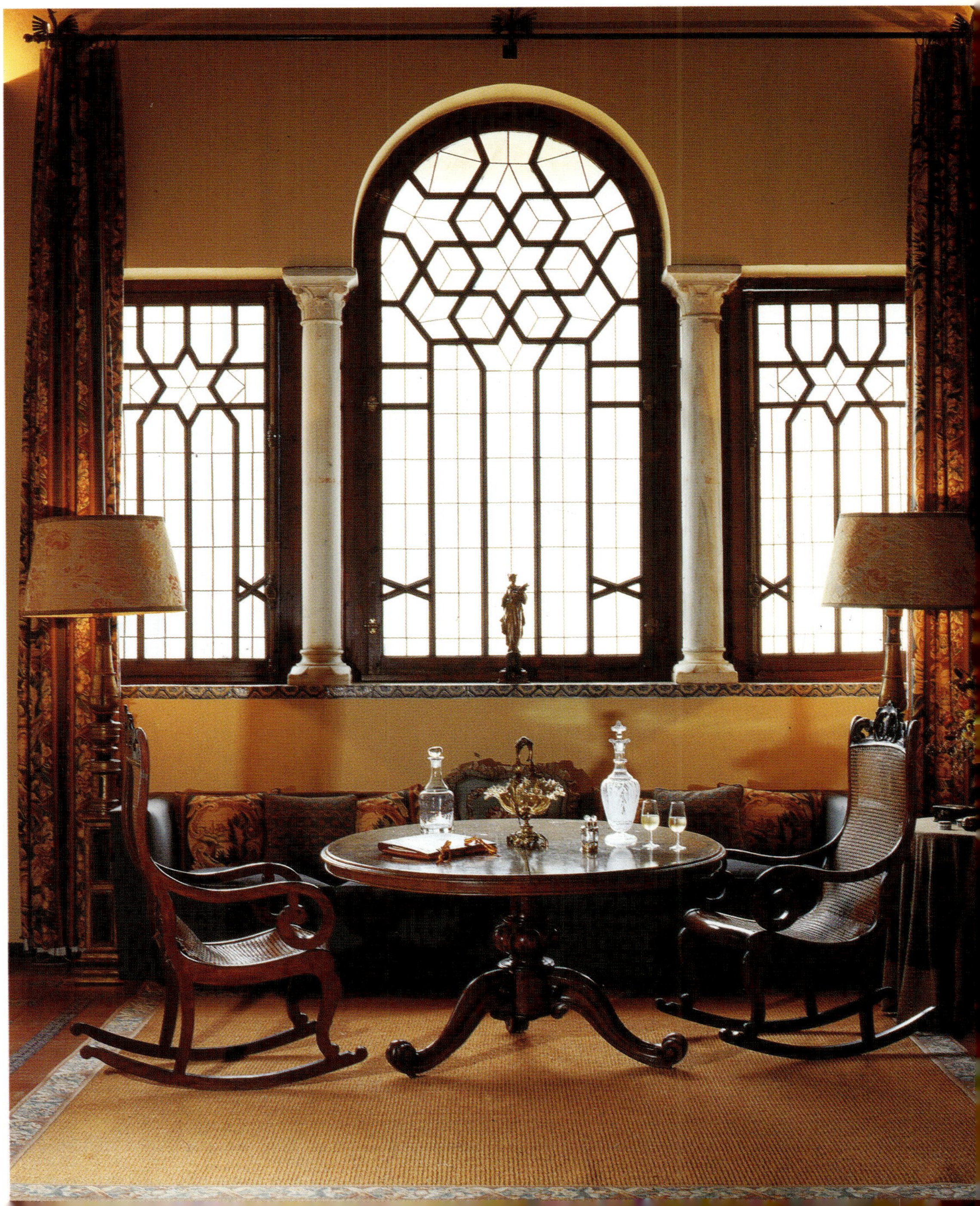

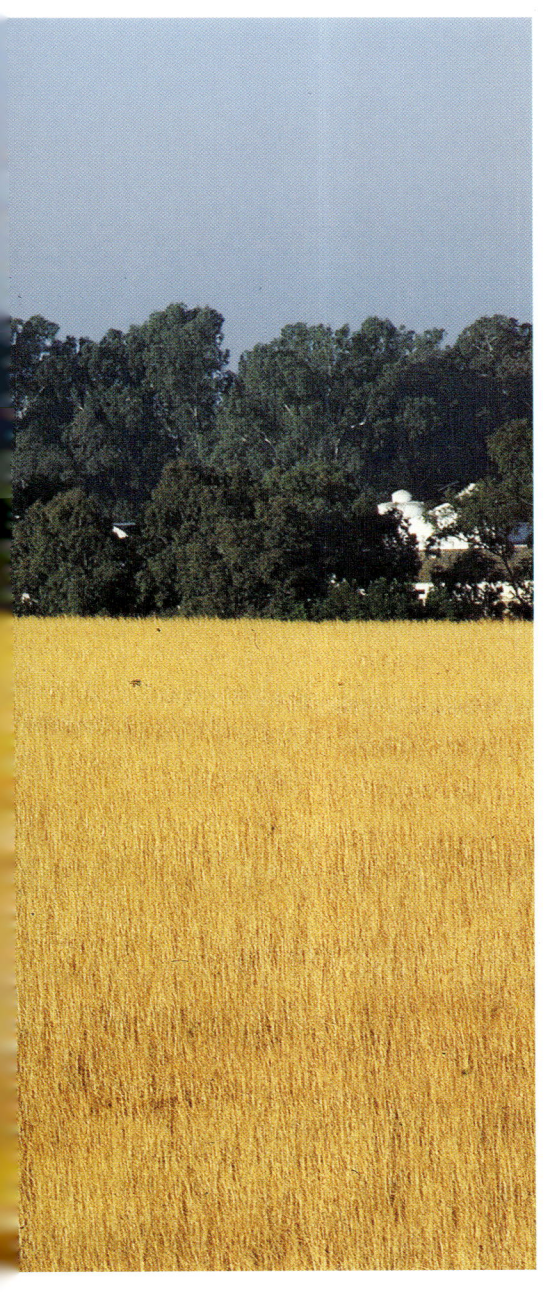

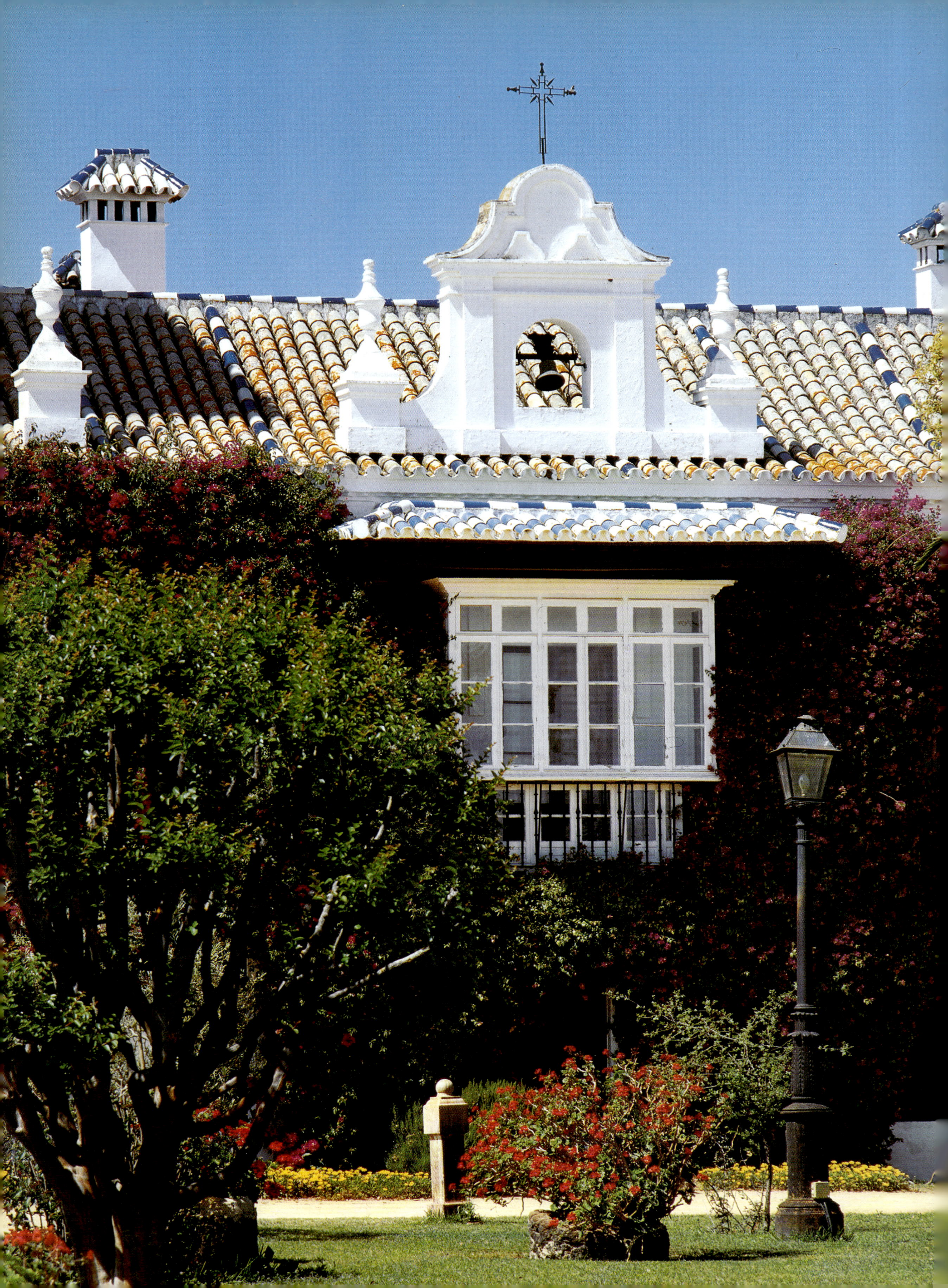

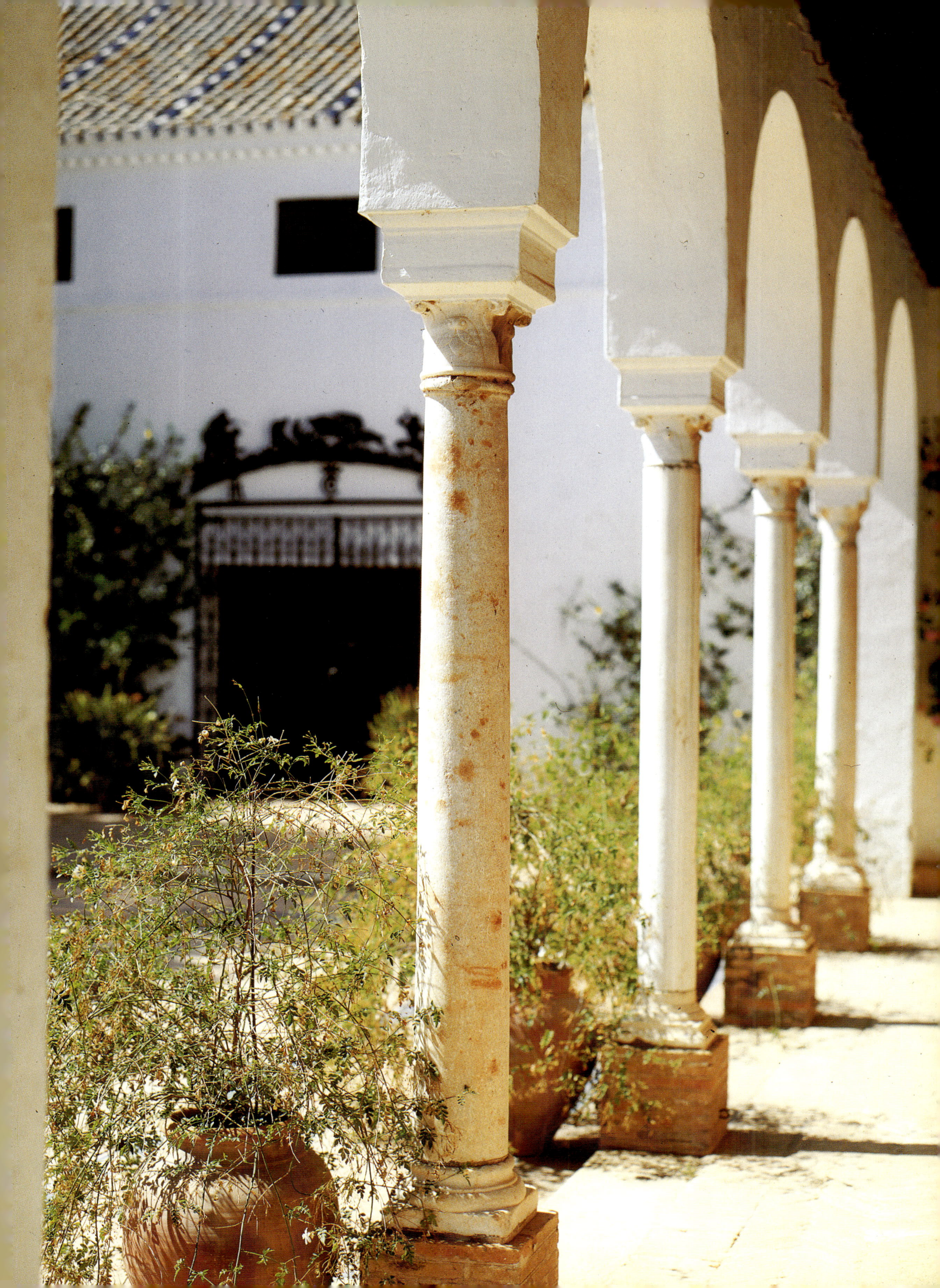

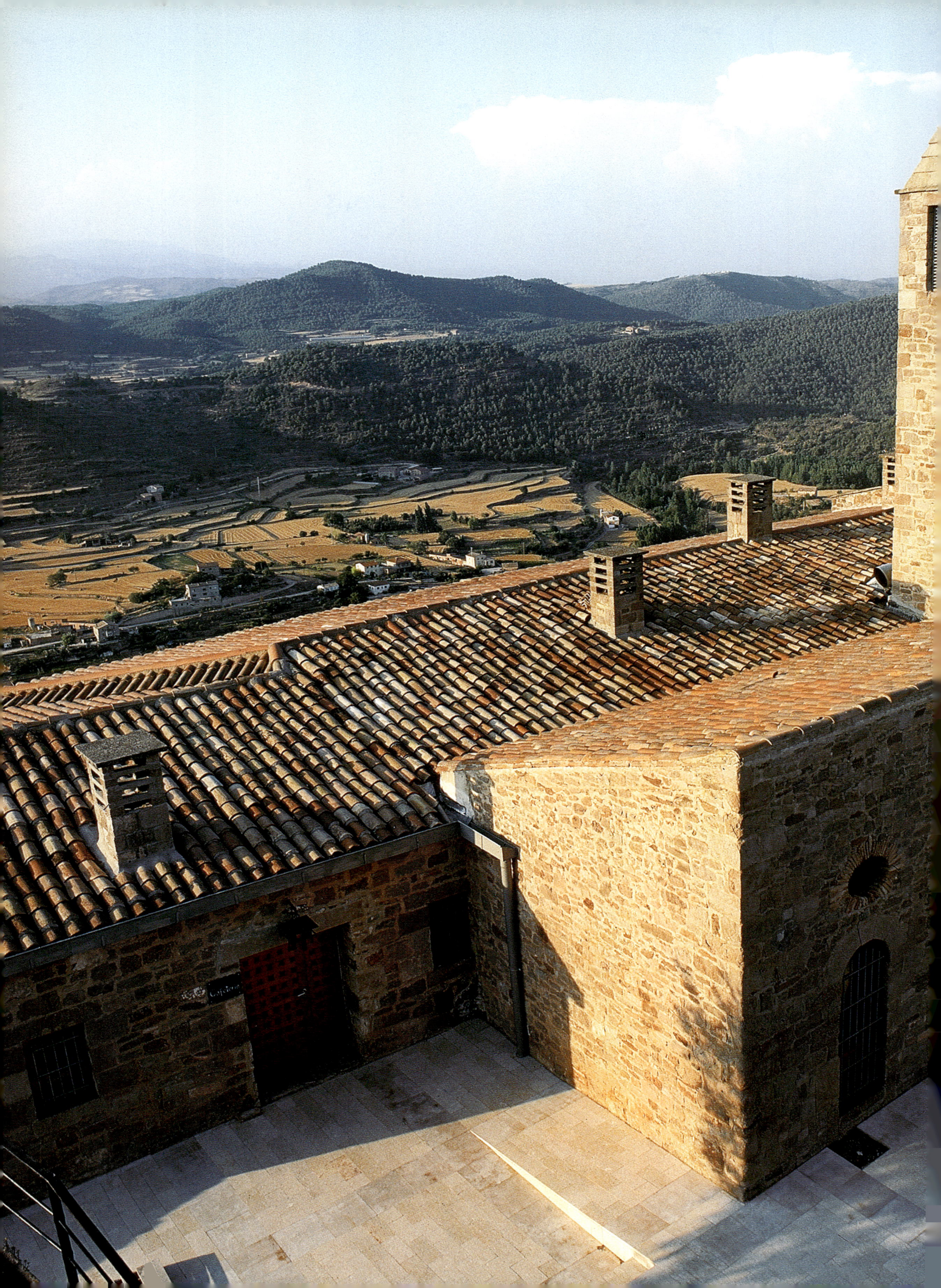

Parador de Duques de Cardona

This harsh area, already known to the Romans, has ,never had trouble defending itself, if only for the impressive fort at Cardona that proved to be invincible during many battles, and has always remained intact.

Luis of Aquitania, heir to Charlemagne, started construction of the castle in 798 and the feudal lords who came after him finished his work. The castle became the property of Ramón Floch, Duke of Cardona and Superior Marshal of Aragón. During the 13th century, the castle was home to the noble Cardona family. An eternal home, as it happens - their remains rest in the crypt of the church. But the most notorious guest at the castle was no doubt San Ramón Nonato, about whom many wonderful stories circulate.

The castle is situated on top of a high hill, and this elevated position allows the guests a fabulous view, far into the distance. At the foot of the mountain flows the river Cardoner, which reflects the castle in often strange ways. The Minyona tower, a wonderful architectural feat from the 11th century, plays a central role in a legend about forbidden love between the daughter of count Ramon Folch and a dashing Moorish gentleman, resulting in the incarceration of the girl. This tragic legend tickles the imagination of visitors and has made room 712, right next to the tower, the most popular of all.

The castle, which became a Parador in 1976, contains a well-preserved Roman temple, considered as the symbol of the city, now the collegiate chapel of San Vicente, consecrated in 1040.

For visitors who have roamed the labyrinthine corridors, seen the moats and the tall towers and are fascinated by this medieval miracle, there are many more wonderful sights to seek out in the area: the strangely-formed salt mountain (Montaña de Sal), with its wonderful caves, the Iberic remains of the city of Solsona, the statue of La Moreneta in the cloister of the convent of Monserrat, and the lakes, rivers, hills and winter sports venues where a range of sports can be practiced.

All this, of course, becomes even more memorable if you can discuss it over a pleasant evening meal. This hotel is certainly the perfect place to be and a prime example of wonderful Catalan cuisine. Taste a wonderful dish of different kinds of dried meats, or the beautiful wild forest mushrooms, as a starter, then choose a trout Cardener, or the wonderful Catalan sausage. Finish off with a typical dessert of cream cheese and honey or some tasty Catalan cake. Parador de Cardona is, without a doubt, a paradise for hedonists!

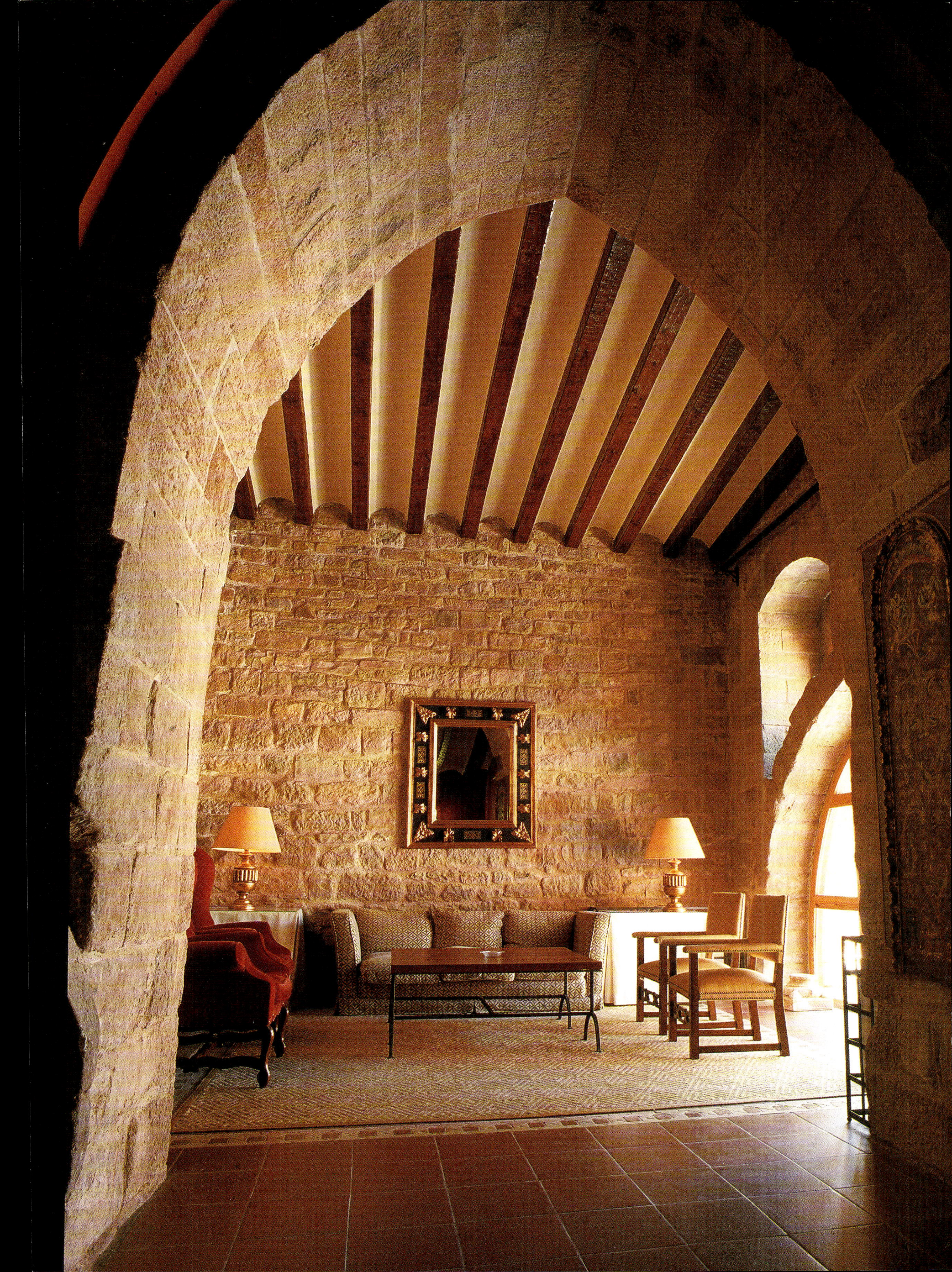

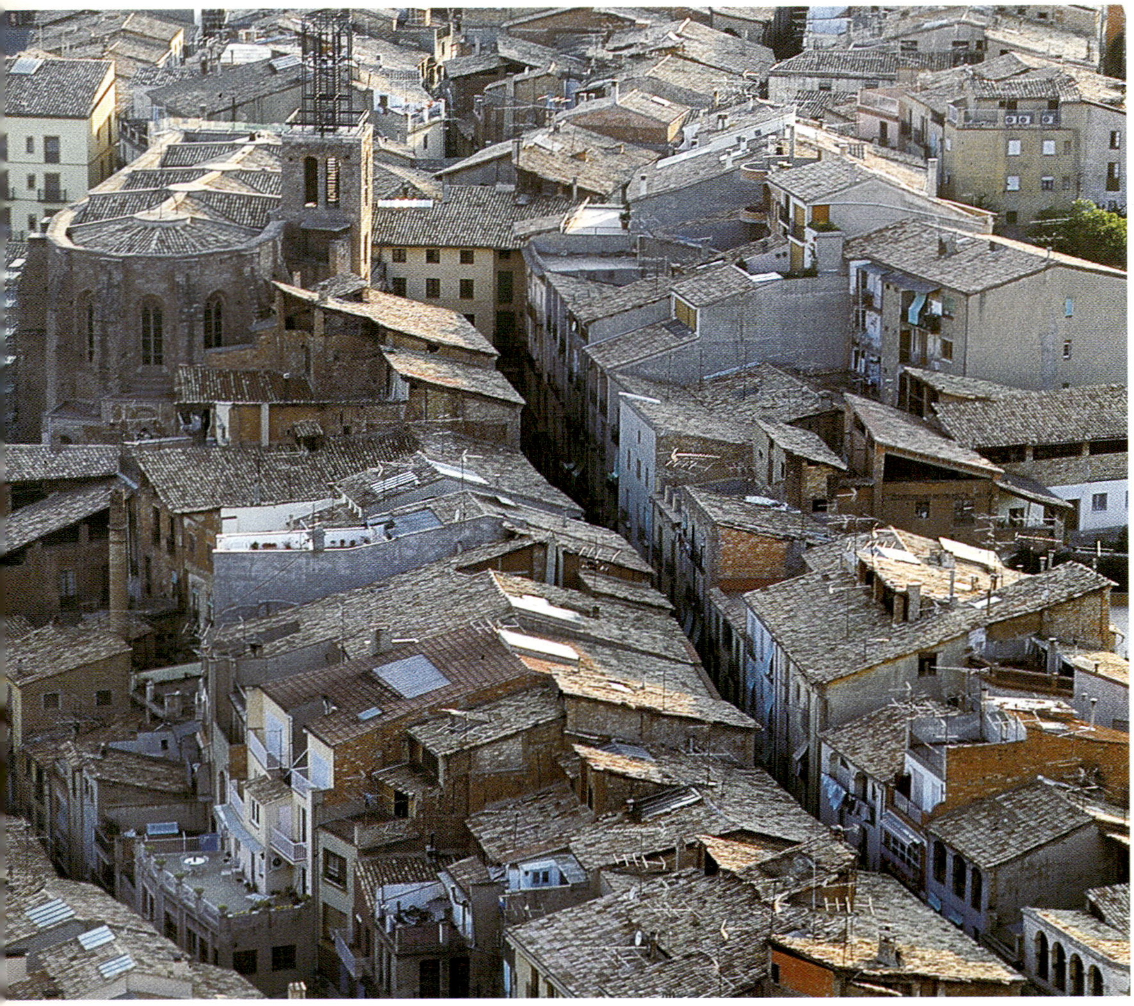

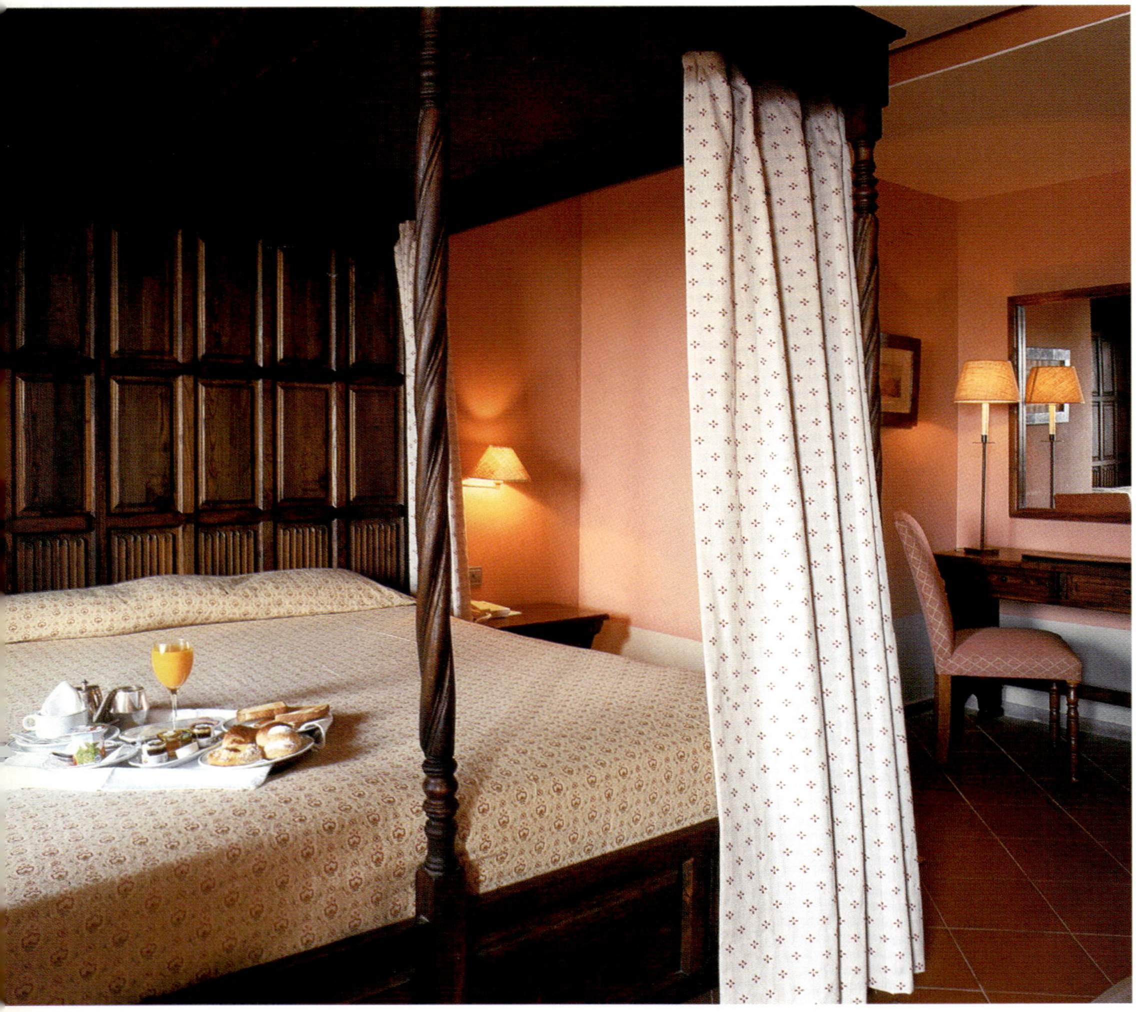

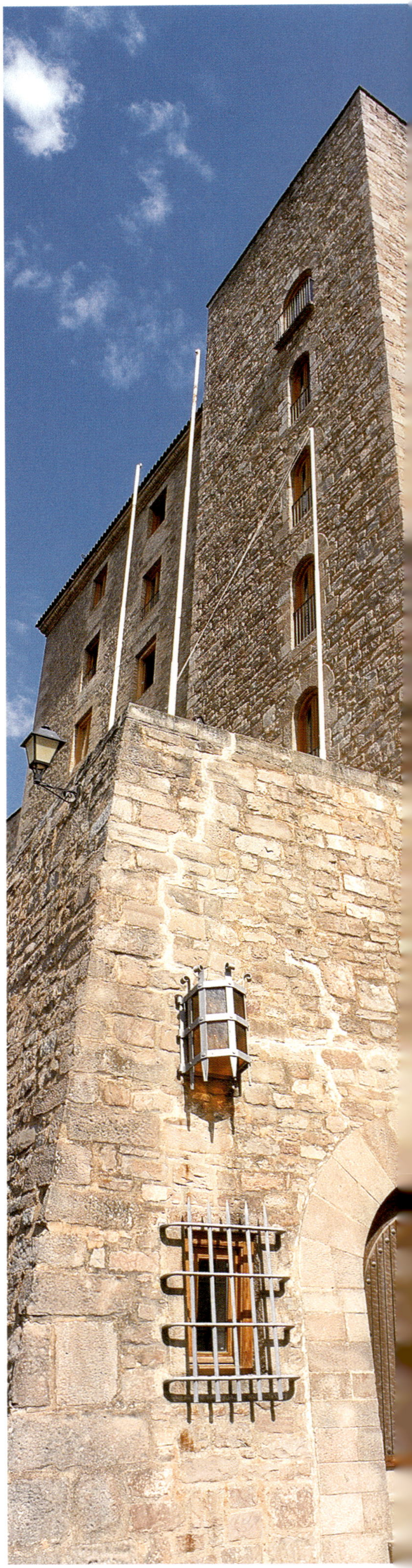

181

CASA DE CARMONA

- **Room amenities:** 33 rooms (1 suite 16 deluxe doubles, with airco, satellite TV, video, compact disc and stereoradio, direct dial phone, minibar, antiques... Bathrooms with hairdryer, bathrobe, lotions.
- **Facilities:** 24h room service, massage, laundry/ dry cleaning, hairdresser and manicure, hotel doctor and fax. Beauty salon, gymnasium. 2 rooms for disabled.
- **Activities on property:** Swimming pool
- **Sightseeing:** Seville and Andalusia.
- **Credit cards:** Visa, Amex, Diners, Mastercard/ Eurocard.
- **Restaurant:** Situated in the former stables of the palace and decorated with paintings. Int'l and Andalusian cuisine, gourmet and traditional à la carte. Air-conditioned

Plaza de Lasso Pag. 10
41410 Carmona/ Sevilla
Ph. (34) (0) 95/ 419 10 00
Fax.(34) (0) 95/ 419 01 89
e-Mail:reserve@casadecarmona.com.
Website www.casadecarmona.com

- **Location:** Seville Int'l Airport 20kms. Seville train station 30kms. From Seville and airport take highway NIV dir. Cordoba/ Madrid, after 25kms first exit Carmona, follow signs "Centro Historico" and follow orange signs to the Casa de Carmona.
- **Season:** Open all year round.

PARADOR DE JAÉN

Castillo de Santa Catalina Pag. 18
23001 Jaén
Ph. (34) (0) 953/23 00 00
Fax. (34) (0) 953/23 09 30
Website www. Parador.Es

- **Room amenities:** 8 single rooms, 31 double rooms and 6 suites.
- **Facilities:** Convention rooms.
- **Activities in the vicinity:** Mountain biking, trekking, swimming.
- **Sightseeing:** Jaén (All baths, cathedral, palaces, Sierra Magina Nature Reserve), Baeza (former university, cathedral), Úbeda (Templo de Santa Maria de los Reales Alcázares).
- **Credit cards:** Visa, Amex, Diners, Agil.

- **Restaurant:** Yes.
- **Location:** The parador is located on top of the Cerro de Santa Catalina, just 5km from the capital, the main accesses are by N-323 main road from Bailén-Motril and N-324 from Cordoba
- **Season:** Open all year round.
- **Affiliation:** Paradores

MAS DE TORRENT

17123 Torrent Pag. 24
Ph. (34) (0) 972/ 30 32 92
Fax.(34) (0) 972/30 32 93
e-Mail: mtorrent@intercom.es
Website http:/www.mastorrent. com

- **Room amenities:** 30.
- **Facilities:** Rooms with airconditioning, direct phone line, satellite TV, minibar, car park in the hotel.
- **Activities on property:** Swimming pool, tennis, squash, cycling.
- **Activities in the vicinity:** Golf Empordá 27 holes.
- **Sightseeing:** Costa Brava, Gerona.
- **Credit cards:** All major cards.

- **Restaurant:** Regional and international cuisine.
- **Location:** 36km east of Gerona via the A7, off n°6, direction Palamós: on the motorway direction Pals. You will find Torrent 800m further on.
- **Season:** Open all year round.
- **Affiliation:** Relais & Châteaux.
- **Accolades:** 5 stars

SANTO MAURO

Zurbano 36 Pag. 30
28010 Madrid
Ph. (34) (0) 91/ 319 69 00
Fax. (34) (0) 91/ 308 54 77
e-Mail:.santo-mauro@ac-hoteles.com

- **Room amenities:** Colour/ satellite TV, air conditioning, hif-fi compact disc, minibar.
- **Facilities:** Swimming pool, terrace, massage, gymnasium, laundry service, private car park, private meeting rooms.
- **Activities in the vicinity:** Restaurants, bars, museums, cinemas, theatres, etc.
- **Sightseeing:** El Prato art Museum, Botanical Gardens.

- **Credit cards:** Visa, Mastercard, Amex, Diners.
- **Restaurant:** Belagua
- **Season:** Open all year round.
- **Affiliation:** AC Hoteles.
- **Accolades:** The Best Hotel of Madrid 1992 Preferente Magazine. Th Best Hotel of Madrid 1998 Grupo Gourmet. The best breakfast of Madrid 1998 Grupo Gourmet.

PARADOR DE SIGÜENZA

- **Room amenities:** 3 single rooms, 64 twins, 10 doubles, 4 suites.
- **Facilities:** Air conditioned rooms with direct telephone line, satellite TV and minibar. Convention rooms.
- **Activities in the vicinity:** Mountain bikes, trekking, horse riding, 4x4.
- **Sightseeing:** Sigüenza (cathedral), Plaza Mayor (with portico), Medinaceli (Roman arch, collegiale church), Atienza ("Fiesta de la Caballada": held since the 12th century), Santa Maria de Huerta.
- **Credit cards:** Visa, Amex, Diners, Agil.
- **Restaurant:** Yes. Regional cuisine.

Plaza del Castillo s/n   Pag. 36
19250 Sigüenza
Ph. (34) (0) 949/39 01 00
Fax. (34) (0) 949/ 39 13 64
Website www.Parador.es

- **Location:** Dominating the town of Sigüenza. It can be reached easily from Madrid and Zaragoza along the N-II. At km 104 turn off along the local road, 20km from Sigüenza, or else, at km 119, at the turning for the Valle de Pelegrina, 12km from Sigüenza, or at 136, at the turning for Alcolea, 18km from Sigüenza. The Parador is located 75km away from Guadalajara.
- **Season:** Open all year round.
- **Affiliation:** Paradores
- **Accolades:** 3 stars.

LA CALA GOLF RESORT

- **Room amenities:** Satellite TV, minibar, hairdryer, telephone, airconditioning, terrace, safe.
- **Facilities:** Hotel *****; Club House, Golf Academy, golf course (42 holes), property development, sports facilities, tennis, squash, fitness centre, indoor & outdoor swimming pool.
- **Activities on property:** Biking.
- **Activities in the vicinity:** Horse riding, beach sports (7km)
- **Sightseeing:** Mijas, Malaga, Ronda, Fuengirola.
- **Credit cards:** Visa, Amex, Access.

Appartado de Correos 106   Pag. 40
La Cala de Mijas
29649 Mijas/ Malaga
Ph. (34) (0) 952/ 669 000
Fax (34) (0) 952/ 669 039
e-Mail: Lacala@lacala.com
Website http://www.lacala.com

- **Restaurant:** 2 restaurants: La Terraza and Los Olivos.
- **Location:** 7km from the beach, in the countryside.
- **Season:** Open all year round.
- **Affiliation:** Relais du Golf.
- **Accolades:** 5 stars.

FINCA CA N'AI

- **Room amenities:** 11 junior suites.
- **Facilities:** Air conditioning, minibar, safe, terrace, telephone, hairdryer, bathrobe.
- **Activities on property:** Swimming pool, heated whirlpool, garden with more than 1000 orange trees.
- **Activities in the vicinity:** Watersports in Puerto (3kms), tennis, golf (15rnin)

Cami de Son Sales,50   Pag. 44
07100 Soller/ Mallorca
Ph. (34) (0) 971/ 63 24 94
Fax (34) (0) 971/ 63 18 99
e-Mail: integral@redestb.es
Website http://www.todoesp.es/ca-nai

- **Sightseeing:** Ideal for walking and mountain trekking.
- **Credit cards:** All.
- **Restaurant:** A la carte.
- **Season:** 01/02 up to 15/11
- **Affiliation:** "Reis de Mallorca".
- **Location:** 3kms from Puerto (port) and 4kms from Soller. Between Puerto and Soller direction Deya, Valldemossa, 1st street to the right.

PARADOR DE LEON

- **Room amenities:** 170 twins, 15 double rooms, 15 suites.
- **Facilities:** Satellite TV, direct telephone line, elevator, convention rooms.
- **Activities in the vicinity:** Horse riding, alpine skiing, tennis, hunting, golf.
- **Sightseeing:** León, Valporquero, Astorga and "maragata" area, Castrillo de los Polvazares, Las Médulas, El Cares Route.
- **Credit cards:** Visa, Amex, Diners, Agil.
- **Restaurant:** Air-conditioned.

Plaza de San Marcos 7   Pag. 49
24001 León
Ph. (34) (0) 987/ 23 73 00
Fax. (34) (0) 987/ 23 34 58
Website www.Parador.es

- **Location:** On the Plaza de San Marcos, in the old city. From Madrid, take the N-VI road, after passing Valladolid and Benavente, at 130 and 66km respectively. From Oviedo (120km), it is reached by the N-632 or along the A-6 motorway.
- **Season:** Open all year round.
- **Affiliation:** Paradores.
- **Accolades:** 5 stars.

LA BOBADILLA

- **Room amenities:** 60.
- **Facilities:** Air conditioning, direct telephone line, satellite TV, minibar. Car park at the hotel.
- **Activities on property:** Swimming pool (indoor and outdoor), tennis, horse riding, sauna, spa, bicycles.
- **Activities in the vicinity:** Golf.
- **Sightseeing:** Granada, Antequera, Loja, Los lnfiernos de Loja.
- **Credit cards:** All major cards.
- **Restaurant:** Local and international cuisine.

La Bobadilla Pag. 52
PO Box144
18300 Loja -Granada
Ph. (34) (0) 958/ 32 18 61
Fax.(34) (0) 958/32 18 10
e-Mail: info@la-bobadilla.com
Website www.la-bobadilla.com

- **Location:** 76km east of Granada by the A92 (Granada/Sevilla), turn off n°175: Villanueva, Iznájar, Salinas.
- **Season:** Open all year round.
- **Affiliation:** Leading Hotels of the World.
- **Accolades:** 5 stars.

CASA IMPERIAL

- **Room amenities:** Deluxe
- **Facilities:** Cafetaria, bar, restaurant (also service in the courtyards), 24h room service.
- **Activities in the vicinity:** Visit to Casa Pilato, shopping, sightseeing
- **Sightseeing:** Seville and surroundings.
- **Credit cards:** AE, Visa, MC, Diners Eurocard, JCB.

C/ lmperial 29 Pag. 56
41003 Sevilla
Ph. (34) (0) 95/ 450 03 00
Fax (34) (0) 95/450 03 30
E-Mail: info@casaimperial.com

- **Restaurant:** Yes
- **Location:** In the old city centre.
- **Season:** Open al] year round.
- **Accolades:** 5 stars

HACIENDA NA XAMENA

- **Room amenities:** Minibar, safe, sea views, balcony or terrace, hairdryer, fuil bathroom, TV.
- **Facilities:** 3 swimming pools, solarium, tennis court, 3 restaurants, bar, meeting facilities, gardens.
- **Activities on property:** Tennis, swimming pools, walking paths.
- **Activities in the vicinity:** Watersports, mountain bikes.

San Miguel Pag. 62
07815 lbiza Baleares
Ph. (34) (0) 971/ 33 45 00
Fax. (34) (0) 971/ 33 45 14
e-Mail: htl.hacienda@v/c.servicom.es
Website www. relaischateaux.fr/xamena

- **Sightseeing:** Ibiza town.
- **Credit cards:** AX, MC/EC,Visa and Diners.
- **Restaurant:** 3 restaurants, from terrace-grill to gourmet restaurant.
- **Location:** Seafront, high on a cliff. Very quiet location. 22 km north-west of lbiza town. Direction San Miguel.
- **Season:** End of April to the end of October.
- **Affiliation:** Relais & Châteaux.

PARADOR DE ZAFRA

- **Room amenities:** 37 twin rooms, 7 double rooms, 1 suite.
- **Facilities:** Satellite TV, direct telephone line, minibar, convention rooms.
- **Activities on property:** Swimming pool.
- **Activities in the vicinity:** Swimming, trekking, horse riding, hang gliding.
- **Sightseeing:** Zafra (Santa Clara Convent, Marqués de Solanda house-palace), Ducado de feria Route, the Templars Route.

PI Corazón de Maria 7 Pag. 68
06300 Zafra (Badajoz)
Ph. (34) (0) 924/ 55 45 40
Fax.(34) (0) 924/ 55 10 18
Website www.Parador.es

- **Credit cards:** Visa, Amex, Diners, Agil.
- **Restaurant:** Yes.
- **Location:** in the centre of the town. Zafra is between Seville and Mérida, along the "Ruta de la Plata", taking the main N-630 road, 141 km from Seville and 60km from Mérida and 73km from Badajoz along the N-432 from Badajoz-Granada.
- **Season:** Open all year round.
- **Affiliation:** Paradores.

ALHAMBRA PALACE

- **Room amenities:** 136 rooms.
- **Facilities:** Rooms with air conditioning, direct telephone line, color TV, room service, minibar, safety box, elevator.
- **Activities in the vicinity:** Golf.
- **Sightseeing:** The cloister (Cartuja), gipsy quarter of Sacromonte, Moorish quarter of l'Albaicin in Granada, Viznar (castle and grave of Federico Garcia Lorca), cathedral of Guadix, Sierra Nevada. Ski in Sierra Nevada (35km) Sport Palace. In summer int'l Festival of Music & Dance Teatro.

Pena Partida 2,4 Pag. 72
18009 Granada
Ph. (34) (0) 958/ 22 14 66
Fax. (34) (0) 958/ 22 64 04 Reservas
e-Mail: H-Alhambrapalace.es
Website
http.www. H-Alhambrapalace.es

- **Credit cards:** All major cards.
- **Restaurant:** Yes.
- **Location:** In the gardens of the Alhambra, facing the Sierra Nevada mountains.
- **Season:** Open all year round.

LA RESIDENCIA

- **Room amenities:** Air-conditioning, hairdryer, direct dial phone, TV + video and CD- player on request.
- **Facilities:** Pools, steam-room, gym, beauty salon, hydrotherapy, tennis.
- **Activities on property:** Tennis, gym, ping pong, mountain biking.
- **Activities in the vicinity:** Walking, watersports.
- **Sightseeing:** Palma city, Valldemossa, Soller.
- **Credit cards:** Visa, Master, Amex.
- **Restaurant:** Ei Olivo (gourmet), Son Fony.

Finca son Canals Pag. 78
07179 Deya
Ph. (34) (0) 971/ 63 90 11
Fax.(34) (0) 971/63 93 70
e-Mail: residencia@relaischateaux.fr
Website
www. relaischateaux.fr/residencia

- **Location:** Mountain village near coast. NW Mallorca.
- **Season:** Open all year round.
- **Affiliation:** Relais & Châteaux.
- **Accolades:** Condé Nast Traveller 13th Best Holiday hotel (world) 1998 and 13th Best of the Best (world) 1999.

PARADOR DE CARMONA

- **Room amenities:** 3 single rooms, 51 twins, 9 double rooms.
- **Facilities:** Satellite TV, direct phone line. Convention rooms.
- **Activities in the vicinity:** Swimming, golf.
- **Sightseeing:** Carmona (museum and Roman necropolis), Seville (La Giralda, cathedral, el Alcázar, "Torre del Oro". Fine Arts Museum), Ecija, Osuna, ruins of Itálica).
- **Credit cards:** AE, Visa, MC, Diners Eurocard, JCB.

Alcazar s/n Pag. 84
41410 Carmona, Seville
Ph. (34) (0) 95/ 414 10 10
Fax.(34) (0) 95/ 414 17 12
Website www.Parador.es

- **Restaurant:** Yes.
- **Location:** 30km from Seville. Take the E-05 Autovia de Andalucia, from Seville to Cordoba or vice versa.
- **Season:** Open all year round.
- **Affiliation:** Paradores

CLARIS

- **Room amenities:** 120 rooms with direct dialing telephone, safe, satellite TV & canal soundproofing, airconditioning/ heating, 24h room service.
- **Activities on property:** Sauna, restaurants & meeting rooms, outdoor swimming pool, gym, cocktail bar, Museum of Egyptian Art.
- **Activities in the vicinity:** La Redrera, El Paseo de Gracia, La Sagrara Familia.
- **Credit cards:** Amex, Mastercard, Eurocard, Diners.
- **Restaurant:** 3 restaurants, Aneurdanes, Beluga, Barbecue.

Pau Claris 150 Pag. 90
08009 Barcelona
Ph. (34) (0) 93/ 487 62 62
Fax (34) (0) 93/ 215 79 70
e-Mail: claris@derbyhotels.es
Website www.slh.com/htlclaris/

- **Location:** Located in the centre of Barcelona, close to the Paseo de Gracia.
- **Season:** Open all year round.
- **Affiliation:** Concorde Hotels, Small Luxury Hotels of the World, Design Hotels, Utell. Accolades: 5 stars grand luxe, Privilege Gold of Concorde Hotels

PALACIO CA SA GALESA

- **Room amenities:** 12 rooms (5 doubles, 3 junior suites and 4 suites) all with a/e, individual heating, satellite TV, minibar, safe, tea and coffee making facilities and hairdryer.
- **Facilities:** Heated indoor pool, sauna, sunbed, small fitness centre, terrace overlooking Palma cathedral, car parking bar, library and afternoon complimentary service in the Monet Kitchen.
- **Activities in the vicinity:** Guided walks in the old part of the city.

Carrer de Miramar 8   Pag. 98
07001 Palma de Mallorca
Ph. (34) (0) 971/ 71 54 00
Fax (34) (0) 971/ 72 15 79

- **Sightseeing:** Palma's Bay, Cathedral and historic city.
- **Credit cards:** Eurocard, Visa, Amex, Diners.
- **Restaurant:** No, but restaurant infoguide in each room.
- **Location:** In the centre between the Cathedral and the City hall.
- **Season:** Open all year round.
- **Affiliation:** Reis de Mallorca (Association of Hotels with character and personal service). Accolades: 5 stars

PARADOR DE JARANDILLA DE LA VERA

- **Room amenities:** 10 single rooms, 43 twins.
- **Facilities:** Air conditioned rooms, direct telephone line, satellite TV, minibar, convention rooms.
- **Activities in the vicinity:** Trekking, mountain bike, routes for horse riding, canoeing, bullfights with young bulls, natural swimming pools, tennis.
- **Sightseeing:** Jarandilla de la Vera (roman bridge), El Raso, El Jerte, Plasencia, Monfragüe Nature Reserve, La Vera.
- **Credit cards:** Visa, Amex, Diners, Agil.

Avda Garcia Prieto 1   Pag. 104
10450 Jarandilla de la Vera
Ph. (34) (0) 927/ 56 01 17
Fax.(34) (0) 927/ 56 00 88
Website www.Parador.es

- **Restaurant:** Yes. Local specialties.
- **Location:** In the centre of town. Madrid 232km along the main 530 road (N-V), turning off at Navalmoral de la Meta. Plasencia is 59km away following the local road and Cácares is 150km away on the N-630.
- **Season:** Open al] year round.
- **Affiliation:** Paradores.

HACIENDA BENAZUZA

- **Room amenities:** Mineral water, mignardises fruit basket.
- **Facilities:** Room service 24h, deluxe cars with chauffeur, heliport, air conditioning, heating, laundry, ironing service etc.
- **Activities on property:** Tennis, paddle tennis, outdoor swimming pool.
- **Activities in the vicinity:** Horse riding, golf
- **Sightseeing:** Excursions to Seville and Andalusia.
- **Credit cards:** All major cards accepted.
- **Restaurant:** "La Alqueria": international and mediterranean cuisine (Arabian and Andalusian specialtjes), "La Alberea": at the poolside (open in season).

C/ Virgen de las Nieves   Pag. 108
41800 Sanlucar la Mayor - Seville
Ph. (34) (0) 95/ 570 3344
Fax.(34) (0) 95/ 570 3410
e-Mail: hbenazuza@arrakis.es
Website www.hbenazuza.com

- **Location:** 20min. from the centre of Seville.
- **Season:** Low season: January - February up to mid-March. Mid-November and December, first two weeks of July. Mid-Season: Mid-March up to the end of June, Mid-August. High season: Week of Easter and April Fair in Seville.
- **Affiliation:** One of the members of the Leading Hotels of the World.
- **Accolades:** Several gastronomy awards.

MAS PAU

- **Room amenities:** 7
- **Facilities:** Rooms with air conditioning, direct telephone line, satellite TV, minibar.
- **Activities on property:** Swimming pool, car park at the hotel.
- **Activities in the vicinity:** Golf.
- **Credit cards:** All major cards accepted.

Carretera de Figueras a Olot   Pag. 116
17742 Avinyonet de Puigventós
Figueras
Tel. (34) (0) 972/ 54 61 54
Fax. (34) (0) 972/ 54 63 26
e-Mail: Maspau@gm.es
Website www.maspau.com

- **Restaurant:** Closed on Sunday evenings and Mondays; in summertime closed Mondays at noon.
- **Location:** 58km south of Perpignan, 42km from Gerona by the A7, turn off in Figueras, then take direction Olot.
- **Season:** Closed from January 15 up to March 15.

LANDA PALACE

- **Room amenities:** 36 rooms. All with colour TV, direct telephone, hairdryer and most with jaccuzzi. 6 of the rooms in the medieval tower, 6 overlooking the Plaza Mayor, with terraces, 3 on the top floor, designed as old mansards and the rest overlooking gardens, pool and the Castilian countryside.
- **Facilities:** 5 meeting rooms. Outdoor pool and impressive gothic indoor pool.
- **Activities in the vicinity:** Golf (30kms) and tennis in town.
- **Sightseeing:** Wonderful gothic cathedral, Las Huelgas, monasteries, Arco de Santa Maria (old town hall)...
- **Credit cards:** Visa, Eurocard, Mastercard.
- **Restaurant:** One for lunch in rustic, elegant style. In the evening dinner is served in the luxurious

Carretera de Madrid-Irún, km235
09001 Burgos
Ph. (34) (0) 947/20 63 43
Fax. (34) (0) 947/ 26 46 76
e-Mail: landapal@teleline.es

Pag. 120

"Salón Real", formal and cultivated, with stone-walled ceiling from whith a huge iron lamp -a real piece of art- hangs down. Breakfast in "Salón Roble" with fresh bakery and home made pastries.
- **Location:** At km 235 N1 (E5), linking Madrid with French border at Irún.
- **Season:** May 1 - October 31.
- **Accolades:** Among many others: Placa al Mérito Turistico, Categoria de Plata, granted by the Spanish Ministery of Tourism, Royal Lodging Place, granted by the House of H.M. the King Juan Carlos I 1977, Hotel of the Year 1996....

PARADOR DE ZAMORA

- **Room amenities:** 41 twin rooms, 5 double rooms, 6 suites.
- **Facilities:** Direct telephone line, TV, minibar, convention rooms.
- **Sightseeing:** Zamora (cathedral), Las Dueñas Convent. Arribes del Duero, Sanabria Lake, Campillo, Toro (Santa Maria la Mayor Collegiate church), La Hiniesta (church with gothic architecture).
- **Credit cards:** Visa, Amex, Diners, Agil.
- **Restaurant:** Yes. Castilian specialties.

Pl de Vidato 5
49001 Zamora
Ph. (34) (0) 980/ 51 44 97
Fax. (34) (0) 980/ 53 00 63
Website www.Parador.es

Pag. 126

- **Location:** Zamora is located on the right bank of the Duero, at the foothills of the western Castilian mountains, 62km north of Salamanca by the N-630.
- **Season:** Open all year round.
- **Affiliation:** Paradores.
- **Accolades:** 4 stars.

PUENTE ROMANO

- **Room amenities:** 226 rooms.
- **Facilities:** Rooms with airconditioning, direct telephone line, satellite TV, minibar, safe.
- **Activities on property:** Watersports, sauna, gymnasium and Turkish baths at the Puente Romano Tennis and Fitness Club
- **Activities in the vicinity:** 27 golf Clubs, horse riding.
- **Sightseeing:** Gibraltar, Ronda, Mijas, Granada, Sevilla, Jerez, Puerto Banus.
- **Credit cards:** All major cards accepted.

Carretera de Cadiz, km 177
29600 Marbella
Ph. (34) (0) 95/ 282 09 00
Fax (34) (0) 95/ 277 57 66
e-Mail: Hotel@puenteromano.com
comercial@puenteromano.com
Website www.puenteromano.com

Pag. 130

- **Restaurant:** Beach Club Restaurant, swimming pool, bar, 'Café del Mar', Bar Cascada, La Plaza Romana open air restaurant, Café El Puente, Roberto Italian restaurant.
- **Location:** 56km south west of Malaga on the N340. Between Marbella and Puerto Banus. Season: Open all year round
- **Affiliation:** Leading Hotels of the World, Utell.

PARADOR DE GRANADA

- **Room amenities:** 33 twins, 1 double room and 1 suite.
- **Facilities:** Air conditioned rooms, direct phone line, minibar. Convention rooms.
- **Sightseeing:** Granada (Alhambra, Generalife and Carmen de los Mártires, cathedral and royal chapel), La Alpujarra, Sierra Nevada.
- **Credit cards:** Visa, Amex, Diners, JCB, Agil.
- **Restaurant:** Yes.

Real de la Alhambra s/n
18009 Granada
Ph. (34) (0) 958/ 22 14 40
Fax. (34) (0) 958/ 22 22 64
Website www.Parador.es

Pag. 136

- **Location:** In the gardens of the Alhambra in the city centre of Granada.
- **Season:** Open all year round.
- **Affiliation:** Paradores.
- **Accolades:** 4 stars.

SAN ROMAN DE ESCALANTE

- **Room amenities:** TV, minibar, heating, airconditioning, phone, safety box, hairdryer, bathrobe.
- **Facilities:** Open air parking, garden, forest, facilities for disabled, XII century chapel, antique shop.
- **Activities on property:** Walking
- **Activities in the vicinity:** Golf, tennis, bike hire, watersports, hill walking, horse riding, angling.
- **Sightseeing:** Castro Urdiales Laredo, small fishing villages, Santander, Guggenheim Museum in Bilbao.
- **Credit cards:** All.
- **Restaurant:** In the restaurant clients can taste different kinds of local fish, as well as a very special cuisine, traditional and modern, local and international wines.

Carretara, Escalante km 2   Pag. 142
39795 Escalante
Ph. (34) (0) 942/ 67 77 45
Fax.(34) (0) 942/ 67 76 43
e-Mail: escalante@relaischateaux.fr
Website www. relaischateaux.fr/lagrimos

- **Location:** 2kms from the small village of Escalante. Situated in very beautiful surroundings in the countryside.
- **Season:** Low season from October to Easter. Mid-season from Easter to June 30. High season Easter, July and August. Closed from December 20 up to January 20.

PARADOR DE SANTIAGO

- **Room amenities:** 12 single rooms, 104 twins, 14 doubles, 6 suites.
- **Facilities:** Satellite TV, direct telephone line, minibar, elevator, parking, meeting rooms.
- **Activities in the vicinity:** Horse riding, parapente, rafting, sailing, canoeing, kayak, golf, fishing, tennis, swimming
- **Sightseeing:** Santiago de Compostela, La Coruña, Vigo, Baiona, Finisterre and Costa do Morte.

Plaza do Obradoiro, 1   Pag. 146
15705 Santiago de Compostela
Ph. (34) (0) 981/ 58 22 00
Fax. (34) (0) 981/ 56 30 94
Website www.Parador.es

- **Credit cards:** Visa, Amex, Diners, Eurocard, JCB, Agil
- **Restaurant:** Yes.
- **Location:** In old Santiago, facing the cathedral. From La Coruña you reach Santiago along the main N550 road, passing through Õrdenes, or along the A9 motorway towards Pontevedra (65km). Both roads take you to Noia, 34km from Santiago, Padrón 22km and Pontevedra 59km.
- **Season:** Open all year round.
- **Affiliation:** Paradores
- **Accolades:** 5 stars.

MARBELLA CLUB

- **Room amenities:** Minibar, safe deposit box, hairdryer, satellite TV, in-house video films.
- **Facilities:** 2 swimming pools.
- **Activities on property:** Swimming, watersports, very soon there will be a spa at the Marbella Club.
- **Activities in the vicinity:** Tennis, own golf course
- **Sightseeing:** Gibraltar, Ronda, Mijas, Granada, Sevilla, Jerez, Puerto Banus.
- **Credit cards:** All major credit cards accepted.

Bulevar Principe   Pag. 150
Alfonso von Hohenlohe s/n
29600 Marbella
Ph. (34) (0) 95/ 282 22 11
Fax.(34) (0) 95/ 282 98 84
e-Mail: Hotel@marbellaclub.com
Website www.marbellaclub.com

- **Restaurant:** Each buffet open for lunch all year round. Grill restaurant open for dinner all year.
- **Location:** 45 minutes from Malaga. Between Marbella and Puerto Banus.
- **Season:** Open al] year round.
- **Affiliation:** Leading Hotels of the World.

VILLA REAL

- **Facilites:** 115 rooms with direct dialing telephone, safe, minibar, satellite TV, canal+ & pay TV, fax-modem connection, background music, air-conditioning/ heating, 24h room service.
- **Activities on property:** Sauna & hairdresser, restaurant & meeting rooms, ancient art collection, scotch-bar & coffee shop.
- **Activities in the vicinity:** EL Prado museum, the Thyssen Bornemitza Collection, the Museum of Queen Sofia, the Botanical Gardens, the Castellana Av, the Opera and the Parliament.
- **Credit Cards:** Amex, Mastercard, Diners, Eurocard.

Plaza de las Cortes, 10   Pag. 156
29014 Madrid
Ph. (34) (0) 91/ 420 37 67
Fax (34) (0) 91/420 25 47
e-mail: villareal@derbyhotels.es
Website www.slh.com/villreal/

- **Restaurant:** Yes.
- **Location:** In the centre of Madrid, 16km from the Int'l Airport Barajas.
- **Season:** Hotel & restaurant open all year.
- **Affiliation:** Concorde Hotels, Small Luxury Hotels of the World, Utell.
- **Accolades:** 5 stars, Privilege Gold of Concorde Hotels.

GRAN HOTEL BAHIA DEL DUQUE

- **Room amenities:** Minibar, satellite TV, direct phone, room service 24hs, hairdryer, safe, airco.
- **Facilities:** Fitness centre, mini-club, 5 swimming pools, Beauty Centre with sauna and massages, shopping gallery, 3 tennis courts, 2 squash courts, watersports at the Playa del Duque, 19 meeting rooms with capacity up to 950 and an Observatory.
- **Activities on property:** Fitness centre, tennis, squash, ping pong, gym, aerobics, thai-chi, archery, billiards, mountain bikes, putting green, darts, dance lessons.
- **Activities in the vicinity:** 5 golf courses between 5 and 15kms, minigolf, riding, diving, parascending, waterskiing, jet ski, sailing, deepsea fishing, jeep safari, go-karting club, excursions.
- **Sightseeing:** The "Cañadas del Teide" National Park 60min. away, the Cliffs of Los Gigantes, Masca, several fascinating museums and other cultural attractions which include the Tenerife International Festival of Music (February) and the Carnivals of Cruz and Puerto de la Cruz.
- **Credit cards:** Visa, Mastercard, Diners, Amex, Eurocard.
- **Restaurant:** 8 restaurants: 1 buffet "El Bernegal" and 7 à la carte: Spanish "La Tasca", Italian "La Trattoria", French "La Brasserie", gourmet "El Duque", mediterranean "Beach Club", South American "La Hacienda" and "Café La Bahia".

C/ Alealde Walter Paetzmann, Pag. 160
sn 38660 Costa Adeje
Tenerife
Ph. (34) (0) 922/ 74 69 00 en 71 30 00
Fax. (34) (0) 922/ 74 69 25 en 71 26 16
e-Mail: comercial@bahia-duque.com.
Website http://www.bahia-duque.com

- **Location:** 15kms from the south int'l airport "Reina Sofia", just beside the beach "Playa del Duque", 3kms from the centre of Playa de las Américas and 80kms from the capital "Santa Cruz de Tenerife".
- **Season:** High season: Carnival and Easter, 23/10 – 08/11. Mid season: 07/01 – 12/02, 24/02 – 25/03, 06/04 – 09/05, 06/04 – 05/09, 01/08 – 22/10, 09/11 – 23/12. Low season: 10/05 – 31/07 (all 1999 calendar).
- **Affiliation:** Sol-Mélia

ARTS

- **Rooms:** 455 rooms and suites
- **Facilities:** Air conditioning, satellite TV, direct telephone line.
- **Sightseeing:** Barcelona, Costa Brava.
- **Creditcards:** All.

Marina 19   Pag. 166
08005 Barcelona
Ph. (34) 93/ 221 10 00
Fax. (34) 93/ 221 10 70

- **Location:** In the Olympic village, facing the sea. Walking distance of downtown Barcelona.
- **Season:** Open year round.
- **References:** 5 stars.

CORTIJO EL ESPARRAGAL

- **Room amenities:** 12 rooms and 6 suites.
- **Facilities:** Air-conditioning, direct telephone, satellite TV, parking.
- **Activities on property:** Swimming pool.
- **Activities in the vicinity:** Golf.
- **Sightseeing:** Seville, Carmona, Cantillana, Alcala de Guadaira, Sanlúcar la Mayor, the cloister of San Isodoro del Campo in Santiponce and the ruins of Italica.
- **Credit cards:** All.
- **Restaurant:** Yes.

C/ de Merida km 795   Pag. 170
41860 Gerena (Sevilla)
Ph. (34) (0) 95/ 578 27 02
Fax (34) (0) 95/ 578 27 83
e-Mail: el-esparragel@sistel.es

- **Location:** 21 km north of Seville via the SE30, direction Merida up to km 795, turn left for Gerena. The hotel is located 1,5km further on before arriving at Gerena.
- **Season:** Open all year round.

PARADOR DE CARDONA

- **Room amenities:** 2 single rooms, 42 twins, 5 double rooms and 5 suites.
- **Facilities:** Air conditioned rooms, satellite TV, direct telephone line, convention rooms.
- **Activities in the vicinity:** Golf, fishing, trips in carts, horse riding.
- **Sightseeing:** Cardona (historical archives, old quarter, city walls), Solsona (cathedral), Mare de Deu de Queralt Santuary, Montserrat.
- **Credit cards:** Visa, Amex, Diners, JCB, Agil.

Castillo de Cardona   Pag. 176
08261 Cardona
Ph. (34) (0) 93/ 869 12 75
Fax. (34) (0) 93/ 869 16 36
Website www.Parador.es

- **Restaurant:** Yes. Catalan cuisine.
- **Location:** On a hill opposite the town of Cardona, the parador is 85km from Barcelona. The A-18 motorway, leaving Manresa towards Solsona, is the main rneans of access.
- **Season:** Open al] year round.
- **Affiliation:** Paradores.
- **Accolades:** 4 stars.

- 25
- 26 Santiago de Compostela
- 8
- 21 Burgos
- 22
- 5
- 18
- 4
- 28
- Madrid
- 12
- 31
- 1
- 15
- 2
- 24
- 13
- 19
- 10 Sevilla
- 9
- Granada
- 6 Malaga
- 23
- 27

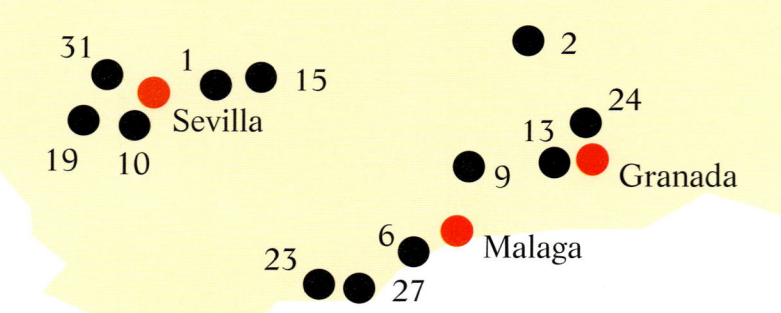

TENERIFE
- 29

#	Name	#	Name
1	Casa de Carmona	17	Palacio Ca Sa Galesa
2	Parador de Jaén	18	Parador de Jarandilla de la Vera
3	Mas de Torrent	19	Hacienda Benazuza
4	Santo Mauro	20	Mas Pau
5	Parador de Sigüenza	21	Landa Palace
6	La Cala Golf	22	Parador de Zamora
7	Finca Ca N'ai	23	Puente Romano
8	Parador de León	24	Parador de Granada
9	La Bobadilla	25	San Roman de Escalante
10	Casa Imperial	26	Parador de Santiago
11	Hacienda Na Xamena	27	Marbella Club
12	Parador de Zafra	28	Villa Real
13	Alhambra Palace	29	Gran Hotel Bahia del Duque
14	La Residencia	30	Arts
15	Parador de Carmona	31	Cortijo El Esparragal
16	Claris	32	Parador de Cardona

With special thanks to

IBERIA

Avenue Louise 54
1050 Brussels
Ph. 00 32 (0)2 548 94 90
Fax 00 32 (0)2 502 18 43

Published in this series

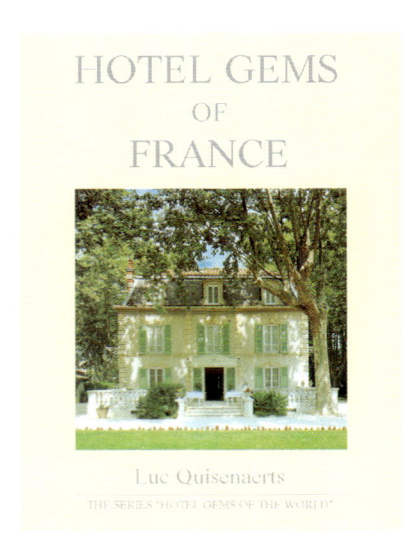

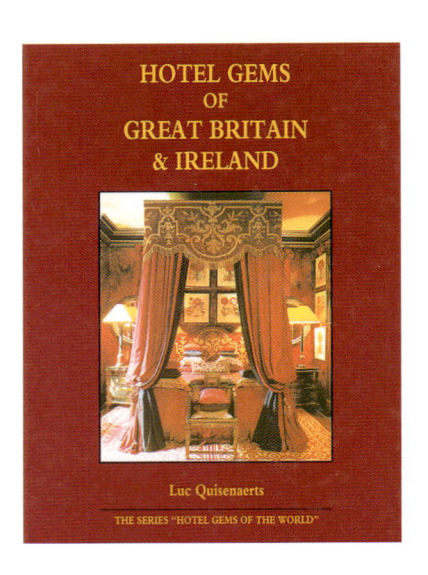

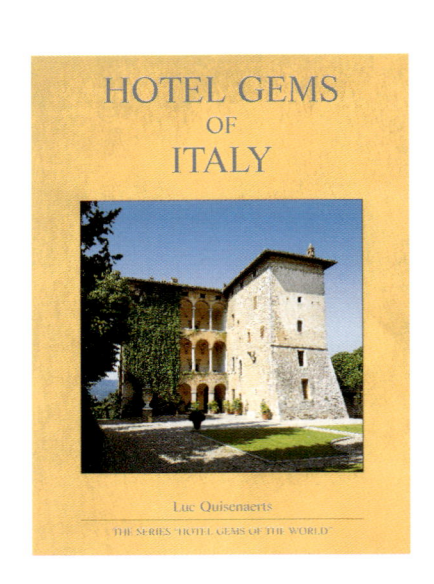

Editions in English, French,
German and Dutch.